T0113433

# INNOVATIVE SCHOOL PRINCIPALS
# AND RESTRUCTURING

*Restructuring is an international phenomenon, and great stress is placed on the* role of the innovative principal in the process. To date, studies have concentrated on *innovative practice or the schools themselves, and there is little* published material which considers the crucial nexus of the interrelationship between principal and school. This book offers insights into the ways in which six principals go about leading the change process in their schools, and looks for ways of understanding why and how principals behave and think in the way they do. The book's edited topical life history approach identifies key events, experiences and significant others in the lives of the case study principals, and shows how these have shaped the way they implement changes to curriculum, teaching and learning in their schools.

**Clive Dimmock** is Associate Professor of Education at the Chinese University of Hong Kong and Senior Lecturer in Educational Management and Administration at the University of Western Australia.
**Tom O'Donoghue** is Senior Lecturer in Curriculum Theory at the University of Western Australia.

# EDUCATIONAL MANAGEMENT SERIES
## Series editor: Cyril Poster

# INNOVATIVE SCHOOL PRINCIPALS AND RESTRUCTURING

Life history portraits of successful managers of change

*Clive Dimmock and Tom O'Donoghue*

Routledge
Taylor & Francis Group

LONDON AND NEW YORK

First published 1997 by Routledge

Published 2017 by Routledge
2 Park Square, Milton Park, Abingdon, Oxon OX14 4RN
711 Third Avenue, New York, NY 10017, USA

*Routledge is an imprint of the Taylor & Francis Group, an
informa business*

Copyright © 1996 C.A.J. Dimmock and T.A. O'Donoghue

Typeset in Garamond by Routledge

*British Library Cataloguing in Publication Data*
A catalogue record for this book is available from the British
Library

*Library of Congress Cataloguing in Publication Data*
Dimmock, Clive A. J.
Innovative school principals and restructuring: life history
portraits of successful managers of
change / C.A.J.
Dimmock and T.A. O'Donoghue.
p. cm. – (Educational management series)
Includes bibliographical references and index.
1. School management and organization–Australia. 2. School
principals–Australia. 3.
Educational change–Australia.
I. O'Donoghue, T. A. (Tom A.), 1953–. II. Title. III.
Series.
LB2979.D556 1996
371.2' 00994–dc20    96  17619
CIP

ISBN 978-0-415-13899-4 (pbk)

# CONTENTS

# ACKNOWLEDGEMENTS

We express our sincere gratitude to the six principals on whom the case studies reported in this book focus. Without their kind and patient cooperation the book would never have been brought to fruition. We are indebted to many generations of students. We would like to mention in particular our post-graduate students at the University of Western Australia in 1995 with whom we shared many ideas and analyses, particularly Sally Burgess, David Hayter, Kathryn Saville and Diana Van Straalen. Finally, we gratefully acknowledge receipt of an Australian Research Council Grant through the auspices of the University of Western Australia under their 'small grants' scheme. This grant greatly assisted in the production of the study.

# 1

# INTRODUCTION

Educational restructuring is taking place in much of the world, with a deregulated, decentralized system replacing central planning, control and supervision (Cistone, 1989). This change is associated with such notions as school-based management, school-based budgeting, and the community management of schools (Lawton, 1992, p. 139). There is no shortage of prescriptive theories as to why educational systems should be restructured (Purkey and Smith, 1985; Caldwell and Spinks, 1988; Timar, 1989). At the same time, it is important to note that the process can take different forms in different contexts, having been enacted at the national level in the United Kingdom and New Zealand and at the district level in Canada (Hess, 1991).

There is also no shortage of explanations as to why restructuring is emerging as a worldwide phenomenon. These explanations have been offered in various countries either to initiate restructuring processes or to legitimize those already begun. Restructuring in some countries has also involved significant curriculum changes. In the United Kingdom, for example, while the administrative changes reflect the deregulatory, market-oriented solutions economists might dictate, even to the point of allowing schools to opt-out of their Local Education Authorities and to collect funds from the central government, concurrently a core National Curriculum has been introduced which provides the central government with control over the subject-matter content of education (Lawton, 1992).

Australia has been no exception to the general international trend towards restructuring in education. Here, two related policy initiatives are shaping change in schools (Dimmock, 1995). The first policy initiative, which is eventuating in 'macro-reforms', involves a shift from centralized governance to decentralized, school-based management. The focus is on change at the whole-school level, primarily affecting governance, management and administration rather than classroom activities of teaching and learning (Chadbourne and Clarke, 1994). The second policy initiative, which is eventuating in 'micro-reforms', concerns school restructuring in order to reform the technical core activities of teaching and learning. The focus of this second initiative is on introducing more flexible, responsive and student-oriented service delivery by targeting change in work organization, pedagogical practices and learning processes.

In Australia, as elsewhere, particular emphasis is placed on the role of the school principal in the translation of these policy initiatives into practice. However, while advice to principals has been plentiful, relatively little of it has been based on contemporary studies. This is not to deny the existence of a significant body of literature on the principalship. Rather, it is to argue that further studies are necessary at the present time, since the context within which contemporary school principals must operate has changed markedly over the last few years. Ribbins and Sherratt (1992, p. 160) take up this matter within the context of England and Wales, arguing that there is a need to know much more about how schools are responding to the demands which have been placed upon them over the last few years. They argue that there are various ways of achieving this. Their own approach involves an in-depth longitudinal study of headship and is close to being an action research project with the role of the experienced researcher approximating that of a consultant. A challenge now for other researchers is not only to adopt the approach of Ribbins and Sherratt (ibid.), but also to adopt other approaches in studying school leadership and restructuring in a range of contexts.

This book is concerned with a research project which attempted to meet this challenge in three respects. The research approach adopted in the project was that of the edited topical life history. Such biographical and life history approaches in educational studies are not new. Twenty years ago, Abbs (1976) demonstrated the usefulness of autobiographical approaches in teacher education. More recently, Evetts (1989, p. 89) argued that life history accounts and biographies have become 'an increasingly popular source of sociological data'. She goes on to highlight Plummer's (1983) contention that in sociology, research which highlights the actual human subject must provide the necessary counterbalance to positivistic emphases on structure and systems.

In adopting the edited topical life history approach in the study of principals who are promoting restructuring initiatives in the areas of curriculum, teaching and learning, the present authors were attempting to take one step further Ribbins and Sherratt's (1992, p. 153) proposal that studies of the principalship can benefit from adopting a biographical and autobiographical approach. What was sought was not only to develop accounts of schools and the role of the principals within them which integrate the perspectives of both the principals and the researchers, but also to provide accounts of these roles by examining the socializing influences relevant to the formation of the principal over the full life experience. Such an approach, as Sikes, Measor and Woods (1985, p. 13) have put it, 'is holistic, that is to say, concerned with a teacher's total life and career, and not just a segment or aspect of it'. These authors conclude by arguing that 'for a full understanding of teacher interests and motives, we need as near complete a biographical picture as we can acquire' (ibid.).

A number of cases have been made for adopting this approach in studying the lives of teachers. Waring (1979) has argued that the understanding of curriculum innovation is not possible without a history of context and she has alerted us to the importance of considering the extent to which the interpretation and execution of curriculum briefs reflect the background and personalities of the curriculum organizers chosen. Goodson (1992, p. 6), in examining the literature on teacher socialization, has also made a convincing case by highlighting the fact that the period of pre-service training and early in-service teaching has been designated as the most formative socializing influence. An alternative tradition, he argues, has insisted that the situation is far more complicated than this:

> Many studies in the 1970s and 1980s have focused on the teachers' own experience as pupils which is seen not only as important as the training period but in many cases more important. One way to follow up on this alternative tradition in teacher socialization research requires that we examine those socializing influences relevant to the formation of the teacher over the full life experience.
>
> (p. 6)

Elsewhere (Goodson, 1991, p. 144), he has argued as follows: 'There are critical incidents in the teachers' lives and specifically in their work which may crucially affect perception and practice.' Taken together, these two strands of the argument correspond with Butt *et al.*'s (1992, p. 51) position that 'interpretation of teachers' autobiographies identifies the nature, sources and manner of evolution of the special kind of thinking, action and knowledge that pertains to their teaching.' It is reasonable to argue that this position also pertains to the study of school principals.

Another characteristic of the approach adopted in this book is that it studies the life histories of school principals within a specific context, namely, Western Australia (WA). This recognition of context is important because while there is widespread restructuring of school systems in many parts of the world, the nature of this restructuring and the changing nature of the principalship is not exactly the same in any one of them. Accordingly, the purpose of the individual life histories which were undertaken was not to seek generalizations that could be applied broadly to other contexts. Rather, it was to seek enlightenment for effecting improvement. Such enlightenment can be provided by an examination of each case in its own right.

The third characteristic of the approach adopted in this book is its focus on a number of principals who were considered by educational administrators, peers and staff to be undertaking adventurous change programmes to improve the quality of curriculum, teaching and learning in their schools. Accordingly, the book offers a holistic perspective of restructuring where principals are seen in relation to both the internal and external contexts of their particular schools and also in relation to key events and influences in their own life histories. This

3

approach is novel and justifiable in that it holds potential for developing further the existing knowledge base regarding key relationships between principals, schools and the restructuring process.

The approach also has implications for the professional development of principals. In other words, an analysis of what innovative principals are doing, how they are doing it and why, could prove useful in the development of in-service programmes for others. At the same time, it can alert us to the fact that developing successful principals is not just a case of designing training programmes based on best practice. This is not to argue against the production of such programmes. Rather, it is to contend that on their own they are no guarantee of success.

Finally, it is important to alert the reader to the fact that the principals who are the focus of the case studies are not 'super' principals. Neither are they 'ordinary'. Rather, their leadership is characterized by a strong sense of, and track record in, innovation within system parameters. We believe that such a choice of principals will enable our readers to relate more successfully to their stories.

The book is organized in eleven chapters. Following this chapter, Chapter Two details the general contextual background. Chapter Three is a detailed exposition on life history methodology and on how it was utilized in this research project. The following six chapters outline the edited topical life histories of six principals. Chapter Ten consists of a discussion of the six case studies. Chapter Eleven presents a conclusion and also details some implications of the case studies for the professional development of principals. Throughout the book there are references to many places in WA. Apart from the city of Perth, most of the place names are pseudonyms. Pseudonyms are also used to protect the identity of the case study participants.

# 2

# THE BACKGROUND:
# RESTRUCTURING AND THE
# PRINCIPALSHIP

## INTRODUCTION

Restructuring of school systems has been taking place in much of the world over the last ten years. The focus of research to date has largely been on the administrative dimension of the phenomenon rather than on initiatives aimed at improving curriculum, teaching and learning. There is a growing acceptance internationally that there is a need to address this imbalance. There is also a need for research which takes cognizance of various contextual conditions. Furthermore, while it is widely acknowledged that the part which the school principal can play in managing the processes at the school level is a crucial factor in ensuring its successful implementation, research on the principalship has failed to keep pace with this changing context. Accordingly, there is a need for a variety of studies, like that reported in this book, which are aimed at understanding the various aspects of principals' work as part of current restructuring.

This chapter, by way of background to the study, presents, first, a brief exposition on restructuring *per se*, and the nature and form it has taken within an international, Australian and specifically WA context. This is followed by a general account tracing the changing focus of research on the principalship over the last five decades. Finally, consideration is given to the fact that a number of issues are in need of much greater treatment in the research literature as a result of the advent of the restructuring phenomenon. This provides the setting for the wide research agenda within which the life history project in the remaining chapters can be located.

## A BRIEF EXPOSITION ON RESTRUCTURING

### The nature of restructuring

Restructuring takes the form of a complex set of policies and processes (Malen, Ogawa and Kranz, 1990). It defies easy description and explanation since it assumes a different configuration in the educational systems where it is adopted. None the less, within the context of government school systems, restructuring has a number of common characteristics (Caldwell and Spinks, 1988, p. 5):

- there is a shift of power and responsibility in making certain kinds of decisions from a central authority to individual schools
- each school continues to work within a framework of legislation, policies and priorities determined by the central authority, hence schools remain part of a system
- the decision-making responsibility shifted to schools includes, *inter alia*, the allocation of resources, particularly with respect to human, financial, material and curriculum resources
- restructuring is a process evolving over time rather than an event. This makes it difficult and misleading to claim at any given time that it has happened and that no further change will occur.

The multi-dimensional nature of restructuring has spawned many complex policy issues. Restructuring policies may focus on empowering parents, principals, teachers, local community and employers. Dramatic changes in traditional roles, relationships and cultures are foreshadowed for all participant groups (Malen, Ogawa and Kranz, 1990). It is not surprising, therefore, that some governments have felt the need to introduce new education acts to accommodate the breadth of change envisaged.

At the heart of the restructuring process is the act of shifting decision-making responsibility closer to that level of the organization charged with service implementation and delivery. The reasons for such shifts may be multifarious. They include:

- managerial reasons – a better-quality decision made by practitioners aware of clients' needs; 'better quality' incorporating greater responsiveness of, commitment to, and accountability for, decisions
- economic reasons – people are inclined to be more thrifty when they are given responsibility for handling their own budgets; resource allocation can be more readily aligned with decisions
- political reasons – widening participation in decision making to include formerly excluded or non-participating groups, thereby changing power and influencing relations.

Given the eclecticism and diversity of restructuring, the task of adopting sets of policies which, considered together, achieve coherence, consistency and alignment, is a major difficulty for policymakers and practitioners. An important consequence of this is the inconsistency between aspects of restructuring policies and the incompatibility of effects that result. For example, underpinning the push for restructuring in many systems is the desire for a quality education provision based on principles of equity, effectiveness, participation, responsiveness and public accountability (Caldwell and Spinks, 1988; Department of Education, Queensland, 1990). These may be difficult principles to balance and achieve in concert. Similarly, in promoting effectiveness, there may be a trade-off with equity; in increasing participation, greater difficulty may be encountered in achieving responsiveness.

None the less, a legitimate way to frame restructuring is to consider the five principles which characteristically provide policy direction – equity, effectiveness, participation, responsiveness and accountability. Furthermore, there is a strong argument presented in the relevant literature that principles cannot be considered divorced from the purpose towards which they are aimed, namely, the provision of better-quality teaching and learning in schools. Accordingly, many argue that restructuring can only be justified if, ultimately, it leads to improvement in the quality of teaching and learning. Thus, it is necessary to consider the nature of this argument in some detail. However, before considering the relevant literature, a short exposition on explanations for current restructuring internationally is appropriate.

## Explanations for restructuring

There are at least five major explanations for the emergence of restructuring in education. First, political explanations are based on 'dissatisfaction theory' (Iannaccone and Lutz, 1978). There was a dissatisfied public opinion with standards and achievements in education in the 1980s. Politicians found it politically advantageous, therefore, to advocate better schools, which were more responsive to the needs and expectations of the public. This ideology was compatible with the renewed political strength of business interests in the 1980s.

Second, Caldwell and Spinks (1988), using Garms, Guthrie and Pierce's (1978) arguments, interpreted the politico-economic case for restructuring education as based on four values – equality, efficiency, liberty and choice. These writers contended that centralized budgeting, with relatively uniform resource allocation to schools, impairs the achievement of equality and efficiency, and by implication, choice. Their solution was to advocate school-site management, with lump-sum budgets allocated to schools, a high degree of community involvement in school decision making, and the fostering of diversity within and among schools to ensure choice (Caldwell and Spinks, 1988).

Third, Perrow (1970) used organization theory to suggest that the appropriate pattern of centralization and decentralization for an organization was determined by the nature of techniques and technology required to accomplish the work, and the nature of the organization's clients. Thus, the more schools are seen as organizations catering for diverse student needs, requiring more specialized teaching and learning, and a wider range of cognitive and affective skills, the more political decentralization is likely to be the appropriate structure. The work of Peters and Waterman (1982) showed that excellent companies combined centralization of core values with decentralization of

7

operational functions. Restructuring in education in a number of Australian states has created a situation where decisions regarding the goals and purposes are taken at the centre while decision making about the means by which these will be achieved has been decentralized, and there is accountability to those at the centre with regard to their achievement.

Fourth, the case for restructuring can be weakly justified on the basis of school effectiveness studies. Among the more acclaimed school effectiveness researchers, Purkey and Smith (1985), used meta-analysis to identify thirteen characteristics for school effectiveness. They concluded that in effective schools

> the staff of each school is given a considerable amount of responsibility and authority in determining the exact means by which they address the problem of increasing academic performances. This includes giving staff more authority over curricular and instructional decisions and allocation of building resources.
>
> (Ibid., p. 358)

Finally, a fifth explanation for restructuring focuses on the case for teacher professionalism and empowerment. Caldwell and Spinks (1988) noted that in the United States, for example, reports by the Carnegie Forum on Education and the Economy (1986) and the Holmes Group (1986) both advocated the goal of making schools better places for teachers in which to work and to learn; places where they could exert more professional autonomy and leadership.

## Justifying restructuring on the grounds of improving teaching and learning

Many question the need for the restructuring of school systems. Whether they be parents, principals, teachers or academics, there are many who, complacent or not, appear to be reasonably satisfied with the status quo. Why then, the need for change? Leaving aside the political and economic justifications for restructuring, it is possible to mount a convincing case on educational grounds, and in particular, on the need to reform the core concerns of schools, teaching and learning (Holly, 1990; Murphy, 1991). First, schools are themselves part of turbulent policy environments. Policy goals and statements commonly allude to the main aim of improving student learning outcomes. Many governments have established structures and procedures to render schools accountable for their students' academic performance. Schools are expected to define their purposes in school development plans and to render accountability in terms of student outcomes. Furthermore, system-wide monitoring of standards and student attainments in basic subject and skill areas, such as literacy and numeracy, enable ministries, schools and parents to measure and compare the performances of individual schools against system-wide norms. These demands on schools shift the focus away from a traditional concern with resource inputs to an outcomes orientation. Changing policy expectations thus render the maintenance of the status quo irrelevant, since schools need to search for greater effectiveness in securing improved student learning outcomes.

A second reason for focusing on change in teaching and learning arises out of the changing relationship between schooling and the broad long-term adjustments in society and the economy. For example, there is the argument that the type of workforce needed for the future will require school and college programmes to reflect the competencies and skills required in competitive global economies. Schlechty (1990) refers to the shift of American society in the late twentieth century from an industrial base to an information base and describes his vision of schools to meet this change for the twenty-first century. In an information-based society, knowledge work, namely, work that entails expending mental effort, is the primary mode of work, since information constitutes the main means for its accomplishment. Elmore (1990), adopting such a perspective, has called for major reform of the American school system, arguing that

> in order to sustain our present standard of living and regain our competitive position in the world economy... we will need a better educated work force, which will in turn, mean that schools will have to dramatically improve the way they educate all children.
>
> (Ibid., pp.1–2)

A new wave of educational thinking in the 1990s reinforces this reconceptualization of teaching and learning. American scholars in particular recognize a shift from behavioural psychology, which has been the source of thinking underpinning the traditional industrial model of schooling, to social cognitive or constructivist psychology as the inspiration for a new model of learning and teaching in the post-industrial information society (Cohen, 1988; Murphy, 1991).

Third, there is every indication that present trends in social problems such as alcoholism, drug abuse, crime, vandalism and family break-down will continue to rise in the foreseeable future. An increasing number of school students are likely to be directly or indirectly affected by these trends. If schools are simply to keep pace with, let alone seriously address, these growing problems and their implications for teaching and learning, they will need to shift from their established cultures and practices.

Fourth, there is growing concern that too many students leave school with little or no success in learning after ten or more years of schooling (Goodlad, 1984; Sizer, 1984). Murphy (1991, p. 52), referring to the United States, claims that 'twenty-five per cent of all students physically remove themselves from engagement in learning by dropping out of school'. Of those students who stay, many fail to achieve the school graduation certificate. While it has been customary to blame students for failure to learn, the spotlight is increasingly shifting to the school and its responsibilities to ensure that learning takes place (Chubb, 1988). Many disaffected students report negative attitudes towards school, finding them unfriendly and uncaring places, unreflective of their values, interests and cultures (Cuban, 1989).

A fifth reason arises out of the relative rigidity of schools with respect to changing pedagogical approaches. Some observers claim current schools bear many similarities to their counterparts in the last century. Elmore (1990, p. 8), for example, describes classroom activity for the average student as 'dull, perfunctory and disconnected from what goes on in other classrooms or in the larger community'. Faced with impossible odds of educating batches of thirty mixed-ability children, teachers lower their expectations of student learning or focus on smaller groups of more able students who provide them with some job satisfaction. With notable exceptions, the curriculum is still delivered in regimented ways, for fixed periods of time unrelated to individual students' learning needs, and students still move in lock-step to the next age grade, irrespective of their performance.

Finally, a growing awareness of social justice issues, particularly pertinent for minority groups and the educationally disadvantaged, is adding an extra dimension to the need for schooling to be reshaped. Increasingly, the goal is to improve the learning of all students and to recognize the entitlements of all to a quality learning experience relevant to abilities, needs and interests (Levin, 1987; Slavin, 1988). Pressures for regular and mainstream schools and classes to accommodate students with learning disabilities and behavioural problems serve only to exacerbate the problem, as do policies espousing equity and protection of the rights of minority and underprivileged groups. Schools are increasingly expected, therefore, to cater for the learning needs of all students at a time when the student body is growing more multicultural and diverse. This is particularly apposite in the case of Australia where, as the next section demonstrates, restructuring has been underway in some states since the 1970s.

## THE HISTORICAL BACKGROUND TO RESTRUCTURING IN AUSTRALIA

For three-quarters of the twentieth century Australian state systems of education were characterized by high degrees of centralized control. During this period a number of prominent overseas educators (Butts, 1955; Kandel, 1938) commented adversely on the overly centralized character of Australian state education. The influential Karmel Report (Interim Committee for the Australian Schools Commission, 1973) espoused, as one of its key values, 'the devolution of responsibility to schools':

> The Committee favours less rather than more centralized control over the operation of schools. Responsibility should be devolved as far as possible upon the people involved in the actual task of schooling, in consultation with the parents of the pupils whom they teach and at the senior levels with the students themselves. Its belief in this grass roots approach to the

control of schools reflects a conviction that responsibility will be most effectively discharged where the people entrusted with making decisions are also the people responsible for carrying them out, with an obligation to justify them and in a position to profit from their experiences.

(Ibid., p. 10)

The three major outcomes of the Karmel Report were an erosion of the monopoly of the state bureaucracies (largely through the establishment of the Commonwealth Schools Commission), a move towards decentralized and more personal styles of educational management and a refurbishment of school syllabuses and teaching styles, stressing relevance, child-centredness, personal development and more humane relationships between staff and students. While the Karmel Report provided justification for, and pointed the way towards, devolution and decentralization, its recommendations were heavily dependent on the development of a new tier of bureaucracy at the Commonwealth level, the Commonwealth Schools Commission. The Commission was established to provide for the needs of the disadvantaged and to encourage diversity and innovation in schools, curricula and teaching. It is somewhat paradoxical that this early seeding of the notion of devolution and decentralization was accompanied by a significant increase in bureaucratic governance at the Commonwealth level. This bureaucratic tier had as its major purpose the injection of resources through, *inter alia,* special programmes, such as the Priority Schools Programme and the Innovations Programme. For the next twelve years, up to the mid-1980s, the Schools Commission produced many reports emphasizing collaborative school-based decision making and local community involvement.

In the mid-1980s, a major change in political values swept the whole public sector, including education. A number of national and state government policy documents, including *Quality of Education in Australia* (Quality of Education Review Committee, 1985), were published, all of which were underpinned by a strong politico-administrative ideology that had been sweeping through much of North America and Europe (Pusey, 1991; Wilenski, 1986). Economic rationalism and corporate managerialism were about to shape the restructuring of Australian education.

A major reason for this change in policies derived from economic difficulties in the 1980s, which led to an examination of the contribution made by education to the economy and an assessment of the quality of schooling. The establishment of the Quality of Education Review Committee (QERC, 1985) to gauge 'value for money' from federal expenditure on education and to gear the education system more closely to labour market needs signalled an end to growth in federal spending. The dramatic shift in values between the Karmel Report (Interim Committee for the Australian Schools Commission, 1973) of 1973, and the QERC (on which Karmel sat in 1985), is aptly described by Smart (1988, p. 17): 'Thus, unlike the Karmel Report (Interim Committee for

11

the Australian Schools Commission, 1973), which was primarily concerned with financial and educational inputs, QERC was required to establish that there were identifiable educational outcomes from federal aid'. The change from a concern with inputs during the relatively prosperous 1970s to a focus on outcomes during the financially stringent 1980s is starkly evident.

Soon after the QERC Report came the Government of Western Australia's White Paper, *Managing Change in the Public Sector* (Western Australia. Parliament, 1986), which outlined the problems facing most state governments in the 1980s, namely, balancing community demands for more and improved services with policies of tight budgetary restraint (Dimmock, 1990). The White Paper delineated a number of key principles for reform in the public sector, including responsiveness and adaptability to the needs of the community, flexibility in the use of resources, and accountability and responsibility to government for standards of service and funding. Efficiency and effectiveness became the prime objectives, although there was also some attention given to equity.

During this period, in WA, the newly elected Burke Labour Government had initiated an extensive review of education in what was perhaps the most centralized state education system in the country (Smart and Alderson, 1980). The subsequent report, *Education in Western Australia* (Report of the Committee of Inquiry into Education in Western Australia, 1984) recommended wide-ranging educational reforms, including the provision of greater community participation in school decision making. As a consequence of these pressures the reformist Minister for Education, Robert Pearce, requested the Western Australian Government Functional Review Committee to review the education portfolio in order to streamline the structure of the Education Department and to improve co-ordination and resource management across the portfolio (Western Australia. Functional Review Committee, 1986). The result was *Better Schools in Western Australia: A Programme for Improvement* (Western Australia. Ministry of Education, 1987), a report which developed the rationale that good schools create a good system. This was the blueprint for restructuring the school system in Western Australia, based on devolving authority and decentralizing responsibilities to a future system of self-determining schools with community participation. Emphasis was placed on decentralizing responsibilities to principals and teachers, devolving power to school councils and making school personnel more accountable to both their local communities through school councils, and to government through performance monitoring and auditing. Similar moves to restructure education, in the form of decentralization and devolution, took place in all Australian state education systems in the late 1980s and are still evolving through the 1990s.

In the second half of the 1990s, the 'centre' in WA still retains absolute control over staffing, has considerable power over policy and guidelines (especially for the curriculum) and has devolved much administration to local schools. At the same time, it expects more accountability from schools. In this respect, the system is probably more 'centralized' than ever in the history of education management in WA. In becoming 'decentralized' by offering schools more discretionary powers over how to achieve the state-set goals with respect to the state-set curriculum, however, the forces of decentralization and centralization sometimes coexist in the three major decision-making areas of curriculum, human resources and finance. The WA system is more accurately described as increasing school-based initiatives with regard to methods of learning. It is likely to be a long evolutionary process before political decentralization of curriculum, staffing and finance becomes a reality in WA schools. Devolution, in the form of less empowered school decision-making bodies rather than more empowered school councils, is also proceeding slowly.

Finally, in the WA education system, as in most others, particular emphasis has been placed on the role of the school principal in the translation of restructuring initiatives into practice. However, while advice to principals in this regard has not been lacking, relatively little of it has been based on contemporary studies. This is understandable since, even though a significant body of literature exists on the principalship, restructuring has brought about a situation whereby the school principal must now operate in a context which has changed markedly over the last few years. Accordingly, it is instructive at this point to present, by way of further background, a general account tracing the changing focus of research on the principalship over the last five decades.

## THE CHANGING FOCUS OF RESEARCH ON THE PRINCIPALSHIP

In promoting understanding of the current state of literature on the principalship, and in particular, its relation to recent changes in educational, political, sociological and economic environments, it is instructive to sketch a portrait of the different and recognizable developments which have characterized the field over the past fifty years. Taking this span of time, it is possible to recognize seven major phases as having characterized research on leadership in general and the principalship in particular. These phases have mostly been concerned with such matters as definition of leadership, recognition of its importance, and differences in approach to, and clarification of, successful or effective leadership. In briefly outlining the seven phases, it should be acknowledged that they represent a somewhat general view of the major research drives and are not all-encompassing in respect of the totality of research focusing on leadership and the principalship during the period in question. It has also to be realized that as each phase was succeeded by the next, interest in previous phases of leadership research did not necessarily disappear or die. In the immediate post-World War II period, leadership studies focused on searching for traits which leaders (including school principals), as distinct from non-leaders, displayed. Stogdill (1950), for example, tentatively proposed that leaders are characterized by above-average intelligence, dependability, scholarship, participation and status. However, he added that 'a person does not become a leader by virtue of the possession of some combination of traits. . . . The pattern of personal characteristics of the leaders must bear some relevant relationship to the characteristics, activities and goals of the followers' (ibid., p. 4). In general, the attempt to identify generic traits possessed by leaders failed. There were seemingly as many characteristics as there were leaders. However, a breakthrough in the traits approach came in the 1970s, when attention focused on its application as a means of improving the selection process of future managers. This shifted the traits approach from a concern to compare leaders and non-leaders to comparing leader traits to leader effectiveness (Yukl, 1981). The trait approach continues, but with an emphasis on exploring the relationship between traits and the leadership effectiveness of administrators. A generally accepted result of Stogdill's (1981) research in the 1970s is that personality is an important factor in effective leadership. He argues that the leader is characterized by a strong drive for responsibility and task completion, vigour and persistence in pursuit of goals, venturesomeness and originality in problem solving, a drive to exercise initiative in social situations, self-confidence and a sense of personal identity, willingness to accept consequences of decision and action, readiness to absorb interpersonal stress, willingness to tolerate frustration and delay, ability to influence other persons' behaviour, and a capacity to structure interaction systems to the purpose at hand.

The traits approach clearly has relevance for a study adopting a life history methodology. This is particularly so given that it has moved away from the assumption that 'leaders are born, not made'. Rather, as Hoy and Miskel (1987) state, the approach now takes a more balanced view that acknowledges the interplay of both leader and follower traits within given situations, the characteristics of which may well influence the leadership process. Leadership has thus come to be regarded as a social transactional process between leaders and followers within the particularities of given contexts and situations.

While the early phase of the traits approach in the 1940s and 1950s was seen to have limited validity in leadership research, it was accompanied at about the same time by something of a breakthrough with the emergence of what can be termed 'the second leadership phase'. During the 1940s, Hemphill and Coons (1950) at Ohio State University became interested in leader behaviour. They developed the now famous leader behaviour description questionnaire (LBDQ). The instrument was later refined by others, including Halpin and Winer (1952). A consequence of their research was that two main dimensions of leader behaviour were recognized – initiating structure and consideration. 'Initiating structure' included any leader behaviour that delineated the relationship between the leader and subordinates, and involved defined patterns of organization, channels of communication and methods of procedure. 'Consideration', on the other hand, included leader behaviour that indicated friendship, trust, warmth, interest and respect in the relationship

14

between the leader and members of the work group. Among the many conclusions drawn from the research was that effective leader behaviour, unsurprisingly, tends to be associated with high performance on both dimensions. Subsequent studies using the same instruments with principals confirm that effective principal leader behaviour, as judged by degree of acceptance of leader behaviour among followers, tends to be associated with both high initiating structure and high consideration behaviour on the part of the principal (Kunz and Hoy, 1976). From the 1960s on, Blake and Mouton (1985) refined the two-dimensional approach to leader behaviour. Through their leadership training seminars they presented their 'managerial grid', consisting of two dimensions – a concern for people along one axis, and a concern for production along the other. The grid, a 9 × 9 graph, depicted eighty-one possible combinations of leader behaviours. The grid extended the Ohio State University studies by recognizing more leadership behaviours and styles. It confirms that high performance on both dimensions is the optimum leadership pattern. These two dimensions to leadership, which still find widespread acceptance in the literature, remain the bases of much theorizing, research and writing on leadership in general and the principalship in particular.

The two-dimensional approach to leadership studies led to the emergence of a third phase in the 1970s, in which there was a spawning of theories and empirical research on leadership style, appropriate styles for particular situations and leaders' capacities to adapt their styles to those contexts. Most of these theories were developed with corporate leaders in mind, but they soon provided a rich source of ideas for application to school principals. Among the most influential of these are the so-called 'contingency' theories, including Fiedler's (1973) work, and 'situational' theories, of which Hersey and Blanchard's (1977) is particularly noteworthy.

Contingency theories of leadership maintain that leadership effectiveness depends on the fit between personality characteristics and behaviour of the leader, and situational variables such as task structure, position power and subordinates' skills and attitudes. Thus, there is no one 'best' leadership style. The contingency approach attempts to predict which types of leaders will be effective in different types of situations. The gist of Fiedler's theory is that leadership style is determined by the motivational system of the leader and group effectiveness is a function of the leader's style and the situation's favourableness; that is, group performance is contingent on the leader's motivations and on the leader's control and influence in the situation. The leadership situation is viewed as an arena in which the leader seeks to satisfy both personal needs and to accomplish organizational goals (Hoy and Miskel, 1987). Support for Fiedler's theory has materialized from studies of school principals utilizing the approach. Such studies have found that in schools where principals are well supported by teachers, a task-oriented style is associated with group effectiveness. In schools with principals less well supported by teachers, there is a tendency for a relationship-oriented style to be associated with school effectiveness.

The situational theory of Hersey and Blanchard, developed in the 1970s and since refined, supports the idea that leader behaviour and style must be responsive to the 'maturity' of the follower group. In other words, leaders should vary their style of leadership according to the experience and competence of the individuals and groups for whom they are responsible and with whom they have to work. Thus, when the group is immature, a task-oriented leadership style is most effective; when the group is moderately immature, a high task–high relationship style is most appropriate; when the group is moderately mature, a relationship-oriented leadership style is most effective; and when the group is very mature, a delegating style (low task–low relationship) is most appropriate. As group maturity changes over time, so should the leader's style. While the situational theory remains particularly popular and influential in principals' training programmes, there have been few empirical studies to test the validity of the theory.

Concurrently with the development of style theories in the 1960s and 1970s, a fourth phase of leadership research witnessed the development of an expansive literature, largely of a sociological nature, which applied role theory and its well developed conceptual framework to the principalship. Undergirding this approach was the realization of a dramatic transformation taking place at that time in the role of the headteacher. The traditional role had been one of benevolent patriarch; the all-powerful male father figure caring for and controlling his 'family', the school. By the 1960s, the traditional model was breaking down. The model of the business manager was proposed as its replacement. Adopting such a perspective, Hughes (1976) sought to recognize the secondary school principal as a professional in an administrator role. Appealing to the earlier work of Abrahamson (1967), Blau and Scott (1963) and Etzioni (1964), he identified two antithetical sets of cultures, the one aligned to professional codes of conduct and beliefs, the other aligned with administrator values and behaviours. For Hughes, developments in the principal's role were tending to place secondary school principals in particular in a dilemma; they were at one and the same time leading professionals and chief executives of professionally staffed organizations. The only solution, according to Hughes, was for principals as professionals to become administrators. This dichotomy is still regarded as relevant to an understanding of the principal's role in the 1990s. It is currently highlighted in the tension acknowledged by principals to exist between their role as educational leader on the one hand and as business leader on the other. The raised expectations placed on schools to achieve better-quality teaching and improved student learning outcomes on the one hand, and the added responsibility placed on principals as a result of restructuring, school-based management and devolved financial and personnel responsibilities on the other, has, if anything, exacerbated this dilemma.

While the educator–administrator dichotomy in the principal's role continued to attract attention during and beyond the 1980s, it was somewhat overshadowed by the emergence of a fifth phase, which had as its research agenda the concept of the principal as instructional leader. In one sense, and with hindsight, this could be interpreted as a reaction to the emphasis being placed at that time on the business management aspect of the principalship. However, the instructional leadership research aligned closely with, and emanated from, the emergence in the late 1970s and early 1980s of what proved to be the influential school effectiveness movement (Purkey and Smith, 1985). One of the major conclusions from school effectiveness studies emphasized the instrumental role played by principals in the success of their schools, provided that they adopted an instructional leadership role.

Many scholars attempted to define instructional leadership behaviours and characteristics. The outcome was usually a long list of responsibilities and skills aimed at providing an effective teaching/learning environment. Since most aspects of schools impact on the teaching/learning environment, principals as instructional leaders were exhorted to take on responsibility, either directly or indirectly, for functions as diverse as clinical classroom supervision of teachers, feedback to students and teachers, provision and allocation of resources in ways which would support effective instructional practices, appropriate staff selection and development and the creation of a supportive and positive school climate. Very little, in truth, was excluded. Eventually, dissatisfaction with, and growing awareness of the limitations of, instructional leadership research, led Hallinger and Murphy (1987) to the conclusion that research designs linking principal leadership and school effectiveness were weak in the following ways: they were unclear as to whether effective schools made strong principals or vice versa; they were snapshots in time and as such failed to look at the longitudinal process by which principals promote change in student and teacher achievement; they were biased in their sampling procedures, concentrating mostly on poor, urban, elementary schools; and they rarely defined instructional leadership in concrete operational terms. At its worst, the instructional leadership research prescribed long lists of behaviours for principals to adopt, regardless of their contexts, in the pursuit of school effectiveness and improvement. It became difficult to escape the view that these limitations of the research base created obstacles to drawing firm conclusions about the impact of principal instructional leadership.

As the 1980s drew to a close, two further developments in research on the principalship were discernible. Both of these developments were significant in that they represented a shift away from a school effectiveness orientation to, first, a school improvement focus, and then, second, a restructuring orientation. Both developments can accurately be regarded as constituting a sixth phase of principalship research, since they are both underpinned by the key notion of the principal as manager of change, itself an endemic feature of improvement and restructuring. Shifting the focus of principal leadership research from instructional leadership to leadership of change and innovation not only coincided with a growing awareness of the limitations of school effectiveness/principal effectiveness studies, but with a strong surge of government policies around the world to change, improve and restructure schools. The research agenda with regard to the principalship responded accordingly. Focus on the principalship was redirected to the need for, and abilities of, principals to lead the change process in their school communities. The underlying motives for schools to restructure were multifarious, as indicated elsewhere in this chapter.

Central to the realization of the growing importance of the principal as leader, manager and agent of change is the emphasis placed in this particular wave of principalship research on transformational leadership. Leithwood, Begley and Bradley Cousins (1994) define transformational leadership as 'the ability to empower others, something often accomplished from the rear of the band', with the purpose of transforming, that is, accomplishing, a 'major change in form, nature and function of some phenomenon'; in a leadership context, it 'specifies general ends to be pursued, although it is largely mute with respect to means' (ibid., p. 7). They continue:

> from this beginning, we consider the central purpose of transformational leadership to be the enhancement of individual and collective problem-solving capacities of organisational members; such capacities are exercised in the identification of goals to be achieved and practices to be used in their achievement.
>
> (Ibid., p. 8)

Bennis and Nanus (1985, p. 217) describe transformative leaders as shaping and elevating the motives and goals of followers. They go on to emphasize the collective nature of transformational leadership and the symbolic relationship between leaders and followers. It is collective and symbolic in the sense that leaders must focus on organizational goals, while at the same time taking account of the needs and wants of their staff. Ultimately, as Coleman and LaRocque (1989) recognize, transformational leadership is about culture-changing and the strategies employed by leaders to secure it. Contemporary research on transformational leadership thus focuses on these aspects in regard to school improvement.

Concurrent with the research focus on the principal as transformational leader is the emergence of a socio-psychological approach to research on the principalship, exemplified by various cognitive studies (Hallinger, Leithwood and Murphy, 1993). This current focus grew from a realization of the limitations of previous research foci on principal behaviours and practices which ignored the matter of how leaders adapt to the complex contexts in which they work. What was needed was an understanding of the thinking that accompanied such practices and behaviours. Consequently, a thrust of contemporary principal research draws its inspiration, in particular, from the field of cognitive psychology. In attempting to understand how principals think and make sense and meaning of their work environment, that is, their social construction of reality, this research is drawing on broad perspectives such as symbolic interaction, as well as more specific fields, such as the psychology of learning, cognitive theory underlying problem solving, the creation of knowledge and its daily use and the importance of context. By taking cognizance of principals' intentions, beliefs, values, knowledge and actions, the approach is beginning to address the 'why' and 'how' questions, as well as the 'when' and 'where', as to why principals do what they do.

A strong appeal of such research is the diverse outcomes to which it apparently leads. Not only does it begin to open up areas of investigation, such as why and how principals do what they do, the problems and dilemmas experienced in performing their work and how they set about solving or coping with such problems, but it also holds considerable promise for contributing to the reshaping and improving of training programmes aimed at preparing better administrators. On the cautious side, there are possible limitations to the sociopsychological approach. As Cuban (1993, p. xi) has observed, there may be a danger of reductionism:

> What administrators do depends on what they think. While such a position is a worthy corrective to behavioral theories and prescriptions that denied even the merit of an administrator's intentions, values and beliefs, it nonetheless ignores the impact of political, organizational and cultural factors in shaping administrative behavior.

In so saying, Cuban has perhaps provided a clear pointer as to the need for more diverse, comprehensive and eclectic directions for principalship research in future.

In concluding this section tracing the changing focus of research on the principalship over the last five decades, a number of major themes are identifiable. First, much of the literature, which tends to be prescriptive, is not based on empirical findings. Second, a significant proportion of the empirical work which exists has been generated using research methods and conceptual frameworks in the positivist tradition. Third, the tendency for studies to be of a statistical nature dealing with samples of populations is not balanced by in-depth empirical studies of individual principals. Fourth, there has been a tendency to ignore both particular contextual conditions and the holistic standpoint which would take cognizance of the dynamic between the principal and the particular environment. Finally, research on the principalship has failed to keep pace with the contemporary restructuring context. These characteristics of previous research on the principalship have been instrumental in setting the research agenda for the life history project reported in this book.

## EMERGING ISSUES RELATING TO THE PRINCIPALSHIP AND CONTEMPORARY RESTRUCTURING

A host of issues that have arisen as a result of the advent of the restructuring phenomenon are in need of much greater treatment in the research literature. One such issue concerns school-based management and the emphasis placed on the individual school as the fundamental decision-making unit within the education system (Guthrie, 1986). All levels of an education system, from the large central bureaucracies to the school and even parent and community levels, are alleged to benefit from restructuring in the form of decentralization and devolution (White, 1989). Recent Australian history, however, has seen changes led more by political motives for less expenditure and more account-ability in the infrastructure of education (Smart, 1988) than by reasoned and researched arguments related to the educational benefits passed on to students. In this regard, the lack of local research and discussion of overseas research prior to the adoption of major policy change in WA, as elsewhere in Australia, is noteworthy.

Whatever the exact motives may be, there are several major positive outcomes that are cited as arising from decentralization and devolution. Brown (1990), after conducting a series of interviews with principals and administrators, concluded that a change to school-based management implies flexibility in decision making, changes in role accountability and the potential enhancement of school productivity. He argued that flexibility in decision making allows initiatives to be taken and long-term planning to be encouraged, while the ability to respond immediately to educational problems is best achieved if control of the resources needed to make a response is closest to the problem. Because principals and teachers have to implement decisions and live with the consequences, thus, the argument runs, it is preferable to have localized decision making as principals and teachers are best able to diagnose students' needs, since they have direct contact with students and access to local information (Beare, 1983; White, 1989). In a similar vein, Knight (1984) concluded that greater discretion over curriculum development at the school site enabled school staff to select instructional materials and methods and to develop curricula that were most appropriate to the needs of their students. In this way, school-based management promises the ability to improve the quality of teaching and student learning.

It is customary to assume that devolution means that central office staff would have less direct authority over schools, while principals would have more control over many kinds of school resources. In addition, increased staff participation could be expected to bring about enthusiasm, interest, commit-ment and effectiveness. In this regard, White (1989) has argued that devolution may improve self-esteem, morale and efficiency of all school personnel. Devolution may also enhance the professionalism of teachers as it empowers them with the authority, responsibility and accountability associated with a professional rank (Caldwell and Spinks, 1988; Hunter, 1989). Principals also believe that schools would be more productive the more school-based management is adopted (Brown, 1990; Goodlad, 1984).

A key argument of those defending restructuring is that parental participation can encourage staff to be more analytical in school matters, and that one outcome of this is improved communication between the school staff and the local school community (White, 1989). A decentralized and devolved system is believed to be more responsive and adaptive to the needs of the community. It is also believed that as schools experience more responsibility for curriculum decision making, improvements in teaching and learning will result. Studies by Brown (1990) and Kowalski (1980) found that many teachers acknowledged the value of the broader perspective offered by members of the wider educational community in their contribution to school affairs.

Notwithstanding the many benefits which, it is argued, can arise from decentralization and devolution, there is much confusion and anxiety associated with the transition period involved in bringing it about. The process of changing to school-based management may create confusion in roles and responsibilities (White, 1989). Principals in devolving systems may assume, for the first time, dual accountabilities both to central office administrators and to the community. As the shift from a hitherto centralized system to school-based management is an evolutionary process, the roles and expectations of principals, teachers and parents are necessarily in a state of continuous flux. Principals, teachers, parents and students may have difficulty adapting to new roles and new lines of communication and consequently may experience considerable role ambiguity. The process of adaptation demands new skills which many participants do not possess. More than a century of exclusion from educational policymaking in an otherwise tightly centralized system has left a legacy of community and parental inexperience which often seems to result in feelings of inadequacy and a reluctance currently to become involved now that opportunity presents itself (Smart, 1988).

Accordingly, the restructuring process has marked implications for the principal who is expected, perhaps for the first time, to draw on a multitude of roles and skills, particularly in the personnel field, rather than rely on bureaucratic direction, as in the past (Handy, 1985; Duignan, 1990). Technical skills such as school-based budgeting techniques, short-term and long-term goal setting and policy planning, time management and the art of delegation must be mastered if the ever-increasing demands of a more devolved education system are to be successfully met. Also, school-based management may lead to a power struggle between principals, teachers, parents and students (White, 1989). Although the principals' decision-making arena has expanded, they are now required to work with new participants who may hold very different values. This calls for heightened political and negotiating skills on their part in order to achieve consensus between diverse groups, leading forcefully from the front on some occasions and steering quietly from behind on others.

There is also a fear that an emphasis on productivity and efficiency may turn the principal and teacher into technicians (Brown, 1990). Some teachers anticipate that there will be a shift in the principal's role, from the supervision of instruction to supervision of the fiscal operation of the school. A loss of collegiality and professionalism may result as principals become more like business managers. Accordingly, despite the rationale for, and much acclaimed benefits of, decentralization, it is not difficult to envisage the problems in moving from an entrenched centralized system. Community and parental inexperience and feelings of inadequacy in relation to participation in school affairs, and changes in the tasks and roles of principals and teachers would suggest that the achievement of self-governing schools is likely to be a long, challenging and evolutionary process. The simultaneous demands for excellence and quality, for economic restraint and accountability, and for an adaptive and responsive system able to meet the needs of a rapidly changing technological society, also contribute to the complexity of the change process.

Finally, there have been relatively few research studies on the reactions of teachers and principals to the current trends towards devolution of control to individual schools in government systems. Little has been written about the experiences and reactions of those who have adopted and implemented school-based management responsibilities. It is likely that greater knowledge of the reactions of teachers and principals, who are expected to implement policy at the school level, will provide insight into the difficulties of transforming entrenched attitudes and practices.

Overall, most studies of principals' and teachers' reactions to restructuring reveal an acceptance of the general philosophy and set of ideas underpinning it. There is some evidence to suggest that many would not wish to return to pre-restructuring times. At the same time, some express dissatisfaction with the political agenda, the pace of change and the lack of resources provided to support their efforts. It also has to be admitted that the research base in support of restructuring in the form of school-based management aimed at improving the quality of teaching and learning is extremely sketchy. What can be acknowledged, however, is that decentralized rather than centralized systems seem to provide greater scope and opportunity for much-needed reform in curriculum, teaching and learning to take place. Whether or not these opportunities are seized, however, is another matter.

## CONCLUSION

This chapter has centred on the phenomenon of restructuring which has been taking place in many school systems throughout the world, including those in Australia, over the last ten years. Among its themes, it has highlighted the importance of the role of the school principal in managing processes involved in restructuring in order to ensure its successful implementation. It is also argued that a variety of studies on the principalship are necessary at the present time, since the context within which contemporary school principals must operate has changed markedly with respect to restructuring. A variety of foci and research approaches suggest themselves. The research project outlined in the remainder of this book focuses on the work of six innovative principals in state high schools in WA and how they are responding to the demands placed upon them over recent years. The methodology adopted was that of edited topical life history. Before outlining the results of this project it is appropriate to present an account of this methodology. Accordingly, the next chapter addresses the matter in detail.

# 3

# METHODOLOGY

## INTRODUCTION

The context of the case studies reported in this book, as indicated in the previous chapter, is the educational restructuring which is taking place in Western Australia. Within WA, particular emphasis is placed on the role of the principal in implementing restructuring policies, many of which involve initiatives aimed at improving curriculum, teaching and learning. The centrality of principals in the leadership and management of change puts a premium on the existing knowledge base as to how and why some principals cope more successfully than others. However, studies on the principalship have not kept pace with the changing context within which schools need to be managed. The existing knowledge base appears surprisingly incomplete with respect to the relationship between the principalship, individual principals and the management of restructuring. In particular, there has been little research which has studied the relationships and connections between individual principals, their approaches to managing school restructuring and change and their personal backgrounds and life histories which might provide at least partial explanations for the connections. Meanwhile, the social, economic and political environment within which principals are expected to lead and manage schools is undergoing dramatic change and has been doing so for some time.

Accordingly, the aim of the case studies in this book is to contribute to the existing knowledge base by using the edited topical life history approach to investigate the relationship between principals' life histories and the initiatives they are taking to improve curriculum, teaching and learning in their schools. A number of cases for adopting this approach in studying the lives of teachers has already been made elsewhere (Waring, 1979; Goodson, 1991, 1992). In general, they correspond to Butt *et al.*'s (1992) position that interpretation of teachers' autobiographies identifies the nature, sources and manner of evolution of the special kind of thinking, action and knowledge that pertains to their teaching. It is reasonable to argue that this position also applies to the study of school principals.

To adopt the life history approach to the study of principals is to take one step further Ribbins and Sherratt's (1992, p. 153) proposal that studies of the principalship could benefit from adopting a biographical and autobiographical approach. Thus, what was sought in relation to each of the case studies reported in subsequent chapters was not only the development of an account of a school and the role of the principal within it which integrates the perspectives of both the principal and the researcher, but also an understanding of this role by examining the socializing influences relevant to the formation of the principal over the full life experience. This chapter outlines the theoretical framework underpinning such a research approach. It then goes on to give an exposition on the forms of data collection and analyses which were utilized in the study in the light of this framework.

## THEORETICAL FRAMEWORK

This book highlights the need at a time of educational restructuring to develop in the case of principals a tradition which owes its origins in educational research to a movement of the late 1970s which 'fully opened up the question of how teachers saw their work and their lives' (Goodson, 1992, pp. 3–4). Accordingly, when initially deciding to study the work and effect of a number of principals in WA who are undertaking change programmes to improve the quality of curriculum, teaching and learning in their schools, particular consideration was given to the need to generate a richness of data. This, it was felt, was necessary so that patterns which exhibited the interaction between the creativity of the principals as agents and the structure within which they operated could, if they existed, be identified. Thus, the study took its theoretical impetus from that stream of qualitative research known as symbolic interaction.

At the heart of symbolic interaction are three principles which govern, and in turn are governed by, beliefs about the nature of the self, of meaning and of symbols. The three principles, as formulated by Henry Blumer (1962, p. 2), are as follows:

(1) Human beings do not simply respond to stimuli or act out cultural scripts. Rather, they act towards things on the basis of the meanings that the things have for them. Blumer uses 'things' to cover a range of phenomena, from the concrete (people, material objects and institutions) to the abstract, which includes the situations in which people find themselves and the principles that guide human life. Thus, people are, for Blumer (1969, p. 55), volitional, not mere responding organisms but rather acting organisms who have to cope with and handle factors, and in so doing have to forge and direct their line of action; meanings determine action. However, as Blackledge and Hunt (1991, p. 235) put it, 'in interpretive theory, the term "meaning" is complex and often undefined'. At the same time, this is not to say that it is undefinable. They suggest that it includes the idea of what one aims to do with regard to a particular phenomenon, the significance of the phenomenon to the individual, and the reasons one gives for one's activity. Furthermore, this theory, they

argue, assumes that the meanings are personal to the individual; 'they are not given by culture or society, rather they are constructed from culture by the actors involved' (ibid.).

(2) Because everyday activity usually consists of interaction with other people, we give meaning to the activity of others as well as give meaning to our own action; 'the meaning of a thing for a person grows out of the ways in which other persons act towards the person with regard to the thing' (Taylor and Bogdan, 1984, p. 9). In other words, people learn how to see the world from other people. Woods (1992, p. 338) states that this is a 'continuous process'. Thus, for the symbolic interactionist, the meaning each thing, whether it is abstract or concrete, has for one, is not fixed. Rather, it is constantly adjusted by new information of all kinds. This new meaning has its effect on human acts. Thus, meaning is acquired from one's experience of the world and because one is in constant engagement with the world that meaning may constantly be modified, if not completely changed.

(3) 'Meanings' according to Blumer (1969, p. 2), 'are handled in, and modified through, an interpretive process used by the person in dealing with the things he encounters.' He says there are two steps in this process. First, one points out to oneself the things that have meaning. Interpretation then becomes a matter of handling meanings. One selects, checks, suspends, regroups and transforms the meaning in the light of the situation in which one is placed and the direction of one's action. Furthermore, as Woods (1992, p. 338) points out, while 'our interpretive scheme may be shared by all people, it may be associated with only one group or even be personal'.

Meltzer, Petras and Reynolds (1975, p. 1) summarize the position as follows:

Thus, 'symbolic interaction' is the interaction that takes place among the various minds and meanings that characterize human societies. It refers to the fact that social interaction rests upon a taking of oneself (self-objectification) and others (taking the role of the other) into account.

They go on to argue that the most basic element in this image of human beings is the idea that the individual and society are inseparable units; that while it may be possible to separate the units analytically, the underlying assumption is that a complete understanding of either one demands a complete understanding of the other. They then highlight the following:

In the interactionist image ... the behaviour of men and women is 'caused' not so much by forces within themselves (instincts, drives, needs, etc.) but by what lies in between, a reflective and socially derived interpretation of the internal and external stimuli that are present.

(Ibid., p. 2)

Ritzer (1983) develops the position of Blumer, one of the originators of modern *symbolic interaction*, as follows:

To Blumer, behaviorism and structural functionalism both tended to focus on factors (for example, external stimuli and norms) that cause behavior. As far as Blumer was concerned, both ignored the crucial process by which actors endow the forces acting upon them, as well as their own behaviors, with meaning.... In addition to behaviorism, several other types of psychological reductionism troubled Blumer. For example, he criticised those who seek to explain human action by relying on conventional notions of the concept of 'attitude' ... what is important is not the attitude as an internalized tendency, but the defining process through which the actor comes to define his act. Blumer also singled out for criticism those who focus on conscious and unconscious motives. He was particularly irked by their view that actors are impelled by independent, mentalistic impulses over which they are supposed to have no control.

(Ibid., p. 301)

Ritzer concludes by arguing that Blumer was also opposed to sociologistic theories that view individual behaviour as determined by large-scale external forces: 'such social, structural and cultural factors as "social system", "social structure", "culture", "status position", "social role", "custom", "institution", "collective representation", "social situation", "social norm" and "values"' (ibid.). In short, he was opposed to any theory that ignores the processes by which actors construct meaning.

Consistent with symbolic interactionism, this study of principals adopts a life history approach. The relationship between both approaches is elaborated upon by Goodson (1980–81) as follows:

In general, the life history is congruent with the main theoretical assumption of interactionism that the individual life is not as clear or ordered as many social science accounts, especially those following the experimental model, would have us believe. The greatest strength of the life history lies in its penetration of the subjective reality of the individual: it allows the subject to speak for himself or herself.

(Ibid., p. 66)

Elsewhere, Goodson (1977, p. 160) takes up the same point when he argues that 'the analysis of subjective perceptions and intentions is incomplete without analysis of the historical context in which they occur.' As Woods (1992, p. 367), in a similar vein, has put it, 'strategies are not only two-dimensional ... they have historical referents'. In other words, with regard to the present study, when studying the role of principals in current restructuring situations, we should examine not only their present role and the reasons they and others provide as to why they adopt particular strategies, but we should also seek to explore life history details that might have a bearing on this behaviour. To adopt such a position would appear also to be at one both with

27

Woods (1985a, p. 254) when he criticizes the tendency to look at social events as if they are 'frozen in time', and with Payne (1976, p. 33) when he questions the assumption of many social researchers that the social events, settings and relationships which are all the time created and achieved by the members of society 'have no existence independent of the occasion of their production'.

Elsewhere, Woods (1993) makes the following case, which would appear to clarify the connection between the theoretical position of symbolic interaction and the life history method of research:

> The present has a living connection with the past. Current meanings and interpretations are shown to have grown and developed over time. In tracing teachers' own histories, we acquire a fuller, deeper and richer understanding of them. Examining the interrelationships of incident, thought, people and place that underpin the current person provides a context that is just as relevant as, if not more than, the prevailing social, institutional and situational.
>
> (Ibid., p. 450)

We find an illustration of this process in Aspinwall's (1992) account of her study of one teacher's professional life:

> It was impossible for Sarah to speak of her professional life without referring to her personal experiences. Significant figures and incidents from her childhood, her time at university studying politics, her children's own unhappy time starting school were all deeply influential in her decision to enter teaching and to her image of the kind of teacher she aspired to be. Her life experiences and her personality combined to give her an idealistic and demanding vision of teaching and teachers. This made her present colleagues particularly hard for her to understand and work with.
>
> (Ibid., p. 254)

Minichiello *et al.* (1990, p. 152) highlight the arguments of Schwartz and Jacobs (1979) and Plummer (1983) that there is 'a fundamental affinity between the central tenets of symbolic interactionism and life history research'. Drawing from these arguments, they go on to state that there are three theoretical assumptions which are common to both traditions. The first assumption is that life is viewed as concrete experience. In other words, there is no point in studying abstractions of individuals or of social life. As Cooley (1956, p. 67) has put it, it is important to recognize that 'a separate individual is an abstraction unknown to experience, and so likewise is society when regarded as something apart from individuals.' Minichiello *et al.* (1990, p. 152) go on to argue that the central consequence of being concerned with life as concrete experience is that, as Plummer (1983, p. 54) has put it, 'in every case of study, we must acknowledge that experiencing individuals can never be isolated from their functioning bodies and their constraining social worlds.'

The second assumption highlighted by Minichiello *et al.* (1990) is that life is regarded as an ever-emerging relativistic perspective. In other words, human beings experience the world through their definitions of it. They quote Plummer (1983, p. 56) as follows: 'The reality shifts with a person's life and people act towards things on the basis of their understandings, irrespective of the "objective" nature of those things.' They conclude that if one accepts this theoretical assumption, then the most central and fundamental source of knowledge is the personal document, the life history which elicits "the sense of reality" that human beings hold about their own worlds' (Minichiello *et al.*, p. 153).

The third assumption highlighted by Minichiello *et al.* (1990, p. 152) as being common to the symbolic interaction and life history research traditions is that life is viewed as inherently marginal and ambiguous. This is tied to the two previous assumptions. They continue as follows:

> If we have taken one person's subjective reality seriously in a life history, and then considered it in relation to another person's, then there is always the possibility that ambiguity and incongruity will become evident in their definitions of the same situations.
>
> (Ibid., p. 153)

They conclude that the message to the life history researcher is to move away from studying abstractions and get at the particular, the detailed and the experiential, thus allowing one to grasp the ambiguities and inevitability of different perspectives.

At this point it is instructive to outline Goodson's (1992, p. 6) crucial distinction between the life story and the life history. He elaborates on the distinction thus:

> The life story is the 'story we tell about our life'; the life history is a collaborative venture, reviewing a wider range of evidence. The life story teller and another (or others) collaborate in developing this wider account by interviews and discussions and by scrutiny of texts and contexts. The life history is the life story located within its historical context.

He concludes by reminding us that while a great deal of valuable work on teachers' stories or narratives was carried out in the 1980s by academics, much of it did not embrace contextual or intercontextual analysis.

With regard to the life history, as distinct from the life story, Allport (1942) and Denzin (1989) distinguish between the complete or comprehensive life history and the topical life history. The complete or comprehensive life history is concerned with all aspects of the individual's life from birth. It is usually a long and complex account which focuses on the overall flow of life of an individual. In contrast, the topical life history focuses on only one phase, aspect or issue of the individual's life. Also, the life history, whether a complete or comprehensive life history or a topical life history, may be edited with comments and analysis by the researcher, either interspersed with the narrative or in a combination which includes introductory passages and analytical commentary after the narrative, or incorporated in a combined form. At the same time, as Denzin (ibid., p. 217) points out, all three forms contain three central elements: the person's own story of his or her life; the social and cultural situation to which the subject and others see the subject responding; and the sequence of past experiences and situations in the subject's life.

The life histories developed in relation to the case studies reported in this book are edited topical life histories. The decision that they should be 'edited' was made in the light of Allport's (1942, p. 78) advice that while unique styles of expression, including argot and colloquial phrasing, should remain un-edited, editing for the sake of clarity or to remove repetitious material would seem justified. The 'topic' is the interaction between current restructuring initiatives and the principals' innovations in curriculum, teaching and learning taking place in their schools. The forms of data collection and analysis which were utilized in the study in order to construct such edited topical life histories are now considered.

## DATA COLLECTION AND ANALYSIS

### The selection of the participants

An initial list of principals to be considered as possible participants in the study was drawn up on the basis of their reputations for attempting to promote adventurous change programmes to improve the quality of curriculum, teaching and learning in their schools. The present researchers became aware of these reputations over the period of a year through the consistency of reporting by district superintendents and central office administrators and through evaluation reports by academics, informal contacts with consultants and hearsay from teachers and parents in the schools. Over a period of time corroborative evidence from these multiple sources emerged to facilitate the construction of a final list of principals. Following this, volunteers to participate were sought. In this regard, cognizance was taken of procedures outlined by Woods (1985b). He argues that in seeking volunteers for life history studies there is always an element of pressure, no matter how courteous and non-committal, in the direct approach. He then recommends that one set out a market-stall to groups of teachers and invite offers; 'there is an immediate sense of negotiation in the "offer", for, in the interests of motivation, they should be allowed to work their personal interests into the general framework of the research' (ibid., pp. 14–15). The 'market-stall' would detail the broad aims of the research; the principles of the method; possible outcomes for education; possible outcomes for the teacher personally, 'such as greater understanding of self and career, and an aid to morale' (ibid., p. 15). The latter, he says, may derive from knowledge of varieties of careers and career planning, and the general contextualising of one's own, which might touch on feelings of success and failure, and general job satisfaction. Above all, such a study promises to promote knowledge of self. As Stenhouse (1975, p. 144) argues, 'The outstanding characteristic of the extended profesional is a capacity for autonomous professional self-development through systematic self-study.'

(Ibid.)

Finally, the 'market-stall' would also detail possible outcomes for the researcher and a statement of guarantees, such as anonymity at all times, respect and protection of privacy, and teacher right to correct or withhold transcript.

From the principals who volunteered, the following were selected: Bronwyn, Janet, David, Anne, Simon and Jason. The selection was influenced by a desire to cast widely for a variety of perspectives, rather than to select a random sample or choose a sample that would be representative of a total population. At the same time, a gender balance is reflected in the selection. Diversity is also to be found in the school catchment areas, whose socioeconomic status ranged from middle and higher income urban populations to lower income urban and rural communities. A portrayal of each of the schools will be presented in the case studies in Chapters Four to Nine of this book.

## Data collection and analysis

Data were gathered and analysed concurrently in three stages.

### Stage 1

In this stage, descriptive data were gathered about each school, including its location, its history and the social background of its pupils. The purpose in generating such data was to assist in portraying the context within which each principal was working. Interviews were then conducted with each principal separately. These interviews were aimed at uncovering the principals' thoughts on what they had been doing to improve the quality of curriculum, teaching and learning in their schools, how they had been going about promoting such innovations, and why they felt they had been promoting them.

The semi-structured in-depth interview method (Taylor and Bogdan, 1984, p. 76) was utilized because it is concerned, first, with creating the environment to encourage participants to discuss their lives and experiences in free-flowing, open-ended discussions, and, second, it enables the researcher to interpret their views. In conducting the interviews, general principles as outlined by Spradley (1979) and Measor (1985, pp. 63–73) were followed. These include the following: having a clear purpose, which is made apparent to the participant; explaining why particular questions are being asked; using clear meaningful

31

language; asking descriptive, structural and contrast questions; using open-ended questions to elicit rich qualitative responses; avoiding leading questions; framing the same questions in different time dimensions; using effective probing to obtain further elaboration, explanation and clarification; using cross-checks to investigate possible exaggerations and distortions; allowing the participant to do most of the talking; being non-judgemental and being sensitive to the participant's situation. Rogers' (1951) categories of intervention – evaluative, interpretative, reflective, supportive and probing – also proved helpful in this regard.

The initial interview with each participant lasted approximately two hours. An *aide-mémoire* (Burgess, 1984) was developed around the following headings to enable the participants to frame their thoughts on the improvement of the quality of curriculum, teaching and learning in their schools as part of current restructuring: goals and objectives; enabling factors; constraining factors; dilemmas; stresses and stressors; actions taken; future directions; and feelings in retrospect about the whole process. However, neither the wording nor the ordering of the questions was fixed. Furthermore, the participants were given the *aide-mémoire* prior to the interview in order to give them sufficient time to reflect on the headings. The adoption of such a procedure, it was felt, would facilitate the generation of both a quantity and quality of data which would be unlikely to emerge if reliance was placed on more immediate responses. Furthermore, because school restructuring matters are complex it was felt that the principals needed time to give due consideration to the questions they were being asked. In this way, the subtleties of events and meanings could be explored and captured.

Cognizant of Goetz and Le Compte's (1982, p. 41) argument that 'the optimum guard against threats to internal reliability may be the presence of multiple researchers', the interviews with five of the six principals were conducted jointly by two experienced interviewers so that later, during analysis, they could discuss the meaning of the participants' words until agreement was achieved. As themes arose they were pursued with the participants in 'a lengthy conversation piece' (Simons, 1982, p. 37). In fact, the term 'conversation' is probably a much more appropriate term for the process than 'interview'. As Aspinwall (1992, p. 251) argues, the term 'interview' 'cannot convey the empathy and interest necessary to the process'. On the same matter, Woods (1985b) speaks of acting as a 'catalyst' and Abbs (1974) speaks of considering with imaginative sympathy the formative influences on others' lives. Accordingly, while the term 'interview' is used frequently throughout the remainder of this book, it is to be understood in the sense of 'conversation'.

The conversations were tape-recorded with the participants' consent. While tape-recording, the interviewers also took notes. Woods (1985b, p. 20) has described the purpose of such note-taking as follows:

These are rather like the rough notes made during ethnographic fieldwork, when one is being assailed by a torrent of data. The cryptic jottings made at the time are sufficient to stir the memory later, when one can record the full data or impression at length. Now the tape recorder may capture what is said. But it cannot capture fleeting thoughts and impressions, as something the teacher says prompts first this thought and then that – the second invariably displacing the first from memory. The briefest of notes can aid recall.

In reading over one's notes along with the transcribed interviews, one can identify points on which one wishes the participant to elaborate and points which one wishes the participant to clarify. This elaboration and clarification took place with the participants for modification until they became accepted by them as representative of their position (Lincoln and Guba, 1984, pp. 314–316). Again, this process was guided by a procedure outlined by Woods (1985b, p. 21):

> Initial conversations have to be followed up. In general, the points to look out for are of three kinds. (a) Corrective: These include inconsistencies, non sequiturs, omissions, lack of balance, implausibility, a too 'cut and dried' or 'black and white' account. . . . (b) Checking and in-filling: a copy of the transcript is returned to the teacher and he is asked to comment. Is he happy with it? Does it adequately represent his views? Does it say what he means to say? . . . (c) Progressive: these are hints that are let fall of possible richness of data in areas according with the themes of the research.

In some cases, this meant follow-up interviews after the initial one. Each of these interviews lasted approximately two hours.

Throughout all of the interviews in this and subsequent phases, cognizance was taken of Langness and Frank's (1981, p. 34) contention that 'the key to successful anthropological fieldwork and also to successful life history taking is rapport.' At all times, the aim of the interviewers was to be friendly and objective outsiders and to be cautious, diplomatic, persevering and patient. They also sought to be good listeners, trying not to interrupt and using body language and short expressions to indicate that they were 'interestedly quiet' (Burgess, 1982). The conversations were conducted, where possible, in 'ordinary' teacher discourse although, because of their backgrounds, the principals were occasionally inclined to use the technical language of educational management and leadership. When such occasions arose, the interviewers allowed the participants to converse in this way while being careful not to steer them down a pathway of sociologese which might have interfered with the relaxed rapport which had been established (De Waele and Harré, 1979). The interviewers' familiarity with the general educational culture of state schools in WA and with 'the general job situation and occupational culture' facilitated their understanding of the 'meanings, idioms, nuances, range of views and bases for making judgements' (Woods, 1985b, p. 21) professed by the principals.

Another factor in eliciting rich data focuses more specifically on the relationship between interviewer and participant. In this regard, the person-alities and gender mix of the researchers and participants may be crucial. In certain situations the eliciting of data is enhanced where both interviewers and participants are of the same sex. In other situations either the reverse may be the case or the issue does not arise. This presents researchers with a difficulty since they have no way of knowing from the outset what constitutes the best mix. Accordingly, in this project some of the interviews were conducted by males with males, some were conducted by females with females, some were conducted by males with females and some were conducted by females with males. However, each participant, once the process began, continued through-out the project with the interviewers with which he or she started. At the end of Stage 1 of the research, the total set of transcribed material was analysed following the procedures outlined by Marton (1988, p. 155), with utterances in the transcripts being brought together into categories on the basis of their similarities and categories being differentiated from one another in terms of their variance.

## Stage 2

The next stage in the research was to conduct semi-structured interviews with the participants on their life histories. The decision to engage in this aspect of the research following Stage 1, rather than the other way around, was influenced by Langness and Frank's (1981, p. 39) argument that the taking of an adequate and reliable life history 'involves a degree of intimacy with the informant and a knowledge of the community as well, that comes only with exceptionally good rapport'. They go on to advise not to attempt a life history until one has known the person and been in the field for some time. The nature of the data gathering undertaken in Stage 1 facilitated such a development.

Three weeks before the first life history interview the participants were each given another *aide-mémoire* so that they could have time to reflect on the themes, begin the process of recall and organize their recollections in a chronological sequence. The *aide-mémoire* which was developed for this occasion was strongly influenced by Lancy's (1993, p. 204) suggestions. It centred on the partici-pants' family life, including their role as spouse and parent; personal school history, especially details of their professional training; their relationship with significant others, parents and favourite teachers; their higher education, including institutions attended, subjects taken, likes and dislikes, influential lecturers, and significant events at college; a sense of their daily routines and life-styles; the nature of the schools and the classroom environments in which they taught; the characteristics and backgrounds of the students they taught, especially regarding class and ethnicity; a sense of the climate of the schools within which they taught and the prevailing teaching ethos; classroom routines in which they engaged, including the use of prepared curricula, grouping arrangements, management strategies and the predominant instructional mode; professional development activities undertaken and recreational activities.

The adoption of a set of headings for the *aide-mémoire* reflects the approach of Lemert (1951, pp. 445–446) in his study of the life history of deviants. The contention is that those headings proposed by Lancy (1993, p. 204) are broad enough to be appropriate in investigating the lives of individual school principals. However, they were also accompanied by a consideration of such factors as social class, religion and social and political climate. As Pollard (1980) argues, sensitively handled and portrayed, the influences of these can be seen in the acted-out life and the formulating self. The intention overall was to generate data sufficiently rich to construct the sort of portrait which, as Plummer (1983, p. 69) puts it, would enable us 'to perceive the intersection of the life history of human beings with the history of their society'. The headings of the *aide-mémoire*, along with the broader headings of social class, religion, and social and political climate, can also be seen as constituting a set of uniform standards so that as each new case is developed comparisons can be made across them.

Goodson (1980–81) also argues for such a focus because, as he expresses it,

> The problem ... as with much of interactionism, is that the personal experience and process often gets divorced from the wider socio-historical structure. The life historian must constantly broaden the concern with personal truth to take account of broader socio-historical concerns, even if these are not part of the consciousness of the individual.
>
> (Ibid., p. 67)

He goes on to quote Bogdan (1974, p. 4) who argued that the full life history should allow us

> to see an individual in relation to the history of his time, and how he is influenced by the various religious, social, psychological and economic currents present in his world. It permits us to view the intersection of the life history of men [sic] with the history of society, thereby enabling us to understand better the choices, contingencies and options open to the individual.

Woods (1985b, p. 19) makes the same point when he argues that the 'danger of reductionism and atomism should be guarded against from the beginning'. Quoting Dollard (1935), he states that this can be done in a number of ways, notably by situating personal and career developments within relevant frameworks, such as social class, ethnicity, gender or generation, and within the prevailing socioeconomic circumstances; and by focusing upon the culture of the primary groups within an individual's biography. In order to probe these issues it was necessary for the researchers to familiarize themselves with the general history of WA over the last forty years as well as with the history of education in the state over the same period.

Finally, when exploring each individual's life history, attention was given to the point of Sikes, Measor and Woods (1985, p. 20) that not all teachers necessarily experience smooth career progression; rather, 'a typical career is marked by critical incidents or phases'. Goodson and Walker (1991, p. 147) make the same point as follows:

> The new work on teachers' careers points to the fact that there are critical incidents in teachers' lives and specifically in their work which may crucially affect perception and practice. Certainly work on beginning teachers has pointed to the importance of certain incidents in moulding teachers' styles and practices.

Furthermore, cognizance was taken of Sikes, Measor and Woods' (1985, p. 20) contention that while such incidents can give one's career and one's life 'a beneficial boost', they can also 'deal it a savage blow, or both at the same time'.

## Stage 3

The final stage of the research involved further analysis of the use of the life history data generated from the first interview with each participant. The aim was to explore those life history details that might explain both the manner in which and the reasons why he or she had undertaken adventurous programmes in the area of curriculum, teaching and learning. The decision to engage in this third stage of analysis was influenced particularly by Woods' (1992, p. 374) argument that because the participants' memories, thoughts and perceptions are of unknown scope and depth, even to themselves, accounts should be built up through successive discussions over a period of time. Accordingly, the previous conversations were reviewed for accuracy and completeness.

Cognizance was also taken of Mandelbaum's (1973) scheme for the analysis of life histories. Briefly, Mandelbaum suggests that when analysing a life history we need to consider the dimensions of a person's life, the principal turnings and the person's characteristic means of adaptation. A dimension is 'made up of experiences that stem from a similar base and are linked in their effects on the person's subsequent actions' (ibid., p. 180). They are biological, cultural, social and psychosocial. With regard to the first two, Mandelbaum (ibid.) states:

> The biological factors set the basic conditions for a life course; cultural factors mould the shape and content of a person's career. The cultural dimension lies in the mutual expectations, understandings and behavior patterns held by the people among whom a person grows up and in

whose society he becomes a participant. Each culture provides a general scenario for the life course that indicates the main divisions, tells when transitions should be made, and imputes a social meaning to biological events from birth through death. Each scenario interprets and affects the biological dimension in its own way; each provides its own chart for the progress of a life.

The social dimension, in turn, consists of the social relations the person encounters during his or her life, the roles required of the person, the acts of personal choice characteristic of the group, and the commonly understood ways of working out recurrent conflicts. The psychosocial dimension refers to the individual's feelings, attitudes and subjective world in general. Mandelbaum recognizes that while each of these are individually experienced, each individual's experiences are also likely to be similar in important ways to others in the same culture.

Turnings are the major transitions that an individual makes during the course of a life. These are accomplished when 'the person takes on a new set of roles, enters into fresh relations with a new set of people and acquires a new self-conception' (Mandelbaum, 1973, p. 181). A turning can take place gradually or it can be a single event. Also, it may be either improvised or in some way prescribed.

Finally, adaptations 'are changes that have a major effect on a person's life and on one's basic relations with others' (ibid.). Mandelbaum goes on to argue that individuals change their ways: 'Each person changes his ways in order to maintain continuity whether of group participation or social expectation or self-image or simply survival' (ibid.). He concludes that while some of these new conditions are imposed by the individual's own physical development, others arise from changing external conditions, whether of custom or climate, family or society (ibid.).

With regard to the matter of generalizability, the issue is one of generalizability ultimately being related to what the reader is trying to learn from the case study (Kennedy, 1979). As Lancy (1993, p. 63) has put it, 'This is comparable to the law where the applicability of a particular precedent case must be argued in each subsequent case. The reader must decide whether the findings apply or not.' Stake (1978) makes the same point when he argues that case studies may be in harmony with the reader's experience and thus a natural basis for generalization.

## CONCLUSION

To study the principalship by means of the edited topical life history research approach is to engage in a pioneering exercise. The motivation to adopt this approach arose out of an awareness of the limitations of the existing literature on the principalship, particularly within a context of unparalleled change and restructuring, and a recognition of the tendency to ignore the formative nature of past experiences on principals' present practices. However, the absence of a clear position on the study of the principalship from a life history perspective presented a major challenge to the present authors. As a consequence, the underlying theoretical position and the guidelines for data gathering and analysis which have been presented in this chapter were developed from a wide variety of sources and woven into what we believe is a comprehensive and coherent exposition. The individual life histories presented in the following chapters represent applications of this methodology.

# 4

# BRONWYN EVANS

## INTRODUCTION

The specific background to this book, it will be recalled, is the two distinct policy initiatives currently reshaping change in Australian schools, namely, those taking place at the macro-level, involving a shift from centralized governance to decentralized school-based management and those taking place at the micro-level, concerned with school restructuring to improve teaching and learning. In the early stages of restructuring it was assumed that the macro policy initiatives on their own would lead to the achievement of enhanced learning for all students. However, while these initiatives targeted changes in the administrative and organizational contexts and created an environment conducive to improving teaching and learning, it was increasingly recognized that they have to be accompanied by micro reforms. The National Project on Quality Teaching and Learning (NPQTL) (1993) and the associated National Schools Project are the most substantial of the micro reforms which have taken place so far, and school leadership is seen as crucial in their implementation. Particular emphasis is placed on the role of the principal and questions are increasingly raised about that role in the changing restructuring context. This chapter offers a number of insights which may be instructive in this regard by using the edited topical life history approach to explore the work of one school principal, Bronwyn, who is beginning to establish a reputation for herself in leading a 'successful' NPQTL school.

## THE BACKGROUND

Bronwyn is forty-five years of age and married with two children. She grew up in Perth, at Applecross, but in her youth she spent long periods of time in the country with her grandmother, particularly when her mother was sick. These country visits are remembered by her with great affection. Her schooling is also something about which she has pleasant memories. Indeed, since both of her parents were teachers, with her father going on to become a secondary school teachers' college lecturer, education permeated her life and that of her brother, who is three years younger than her and who is also a teacher. At school, her favourite subjects were mathematics, physics and chemistry, and these were also the subjects at which she excelled. This situation, of course, is a relatively unusual one given that up until lately these subjects at senior high school level tended to be largely the province of boys only.

Bronwyn led a very 'normal' and active life outside of school. She was very much involved in a variety of sports, particularly netball and athletics, and her memory is very strong of 'playing sport every day' and considering this level of activity to be very important at the time. Her personal development was also a well-rounded one. On this, she has fond memories of learning to play the piano and also of becoming a Sunday school teacher at the age of twelve. She attributes her involvement in religious activities when she was young to the influence of her grandmother, who was a devout member of the Church of Christ. At the same time, however, she suggests that she may have reacted negatively to some of this influence, since she now sees herself as having no great interest in religion.

On completing primary school Bronwyn won a half-scholarship to attend Perth's exclusive Methodist Ladies College, but decided instead to attend a local government high school. At eighteen, she enrolled at the University of Western Australia (UWA). Here she did a BA, majoring in psychology, and concurrently trained as a secondary school teacher at nearby Claremont Teachers' College. In this regard, she took what was by now a well-established route towards becoming a teacher in WA, namely, entering into a 'bonding' agreement with the Education Department of Western Australia (EDWA), whereby she was required to teach in their schools for five years after graduation, in return for which she had to pay no fees and received thirty-two dollars a fortnight as a living allowance. She is also adamant that her decision to become a teacher was not one which was made on the basis of a great passion to enter the profession. Rather, it seemed like the best option from the small number available to young women at the time whose circumstances were such that they did not have the necessary finance to pay the fees required for admission to university courses in the other professions. On this, she states,

> As girls in those days we were left out on a bit of a limb. Apart from teaching or nursing, there were very few options open to you. I certainly knew that I did not want to be a nurse. So that only left teaching. I didn't come with a very strong dedication to teaching as a career. I was also influenced by my best friend who, in turn, was motivated by the money side of things and the independence which it gave. It was attractive to get thirty-two dollars a fortnight.

She is also anxious to highlight, however, that her decision was affected by what she terms 'the limited background of girls at the time whereby they were not exposed to other possibilities'.

On graduation in 1970, Bronwyn immediately commenced teaching in a WA rural high school. Here she met her husband and the following year they got married. Then, in 1972, after three years as a class teacher, she became deputy principal of another rural district high school where she and her husband worked for five years. In 1979, she accompanied her husband to Canada as part of a teacher exchange scheme. This overseas experience she sees as having been a major event in her life and particularly in her professional life. Above all else, she sees it as having been a time when her mental horizons were broadened as the exposure to another culture and environment opened up a new range of possibilities for her to explore. They returned to WA the following year and recommenced teaching as classroom teachers. However, Bronwyn's experience stood her in good stead because in 1980 she became deputy principal of a high school in a town in the northwest of WA and was accompanied by her husband, who was appointed as head of the social studies department in the same school. This, of course, was no coincidence. As she put it, 'we have always looked at the rules within the Education Department and worked out how we could abide by them and still organize it so that we could both work in the one district.'

They remained in the northwest for four years, followed by another four years in the same position at a different school. During this period her son was born. This meant that she remained out of work for a total of eighteen months, since she was most anxious to spend time at home, bonding with her son. She recalls this period with great pleasure, stating that she was 'a wonderful mother at home, doing all of the painting with my little boy'. She also lovingly recalls the great support which she received from her husband during this period. At the same time, she makes it quite clear that she never seriously contemplated resigning from the educational world, expressing a belief that once children get to two years of age it is important for them to make little friends and to be playing with them. Her circumstances were such that she was able to organize her son's life in this manner by making use of childcare facilities every day. This then allowed her to return to the workforce as principal at Big Tree Senior High School (SHS).

Big Tree SHS is located in a rural town in the southwest of WA, about three hours' drive from the centre of Perth city in a predominantly farming area. It is a relatively small school with only 500 pupils, but is also characterized by much of the intimacy which is often associated with such a situation. Bronwyn has been active in promoting the notion that the school should aim to provide a learning environment in which students can develop into happy, self-reliant adults who are able to cope with change and new ideas, and who are academically equipped to their full potential. Furthermore, she has placed great stress on making this aim explicit for the school staff, for the parents and for the pupils. Also, she has ensured that each year a whole school approach is taken to address a number of areas of education. Priorities are identified by the staff, are approved by the school council as areas worthy of special emphasis, and are given priority status in the school for a period of up to two years. Accompanying this, school staff hold weekly departmental meetings to ensure that the teaching programmes in their areas progress smoothly and regular meetings of the entire staff are held for the purpose of discussing, evaluating, modifying and developing school policy and activities. As well as successfully introducing these structures, a variety of reforms which Bronwyn guided were beginning to come to fruition at the end of 1993 when this case study was conducted. In particular, time had been made available so that key planning groups which had been established could meet. As well, integrated courses based on more active and collaborative student learning, including problem solving, had been introduced for senior English students. Provision was also made for a certain amount of independent learning by students. Furthermore, it was planned for 1994 to introduce year eight learning teams based on twenty-five students being serviced by a group of three teachers for half a day every day. The notion was that students would work in teams. The school was supported in implementing this reform by external resourcing through an EDWA programme entitled 'Stepping Out' and through the NPQTL project. The latter, it will be remembered, was launched by the Federal Government in February 1991 to restructure the teaching profession, deal with low teacher morale and improve the quality of teaching and learning (NPQTL, 1993). The 'Stepping Out' project is a specific project of the EDWA aimed at improving student outcomes in years six to ten through the specific focus of improving literacy skills.

The claim that Bronwyn has been successful in guiding these and other initiatives aimed at improving the curriculum, teaching and learning in her school, is not based on measured outcomes or products. Indeed, the process has not been underway long enough for long-standing outcomes to be manifested. Rather, success is to be gauged by the significant progress made preparing the ground to establish the preconditions for the restructuring initiatives to be accepted. This involved the introduction of collaborative processes and the building of an appropriate culture and climate for transforming teaching and learning in the school. The apparent success of this early phase of restructuring in the school illustrates the harmonious match between the nature of Bronwyn's leadership and the situational context in which she found herself. The remainder of the chapter now considers this in some detail.

## BRONWYN'S LEADERSHIP STYLE AND HER LIFE HISTORY

Bronwyn is very definitely a school principal with vision. This is significant in light of the findings of the schools effectiveness literature. As Campbell-Evans (1993) recognizes, the adoption of school effectiveness characteristics depends on a number of factors, one of which is that there be a vision of a future for all of the children. This commitment requires leadership, particularly from the school principal. In Bronwyn's case, not only does she have a vision, but she also has a strong sense of how important this is.

Bronwyn's vision focuses very clearly on trying to promote change aimed at improving teaching and learning in her school. Indeed, current restructuring initiatives, as she sees it, are only justified if 'they lead to the improvement of student outcomes'. Furthermore, she claims that she has focused much of her efforts on creating a mindset amongst her staff such that, as she puts it, 'they become mindful of the real justification for change being the improvement of student outcomes'. Accordingly, amongst the initiatives which she has taken has been the engagement of her school community in whole-day activities aimed at developing a school vision based on student outcome statements. In this regard, she is also 'driven by the vision of good schools and leadership in the work and writing of Roland Barthes'. In particular, she is influenced by Barthes' vision of good schools, his views on leadership and his advocacy of creating a 'community of learners and leaders'. Consequently, she speaks of the importance of having teachers in your school who have an appetite to become learners and leaders.

On initial reflection, Bronwyn felt it was natural that 'at forty-five years of age you should have come to a set of beliefs'. However, on being probed she unearthed some possible reasons as to the origins of her predisposition to approach her work in a visionary way. In particular, she spoke of the influence of her parents in this regard. Both of her parents, it will be recalled, were teachers; her father became a trainee teacher after World War II and her mother was trained 'on the job'. A major message to Bronwyn and her brother from their parents was that education is something to be valued very highly and that it is a passport to success. In fact, every time that she and her mother passed the university, and that was quite often since they lived nearby, her mother would impress upon her that one day she would go on to study there. Bronwyn now sends similar messages to her own children. Her belief in the importance of education prompted her in 1994 to take up a new position as a principal of a high school in the Perth metropolitan area so that her son and daughter could have a greater choice of school subjects than was available to them in the rural area in which they lived.

In pursuit of her vision for her school, Bronwyn has not allowed herself to be blinded to various pitfalls which presented themselves from time to time. In particular, she argues that she has learned that restructuring takes time, that 'the first fruits of changes in teaching and learning from the initial push for change took three years'. She goes on to argue that 'at times the slow pace frustrates some, yet it is essential if change is to affect the whole school'. However, she is also quick to recognize that changes that are taking place in WA as a result of restructuring should not be attributed solely to government policy. Rather, she argues, 'a climate supportive of change was already there'. In this regard, she was alluding to the fact that by the late 1980s teachers were still largely operating within the dominant Australian education culture of the 1970s, with its concern for equity and community. That decade, as Angus (1992, p. 389) has pointed out, fostered 'a sense that, by educating the "whole child", schools would develop individuals to their full potential while socializing them into communities of enquirers who would contribute to a just society'. The Schools Commission and the Curriculum Development Centre (CDC), both established by the Federal government, actively promoted the notion of school-based curriculum decision making and supported it through research and funding. The CDC, in its commitment to a social reconstructionist philosophy, also advocated the introduction of a core curriculum (Marsh and Stafford, 1988, p. 55). These developments, with their concern for the personal growth of the individual and for social justice, arguably won the support of teachers and created a culture which predisposed them towards the types of changes envisaged in the restructuring philosophy to which they were exposed in the latter half of the 1980s.

Bronwyn also argues that the general readiness for change was clearly evident at her particular school when she arrived there: 'The teachers admitted that existing secondary school structures were not conducive to learning. The senior staff, in particular, recognized the value of school staff in planning and participating in the whole change process.' All parties, she says, realized that 'quality time' is vital to planning and goal achievement, and they saw the need to seize timely opportunities such as those presented by the NPQTL which encouraged them 'to challenge the regulatory framework and get support to get around the regulations'. Bronwyn also welcomed the opportunity to seize the opportunities which presented themselves. What distinguishes her from many other principals is not only her visionary capacity but also the fact that she is motivated both to capitalize on opportunities which have the potential to allow her to pursue her vision and also to seek them when they are not very obvious. Also, she is very much aware of her motivation in this regard, as evidenced from her regular voicing of the phrase 'you must seize the opportunities'. Furthermore, she adopts a mindset which sees the last seven years of educational developments in WA as being 'times of great opportunity', as 'opening up a whole new way of operating for principals'.

A significant landmark nationally in the 'opening of opportunities' referred to by Bronwyn was the establishment of the Quality of Education Review Committee (QERC, 1985). This committee was established to gauge 'value for money' from Federal expenditure while signalling the end of growth in Federal spending, and to gear the education system more closely to labour needs. The committee's influence was soon felt throughout Australia, including WA, with one of the most centralized state education systems in the country (Smart and Alderson, 1980). In 1987, it will be recalled, EDWA published *Better Schools in Western Australia: A Programme for Improvement*. This report established the overall plan for devolving administrative authority and responsibilities from a previously centralized ministry to the school level. Underpinning the plan was the need to achieve maximum effectiveness through the achievement of goals, while at the same time securing efficiency and economy of resource use (Dimmock, 1990). However, the suspicions of the State School Teachers'

Union of Western Australia (SSTUWA) led to an industrial campaign which did not end until an industrial agreement was reached between itself and EDWA in 1990. A significant outcome was the agreement on full implementation of devolution over a period of five years and a detailed plan for the first phase of implementation.

The implementation plan focused on school-based decision-making groups, school development planning and the monitoring and reporting of school performances. Developments since then have centred largely on the first two of these. A change in 1993 from a Labour to a Liberal government led to the new Education Minister having a discussion paper prepared which proposed that school communities would set and collect fees in 1994, manage their own budgets in 1995 and choose their own staff in 1996. A draft of this paper was leaked to the press and, as a consequence of the outcry which it generated from the State School Teachers' Union, a modified document was published.

Bronwyn, like many of her peers, is not happy with all aspects of these developments. In particular, she does not 'go along with the policy that schools will have a say in staff selection'. Nevertheless, rather than focus on what she sees as negative factors and adopt an attitude of indifference or hostility, she channels her energies into seeking ways by which restructuring presents opportunities which can be harnessed to improve the quality of the curriculum, teaching and learning which pupils are offered. She states that when schools were invited to be involved in the NPQTL she 'knew straight away' that this was her opportunity to develop herself to become the principal she wanted to be. The project, as she saw it, gave her 'the rubber stamp' to implement her belief that 'group decisions in schools are better than those made by individuals'. At the same time, she is also realistic in her recognition that while successful change requires commitment to a set of clear goals, frequent waves of new policies create an unstable context for school restructuring.

'What then', one might ask, 'is the source of Bronwyn's motivation to "seize the opportunity" when it presents itself?' Her view is that, in the first instance, it stems from both parents allowing her in her youth to pursue the wide variety of interests which she developed, while at the same time 'you knew they expected you to come up with the goods'. Associated with this, in her view, is the adventurous childhood which she had. Her grandmother looms large in her account of the provision of this adventure: 'My grandmother was probably an important influence, too. She was a great fisherwoman and I like fishing. It's so relaxing. We used to visit her in Mandurah to go boating and fishing and crabbing.'

Bronwyn considers that this instilling of a sense of adventure in her youth may well go some way towards accounting for her adventurous approach to education at the present time. Along with this, she also experienced a certain amount of responsibility in her youth, having been a Sunday school teacher when she was twelve. However, she is quick to add that whatever seeds were planted within her would not have blossomed if they had not been developed by the influence of her husband. From the beginning of their marriage he encouraged her to explore the variety of career options outside of classroom teaching which existed for somebody like her with a degree in psychology and a teaching qualification. He also encouraged her to follow them up by applying for jobs whenever they are advertised. For that reason, she is adamant that it is not just being married but the particular person to whom she is married which has been important: 'If I had not married John I don't think I would have been adventurous. It was important to have married him and to have done what I did and yet lead a normal life.' Her tendency to be adventurous was also reinforced by experiences which she shared with her husband. She has a very positive memory of both of them going off to Canada for a year on the teacher exchange programme, seeing it as having been a most fruitful event and well worth the planning, time and finance they invested in it. Also, the adventurous investment which she and her husband made a number of years ago (when they bought a motel and a restaurant in a country town and her husband gave up teaching in order to manage it), has been successful and 'opened up a whole new world' for them.

The nature of Bronwyn's relationship with her husband also is such that when opportunities arise for her to broaden her own horizons on educational issues she is able to seize them, even when it means being away from home for a period of time. Lately, she has spent a week at a winter school for principals in Sydney and previously she has attended a summer school at Harvard University on effective schooling. She considers the effort which she has to make to attend such convocations as most worthwhile: 'I like to talk to different people, not just people in the school. It opens up the world for you. You keep up with what is going on.'

Bronwyn also adopts a goal-setting approach as part of her translation into practice of her vision for the school. She does not consider herself very pushy in the way she works, but when she sets her mind to a task, she succeeds. She is also very conscious that she does this 'a lot of the time' through setting goals and, as she puts it, 'trying to work out how I am going to win'. She adds that this is both an ability which she has and an approach which she has used successfully for some time. She gives as an example her success in becoming president of the university netball club when she was a student after first of all setting it as a goal and then deciding that she must go about achieving it in a certain kind of way. More recently, after she had decided to go to the Harvard Summer Institute of Education, she planned how she was going to get there in terms of obtaining the necessary finance and time.

When asked what she thought the source of her goal-setting approach might be, Bronwyn's initial reaction was that she was not sure. On being probed, however, she dwelt at length on her sporting experiences in her youth. She recalled that she had been a fast runner when she was young and had been quite successful in competition: 'You knew you could do it so you always did because you did not want to let yourself down. I liked the taste of success. I think there is a spill-over from my sport.' Amongst the spill-overs, she felt, was an experience while she was in year eleven where only six girls were in a very big mathematics class. Here she 'quietly set her mind' to beat the boys. However, while she had no clear views as to what drove her to behave in this manner, she felt that 'partly it must be inbuilt' and partly that 'it seems quite satisfying to get up and win if you know you can win'.

Bronwyn is also anxious to impress that goal-setting in education is not a simple matter. She expressed her view on this as follows:

> Setting goals to change the climate of the school is very hard and you find yourself asking: 'What am I doing this for?' and 'Why am I doing it?' You go backwards quite a lot I think before you go forwards again.

A key ingredient in assisting her to stay 'on task' even when the nature of the task is not always clear is the fact that she leads an orderly regular life. This provides the necessary environment for her to be goal oriented. In a 'typical day' Bronwyn rises at six o'clock and often goes for a walk. Then, with her children, she eats breakfast and prepares lunch. She arrives at the school around eight o'clock and gets around to talk to the gardeners, the cleaners and any pupils who have come early. She then quickly moves on to deal with administrative work. Over the remainder of the morning she spends about an hour making phone calls to deal with various matters, another hour organizing the cleaners and gardeners, and an hour getting around to speak with the staff and observing what is going on in their classrooms. The afternoon is taken up with 'more paperwork and maybe half an hour on the phone'.

Bronwyn has also organized her working life so that she is able to play a supervisory role in the school to assist in a special programme for ballet students. These students have a reduced academic load so that they can concentrate on their ballet and she supervises them once a day so that they can do homework in school. She thinks that it might be more helpful for the school if, in the future, she gets someone else to do this and she takes on a teaching duty instead. Finally, she usually leaves the school around a quarter past four but regularly returns after tea for meetings.

It is clear that Bronwyn approaches her work in a task-oriented manner, that she makes these tasks very clear for herself and that she pursues them by leading a very ordered and planned day. Yet, she is insistent that her 'pretty ordered life' is not 'a time management thing' and she does not feel pressured by it. In expressing this opinion, however, she is not at the same time being dismissive of the educational management literature. Indeed, she is influenced very much by this literature, particularly as it pertains to school effectiveness, school improvement and pedagogy.

Bronwyn is also a great believer in the importance of teachers informing their work with the latest research findings in education, particularly those which relate to improving teaching and learning. She expressed her policy on this as follows:

The research is very important. I like to hand stuff out to people. If you give people enough information about anything you will bring them around to a different way of thinking and probably a better way of thinking and they might actually do something about it.

This is consistent with the views of a number of authorities that teaching, as a profession, has a knowledge base, that this knowledge is constantly changing and that, as a consequence, practitioners must be kept up to date. On this, Beare (1992, p. 67) states:

The profession recognises that bodies of knowledge are dynamic, so that it can never be assumed that the knowledge or skill base is able to be acquired once by a practitioner and never be updated. Hence, the pursuit of research, the diffusion of knowledge and in-service training are intrinsic to being a professional.

Equally, he states that for the whole of one's occupational life it will be necessary for professionals to read new books, journals and articles relating to their department of learning.

This theme of life-long learning and the notion that the teacher must always be a learner, pervades the literature. However, Bronwyn's arrival at this conviction has not been via the more usual postgraduate studies route. She does not have any formal postgraduate qualifications in education and administration. On this, she relates how, ten years ago, when it looked as if having a postgraduate degree was going to be a prerequisite for appointment as a principal, she enrolled in a masters' degree in educational management, bought all the books and paid the fees. However, she then went home, put the books in the cupboard and decided she was not going to proceed. A major reason she gives for this is that she could not see a clear purpose in the courses and they did not interest her. On the other hand, she attended the Harvard Summer School of Education because when she saw its offerings it dealt, to use Deweyian terms, with her perplexities, issues and problems. As she put it, 'the stuff was all about what I want to be about. It was down to earth and I could identify with it.'

Bronwyn balances her belief in the goal-directed, student outcomes dimension of the school effectiveness literature with a belief in the importance of establishing a caring environment. This is not surprising given the body of literature which expresses teachers' commitment to caring for their students (Belenky et al. 1986; Gilligan, 1988; Holt, 1970; Kozol, 1975; Noddings, 1987; Sichel, 1988) 'in a clear and often passionate way' (Elbaz, 1992, p. 422). Teachers, it is argued, view their relationship and connectedness with their pupils as being at the heart of the educational enterprise. As Lortie (1975, p. 27) has demonstrated, one of the great attractors to teaching is the notion of 'giving service'. This emanates from a motivation to demonstrate one's care for fellow humans and in a way in which people may feel they are making important contributions to their communities or their nation.

The importance which Bronwyn places on a caring environment is also consistent with the findings of the school effectiveness literature. A caring environment plays an important role in such critical issues as students' social and academic competence and teachers' sense of personal fulfilment and decision making. Again, however, an acquaintance with the literature on its own is not sufficient to explain her commitment to 'placing students' welfare at the centre of change'. She speaks about the importance of caring about her family and how this was another reason why she did not pursue her masters' degree: 'I was not prepared to give up the family side'. Also, it will be recalled that lately she has moved to a new position in Perth so that her children can pursue their educational interests, but in a day school with her providing a homely environment for them.

It would seem that the school effectiveness literature legitimizes for Bronwyn the drive to provide a caring environment for the pupils in her school. This, in turn, it can be argued, assists her in the provision of a positive culture to facilitate the improvement of teaching and learning. However, she also highlights another aspect of the school effectiveness literature which serves to guide her in creating this positive climate and in maximizing the possibility of innovations being implemented successfully, namely, the importance of a collegial approach which includes all stakeholders. Again, what is significant is that she is committed to this perspective not only because it is highlighted in the research literature but also because it corresponds with personal experience. Indeed, she highlights and revisits the matter to such an extent that it merits the separate consideration which is now presented.

Bronwyn places great emphasis on involving all stakeholders in her initiatives aimed at improving the curriculum, teaching and learning. She argues that she is 'not interested in administration *per se*' but that she is exceptionally efficient, getting all of her letters and reports written regularly and very quickly. Her voicing of this, however, is punctuated by the statement that 'working with the staff is the main thing'. Furthermore, she does not restrict her belief to the teaching staff only: 'Every day I try to talk to the cleaners and the gardeners and listen to what they have to say. Then I walk around the school to try to talk to the students.'

While Bronwyn is at pains to stress the importance of collaboration in the restructuring effort, however, she also sees her role as central to the process. 'I see myself,' she claims, 'as a key person in tapping into available resources to enable individuals to make change happen.' The NPQTL co-ordinator suggested the project would suit Bronwyn since 'she was keen to ensure reform in work organization'. Bronwyn was duly elected school project co-ordinator by the school's 'quality committee', a position she thought important for the principal to fill: 'I was personally interested in the project and had initiated the idea of joining it.'

49

Bronwyn claims that involving all of the teaching staff in making the case for entry to the National Schools Project enabled them to reflect on how ineffectively time was being used for learning. It took eighteen months for staff to develop a decision-making policy and guidelines working document, which became 'one of the most significant activities of this restructuring'. This enabled a 'shift away from committee structures to key planning groups'. Also, she engaged her school staff in whole-day activities developing a school vision based on student outcome statements and created planning time for the staff to make significant changes to teaching and learning.

A further impetus for change was provided by the involvement and support of the wider community. This was necessary because additional staff planning time had to be gained by closing the school for three and a half days at the end of term and redistributing this as planning time throughout the year. Overall, she feels that her approach has been successful; that there is, as she puts it, 'courtesy in the way people talk to each other and an expectation that people will listen to the views of others'.

For Bronwyn, the dominant feelings arising from leading restructuring in her school are strongly positive. She remarks: 'I enjoy setting things up and facilitating change. Seeing people take on leadership roles is very important.' Interestingly, she claims not to have been particularly stressed by the experience of continued restructuring. Indeed, she appears more concerned about the effects of stress on her staff. She believes that her promotion of leadership by others 'was disturbing for the few who felt safe only when following rules under a bureaucratic style of leadership'. She had to explore many possibilities in order to 'seduce the staff into new ways of working. Some of them felt stressed and, while they wanted the decision-making responsibility and power, they were frightened by what they saw as the enormity and importance of the task.'

It would also be misleading to underplay the degree of uncertainty and risk with which the restructuring process began. For example, she remarks: 'At the start you wondered whether embarking on a journey like this could end up causing factions within the staff.' In fact, the opposite happened and a much more united, cohesive team has emerged. She comments that 'learning to understand where people were at in the change cycle took time. Sometimes you'd be frustrated by people's negative reaction to something'. However, she concludes that three years after working together, she and her staff understand and accept each other better, so much so that 'negative reactions and conflict are much more effectively handled collaboratively and worked through together'.

Bronwyn also articulates clearly why she believes in collegiality. It is her belief that people need to have clear direction and they need to be reminded of it as they go about their daily work. Accordingly, she argues that it is very important when you are working with other people that you have a direction and that people know what it is. Allied to this is her belief in the need to give regular affirmation in group settings and she has now instituted a procedure whereby in administrative meetings 'noteworthy deeds' recently undertaken by the staff are noted and praised where appropriate. Also, she encourages a cooperative spirit by adopting a non-confrontationalist management style. On this, she recalls that one of her teachers went through an aggressive phase, arguing that he was standing up for teacher union issues in showing hostility to her reformist agenda. However, she managed to get him to become a member of the year eight learning team and claims that he is now thoroughly engrossed in that work: 'I spoke positively to him and I gave him responsibility. He is now responding in a very positive way.'

Bronwyn attributes some of her belief in the importance of a collegial approach in running her school to the fact that while she was studying for her first degree in psychology she developed a great interest in human motivation and what makes people behave in particular ways. However, she places an even greater stress on those experiences she had when she was a teacher which impressed upon her that a cooperative approach in schools can lead to an improvement in the curriculum, teaching and learning: 'What I learned as a schoolteacher may be why I am the way I am.' In particular, she recalls that when she and her husband taught mathematics together in one school where they were employed, they taught as a team:

> The kids would get either me or him but we worked it so that we taught the kids as a team – they were exposed to both of us. Students got the best out of us operating in that way rather than working in isolation in each other's classroom. We used to discuss where kids were at and they got a better deal. I learned that if teachers work together pupils benefit.

She also recalled the principal of the school where she first became deputy principal. 'He was,' she said, 'a terrific principal who gave you responsibility and expected you to do the job and to do it well.' Such experiences, she feels, have helped shape significantly the way in which she, in turn, now works with her own staff. Finally, it would be wrong to give the impression that Bronwyn does not have some doubts about the justification for the collegial approach she is cultivating. In particular, she argues that there are times when she feels she is, as she puts it, 'giving away responsibility for which I am being paid'. Also, she is conscious that her role is not a completely democratic one but one that is guided by a notion that she is 'a key person in tapping into available resources to enable individuals to make change happen'. However, these are not issues on which she broods for too long and they tend to disappear when she becomes 'energized and excited' by seeing the commitment of her staff and listening to the 'buzz of staffroom talk about educational issues, pedagogy and what happened in the classroom'.

# 5

# JANET TURNER

Janet Turner, the Principal of Western Coast Senior High School (SHS) in the Perth metropolitan area of WA, is promoting innovations in her school aimed at improving the quality of the curriculum, teaching and learning. She is endeavouring to promote change through the development of an environment which is supportive of her teachers and students as well as of the government body which employs her. She is a person who has a very clear vision of what should be done and she focuses her vision in a manner which brings out the best in people by working with them. Janet believes in working with and developing people, as opposed to dictating to them. She is not governed by predetermined notions of who should be in control but opens up the process to those who have the expertise in curriculum and management to make decisions, who will be affected by them, and who will have to implement them. Her freshness of manner and approach, and her optimism and enthusiasm, are infectious.

As an employee of the WA Government, Janet is committed to its education policies and does what is requested of her in her position as its representative. She does, however, reserve the right to interpret and implement the directives in a way she thinks can best enhance curriculum, teaching and learning. As an active member of the WA Principals' Association she enjoys the opportunities such a position gives her to debate the broader picture of education with her peers, something she feels she would not experience if she restricted her energies to working only within her school environment. Her membership of the association's executive also means that she meets with and debates important policy issues with the state's central education office policymakers, thus giving her association a say in helping to shape the course of education within the state. She believes that such involvement also raises the quality of the leadership which she provides within her school.

In her five years at Western Coast SHS, Janet has guided the school through three distinct stages in her attempts to influence the quality of the curriculum, teaching and learning provided to students. The first stage focused on the need to reassess the culture of the school. The pastoral care system was addressed and changes were made which ensured that it became a system providing for the welfare and support of the students of the school, not as it had been, namely, an administrative and disciplinary role in relation to students. The second stage was concerned with the promotion of initiatives within a 'school development planning' framework. In the third stage the emphasis moved from seeking to promote change through a 'whole school' approach, to one based on individual teachers being facilitated to reflect on their classroom practices, using the leadership capacity of heads of departments and 'teachers in charge'. Before these stages can be examined, however, it is necessary that we step back a little and explore Janet's background in order to appreciate the influences on her life which have helped determine the kind of principal that she has become.

Janet's immediate family is Australian born. Her paternal grandfather's family came from Ireland originally, but he travelled from Ballarat in the Victorian goldfields to Perenjori in the midwest of WA, to pioneer the area with his brother. The population of the state was sorely depleted at this time and the government and the Roman Catholic Church actively recruited migrants with offers of land grants. The brothers, being Catholic, had been asked to come to the area by their archbishop . They cleared the land and farmed it, as did all of their children, except Janet's father who became a bank clerk. He had been sent to New Norcia near Perth as a secondary school boarder and was educated there in a school run by a Catholic religious order. This influence of having been sent away from the country to school and to have achieved educational success led him away from farming as a possible future. He promised his children an education, seeing it as the highest possible gift and achievement: 'Dad always said that he wouldn't leave us with nothing. We would be given a good education.' Janet's maternal grandfather was of Swiss descent and her maternal grandmother was English. They, too, settled as farmers in the WA countryside. Both branches of Janet's immediate family were Catholic. After Janet's parents met and married her father went to fight in World War II. On return, they travelled to the isolated former goldmining town of Cue, before eventually settling in Perth where Janet was born in 1951, the second youngest of six children.

The early years of Janet's life were spent in an eastern suburb of Perth, but her parents decided to move to a western suburb when she was five so that the children could be close to the schools that their father wished them to attend. Janet, like her three sisters, attended a Loreto nuns' convent school while her brothers were educated at a Jesuit school. All of her twelve years of schooling from 1956 until 1968 were with the Loreto nuns. School presented no problems for Janet and she excelled. In fact, she recalls with pride that she completed the year eleven and twelve mathematics course in one year. The curriculum was very academic and Janet studied mathematics and chemistry which were unusual choices for girls at the time in most school systems. Loreto was an upper-middle-class Catholic school and Janet was from a less wealthy family than many of her peers: 'A lot of the girls at school with me were from very rich families. Some of them had parents who were doctors and lawyers. One girl's parents were both doctors.' At the time, a small number of Catholic schools throughout Australia provided curricula which emphasized the humanities and sciences, catering for the needs of upper-middle-class Catholics who desired a university entrance education for their children. It is possible that without the vision and the sacrifices made by her father to send her to Loreto, she might well not have had the opportunity to study mathematics and chemistry.

It is also apparent that she holds her father in high regard for positions he adopted as head of the house, taking full responsibility for the family and its welfare. Janet tells us that he had three jobs for most of his life, working the usual week, followed by two jobs every Saturday from midday to midnight, but he was always at home on Sundays. He continued this practice until the last child's education was complete. He sacrificed promotion within the banking hierarchy, in order to remain in the city and be near the schools chosen for the education of the children.

Janet's father never gave the impression to his children in any way that he harboured any resentment for the personal sacrifices he made in order to provide them with an education. She says:

> It was only when he said that he could now give up the two Saturday jobs, when my youngest sister began university, that I realized why he had three jobs at all. It must have been to pay for all of those school fees at the Catholic schools for his six children.

All six children also experienced equality in the home. This is a notion which Janet now fully supports in her working life and it is reflected in her attitudes to both her students and staff and to their needs. Decision making is the right of all on her present staff when she considers that they have the expertise and interest and are responsible for implementing their decisions. She has deliberately dismantled the structures within her school that empowered, as decision makers, only those with seniority and promotional position, like the heads of departments, the deputies and herself. Her attitude to her staff is that they all deserve equality in terms of the opportunity to participate and she holds that they should not necessarily be excluded from participation if they do not hold promotional positions.

When Janet was in school Catholic education was characterized by the extent to which it was ordered, directive and task orientated, and it had high expectations of its pupils. Various regulations designed to govern the behaviour of the religious teacher in Catholic schools served to reinforce these characteristics and enhanced the quality of teaching and learning. The schoolroom was expected to be a model of neatness and tidiness. The teacher was expected to attend carefully to the preparation of his or her work, and in the case of certain religious orders there was a requirement that a record of the syllabus covered should be written up in great detail at the end of every month. In general, the approach seems to have been one which would find favour with contemporary education theorists who stress the importance of such core leadership elements as 'goal-focused activities' and 'teacher directed classroom management and decision making'.

Although apparently clinical in its application, Catholic education was secure and safe. Spiritual growth through education and personal development through service to others were priorities along with academic achievement. Joining Church organizations which were dedicated to service within the community was encouraged and participation in them was highly praised within the school. Activities aimed at cultivating missionary zeal amongst pupils and encouraging them to join the religious life were also promoted. Janet engaged in some activities that were service related, including visiting people's homes and performing in musical concerts at Christmas aimed at raising money for charity. At school, she was also in the tennis team and the netball team and was a prefect and a house vice-captain. She participated in every aspect of school and Church life, both of which were closely bound. This social involvement has stood her in good stead ever since. She admits to being a people person and likes to work with people. She's a team player.

When Janet's own school matriculation results were publicly announced at the end of her final year of schooling in 1968, family practice resulted in all of the members discussing her options for the future. However, her father recognized their lack of expertise in the circumstance and called in what he considered to be the expert for advice, namely, a family friend who was also a vice-principal at one of the primary-teachers' colleges. As a consequence of that advice, she enrolled for a science degree at the University of Western Australia (UWA).

University proved to be as absorbing for Janet as school had been, but the work load was more demanding and exhausting. In her opinion, she had been well prepared by the school and was committed to very long days and nights for all of her years there. Despite this heavy time commitment, her social life meshed in well with her studies and she mixed mainly with fellow students. Typically, Janet found them exciting and begrudges none of the time given over to study: 'I noticed that the more I progressed with my degree the better the marks became. I think it was because I was specializing in what interested me and the people with whom I studied. We all encouraged each other.'

On finishing university with first class honours in Botany in 1972, Janet did not wish to continue to doctorate level as the routine and repetitiveness of research during her honours year offered her little inspiration. Having consulted her father and accepted his advice, she enrolled for and completed a diploma of education the following year, despite having been offered a scholarship to complete her doctorate. She now had the necessary qualifications to embark on a career as a schoolteacher. She was also not to embark on it alone. During her first year of university Janet met her future husband, Mike Turner, who was also studying for a science degree. They married in 1973 and both moved to Northern Senior High School (SHS) in the northwest of WA, as members of the science staff.

At Northern SHS Janet taught science, biology, human biology, health education and physical education. Her attitude to this situation of teaching a variety of subjects for which she was not qualified was simple: 'If you can teach, you can teach.' She found the experience of teaching across the subjects invaluable and she also enjoyed it. It gave her an insight into the personalities of her students. In this regard, she offers the example of teaching some students who displayed one set of characteristics in a health education lesson and another set in physical education. She viewed her introduction to teaching as an adventure and speaks of the head of department as an outstanding teacher who clearly focused on student needs and was inspirational.

Janet was innovative at Northern SHS. She developed a health education programme there which suited the needs of the students she taught. The existing programme covered such subjects as sanitary landfill, which neither Janet nor her students found the slightest bit interesting or relevant to the environment in which they lived. Theirs was a very hot, very remote, iron-ore mining town. Together, they decided what they wanted to know about and what was relevant, and rejected those aspects of the curriculum laid down by EDWA which they considered irrelevant and replaced them with others.

Janet's experience of teamwork at Northern SHS was also positive, particularly with the other science teachers. As there was no laboratory technician at the school it was the science staff's responsibility, in addition to their teaching load, to prepare experiments and equipment for the lessons. This required extra hours of work. In these tasks they worked as a team and supported each other. This experience, Janet claims, also was invaluable as it gave her an awareness of the elements involved in making science an attractive and worthwhile subject. Her experiences translate now into an understanding and appreciation of the importance of teamwork if curriculum and administrative innovations are to be successful. Throughout her six years in this country town, she also participated heavily in sporting and community life. The friendships which she made in the 1970s have been enduring. Indeed, twenty years later she holidays with a group of friends from this era together with their children.

In 1978, Janet was invited to take the position of acting deputy principal at Northern SHS. She was the most highly qualified woman on the staff and the only one with a university degree. While acting as deputy principal she chose to continue teaching biology and physical education so that she could remain in touch with the students and the teachers. She applied for a permanent position as a deputy principal the following year. At the same time, she applied for entry into the medical faculty at UWA and was offered a place. However, she declined the offer in favour of continuing teaching when she was offered the position of deputy principal in a permanent capacity at Northern SHS. A year later she transferred to Eastern Suburbs SHS in Perth, where she remained until 1986. During her time there, Janet had a year's leave in 1983 when she gave birth to her daughter and commenced studying for a graduate diploma in educational administration.

In 1986, Janet succeeded in her application to become a principal and transferred to Pilbara SHS in 1987. Female principals were very few in number and Janet had needed a lot of encouragement to apply initially in 1985. She had not considered the position for herself until others mentioned it to her. In this, it is significant that she had not measured her own worth in terms of her experience, qualifications and skill. She is self-effacing and modest about her abilities. Once she takes on a challenge, however, her attitude is one of 'I can do that'.

Before 1985, it had been very difficult for women to gain promotion to the level of principal in government schools because few women had achieved a level of 'seniority' which would enable them to apply for this promotional step. One's 'level of seniority' refers to the number of years a person had taught with EDWA as a 'permanently employed' teacher. 'Permanency' was granted after two full-time years of teaching, after an EDWA superintendent had assessed a teacher's competency. The prerequisite for promotion, apart from seniority, was permanency.

The main reason why there were very few female principals was because women had not achieved seniority due to the temporary nature of their employment. Until the 1970s, women in WA had to resign their permanent status when they married, thereby rendering them ineligible for promotion. This practice was not unusual, as all government bodies and banking institutions had the same rules regarding women and marriage. It was accepted by society because it reflected the commonly held attitudes of both men and women that a woman's place was in the home. Indeed, it was relatively unusual to find a woman, who was married with children, in the workforce. Women often resigned from work when they married and they were neither expected nor encouraged to return to the workforce. Superannuation schemes offered women a lower rate of return on their investment and women were discouraged from enrolling in a scheme at all. The argument was that it would not be worth it because they were only going to pull out anyway.

When women employed by EDWA were granted the legal right to permanency regardless of their marital status, their seniority was calculated from the date on which they reapplied for and were granted permanency. None of their previous service was counted. It was for these reasons that, in 1985, EDWA changed the criteria under which women could apply to become principals. Now, it was possible for them to apply for promotion on merit, if they had served as a deputy principal for more than five years. Three people in particular encouraged Janet to apply for the position of principal. The first to press her to apply was the 'regional superintendent', a woman and former government school deputy principal. She recognized Janet's talents and the expertise that she offered. Another person who pushed Janet to apply was her previous principal, a male. It was he who enlisted the third person, Mike,

Janet's husband, to also seek to persuade her to apply. They were successful in their efforts. The interview process was gruelling and Janet admits to feeling great relief at not being selected the first time. She did, however, apply again and was successful. Accordingly, the family, in full support of her, moved to the northwest mining town of Pilbara in 1987.

At Pilbara SHS Janet's first task was to plan for the implementation of EDWA's 'Unit Curriculum' programme within the school, in consultation with her staff. The decision that a unit approach should be adopted in the organization of the curriculum in all WA government schools in seven component areas for lower secondary schools was taken by the Minister for Education. These seven component areas, each of which was accorded equal status, were English, languages and communication; mathematics; personal and vocational education; physical education; practical and creative Arts; science and technology; social studies.

The goals of Unit Curriculum were excellence, equity and relevance, to be achieved through increased curriculum flexibility, more public access, and more explicit teaching and learning goals. To this end, the seven curriculum components were organized into forty hour units of study. Nearly 300 units were prepared by EDWA within the specified component areas and students had time to complete seventy-two units or more during years eight to ten. Units were allocated to a stage of progress from stage one to stage six, with varying entry points for students. In general, progress was to be sequential and students' programmes could include units in a variety of stages at the same time. The associated assessment system was criterion based. Also, unit maps were prepared for each subject showing the allocation of units to each stage. The intention was that students, given appropriate advice and support, would be able to develop their own pathways through the unit maps and plot a learning programme suitable to their needs, interests and abilities.

It was Janet who was the stable force in the three years of her principalship at Pilbara SHS and the guiding force behind the introduction of the Unit Curriculum there, as the deputy principals and senior staff were moving in and out of permanent and relieving positions. In fact, she became the longest-serving principal in that town. At a time in which major policy changes were being implemented, her authority and stability provided those who were planning the changes with a figure to whom they could turn for guidance. Janet was also busy on other fronts. She completed the graduate diploma which she had begun in Perth, using the correspondence mode as she could no longer attend the campus many hundreds of kilometres away. Also, during her tenure at Pilbara SHS, Janet was nominated by EDWA for the 'WA Women in Management Award' which is presented every second year. Although she was not the ultimate winner, she was very flattered by the nomination in recognition of her achievements.

Janet applied for and was appointed to the Principalship of Western Coast SHS in Perth, in 1990, but did not take up the appointment until 1991 after taking a year's long-service leave. Since her arrival at Western Coast SHS Janet has implemented many innovations aimed at improving curriculum, teaching and learning. These will now be considered in detail and in relation to the extent to which they can be attributed to her life history.

Western Coast SHS is located in a suburb on the west coast of the Perth metropolitan area. The catchment area of the school is made up largely of lower-middle-class families, many of whom are buying their own homes. The school is approximately nineteen years old and has at the present time a student population of approximately 850, with sixty-three teaching staff. It caters for students from years eight to twelve and has, in 1995, become a focus school for repeating year twelve students from the surrounding districts. Past enrolments have been as high as 1,200 students. The school staff includes a principal, two deputy principals, a programme co-ordinator, heads of department, youth education officers and teaching staff. The teaching staff is organized into traditional subject departments, including mathematics, English, science, social studies, home economics, design and technology, information technology, physical and health education, art and languages-other-than-English (LOTE). Decision making in the school is participative and takes place through a limited number of committees, including the school council, the subject representative meeting and general staff meetings. The school has a representative student council and a parents and citizens' association which supports the school.

There have been three stages of change and development since Janet's arrival at Western Coast SHS. The first stage was concerned with cultural changes. The main focus was on changing the pastoral care system to ensure that it became a system providing support for the students of the school, rather than discipline as had been its previous function. There was a flow-on effect into many other areas of the school affecting both students and staff, particularly staff participative decision making. Primarily, the focus at this early stage was on the welfare of the students. Amongst the areas addressed were the size of form classes, the duties of year co-ordinators, the involvement of all staff with form classes, and the development of opportunities for all staff to participate rather than just those in promotional positions.

Janet admits that she can and does represent her personal perspective through her interpretation of the role of the pastoral care programme, which may also reflect some Catholic values. This is not, she believes, in conflict with the fact that government high schools are non-sectarian since they promote the valuing of others, courtesy, respect and generosity. Janet, in fact, strongly defends the rights of the parents and students to have an education free from religious influence. She firmly supports the belief that if parents require religious instruction to be provided at school, then they can choose a religious school for their children. Indeed, her own daughter attends a Catholic school.

59

Stage two of Janet's development programme emerged out of the need for the school to generate a school development programme. It, too, commenced in 1991, although EDWA had initiated the process as a directive to all schools in 1990. This development involved the close examination of the school and many of its practices. Time allocations were addressed so that they would meet the needs of the students and the teachers, and the method of reporting on students' performance was reviewed. Accepted ways of approaching and doing things were questioned and changed in many cases. Within the third stage of Janet's development programme, the emphasis moved away from seeking to promote change through a 'whole-school' approach to one based on individual teachers being facilitated in reflection on their classroom practices. Although this stage was begun in response to EDWA's request for 'accountability' of schools, Janet interpreted the request in terms of how it could be harnessed to provide the professional development of her heads of department (HODs) to enhance their leadership. As each new stage emerged, the previous ones continued to develop. Each of the three stages will now be discussed more fully.

When Janet took up her appointment at Western Coast SHS in 1991, the school had not had a stable administration for two years. Janet's predecessor, of whom she speaks highly, had been seconded to take up another position in 1989 and the deputy principal had filled the position. In 1990 Janet and her family had a year's long-service leave and the position was again filled by a temporary principal. The consequence of this situation was that the school merely ticked over with the relieving principal adopting a caretaker role. Little things, Janet noticed, had not been maintained in terms of administrative practices over the two years prior to her arrival. She knew, for example, that the previous permanent principal had a very effective method of managing and filing correspondence. She had adopted his method at Pilbara SHS, having been introduced to it at a professional development course conducted by him on the subject. Little had been done, either, in regard to matters of policy since the last principal had been there. Janet says of the situation: 'It was as if everything was on hold waiting for me. I felt that the staff was waiting for me to do something – anything, and I did not let them down.'

Even though Janet was not expected to take up the principalship of Western Coast SHS until 1991, she made two visits to the school in the November of 1990. During these visits she gathered information, then focused in particular on the system of pastoral care at the school. The students were grouped into form classes of approximately thirty-two students. Each form class was assigned a form teacher and they met daily before school for twenty minutes. The main purpose of the form class was for the teachers to note pupils' absences and to disseminate any information from the administration. Form teachers were required to oversee the reporting on students each semester and ensure that all reports written by other teachers were completed correctly. Form classes provided an organizational structure, too, for certain school events like sports carnivals. Another aim of the form class was to provide pastoral care, based on the notion that the teacher and students would build up a relationship with each other over the year.

Prior to Janet's arrival, the HODs and other senior staff had not been required to participate in form classes. This situation was perceived to be one of the privileges of their position and gave them a little more non-contact time with students. In theory, this was so that they could dedicate a little more time to their administrative duties. The outcome, however, was that the form groups were very large. Janet was concerned about the inequity of this system as it seemed to create a sense amongst staff that some were more privileged than others. She considered that this was bad for morale. She felt that there were significant gains to be made for all concerned by adopting a system of pastoral care in which all staff, including the HODs, participated. She also saw that it would reduce class size to groups of 20–22. At her request, this change was made and was in place when she commenced work as principal in 1991.

Another change which Janet made to the structure of the pastoral care system was in the area of form teachers. From now on, a year eight form class and its teacher, for example, would remain together until that class graduated at year twelve. The teacher, if still in the school, would then begin all over again with a new year eight class. Janet says of this arrangement:

> It is desirable to have a system which provides continuity of form teachers with their form until one or other leaves the school. It contributes to an atmosphere which at best can build mutual trust and respect within the group. It creates a sense of belonging and of family.

She knew that for some students, this form system would provide the only formal opportunity they would have for this kind of relationship. The need for it had been demonstrated to Janet at Eastern Suburbs SHS where she was the deputy principal for seven years. There she found herself working with some very difficult and socially deprived students. The school's catchment area was one in which there was very real poverty and social disfunctionality. One significant incident in particular had been instrumental in forming Janet's attitude to the need for a well-constructed programme of pastoral care. She had cause to go to the home of one of the students in her capacity as deputy principal. The girl had been suspended and both Janet and the principal had escorted her home. What she encountered was a first-hand introduction to the deplorable home lives of some of her students. The home was filthy and in complete disarray. There was rubbish in the house and bedding was strewn everywhere. There was also graffiti littering the internal and external walls of the house.

The experience, Janet claims, drew her attention to the nature of the unseen aspects of all students' personal lives which impact on their school lives and behaviours:

It dawned on me again how important it is never to judge someone. One never really knows the real circumstances. My experiences in that school taught me compassion. I was exposed, however, to both the worst and the best that people could hope to be. The poverty that I encountered in some of the families was staggering. Some students survive well but others certainly do not. But you know, I think I have an idea about what makes the difference – why some survive while others don't. The difference between being the best you can be and the worst, lies in the consistent, stable support by a parent or parents. For others, where this does not exist, the school is their only hope.

Janet helped extracurricularly in what she considered the best way she could, namely, becoming the coach of a netball team and transporting the players to and from the games which they played each week.

Janet's initial pastoral care initiatives at Western Coast SHS were such as to involve many more than herself. Her pursuit of more staff involvement and smaller form classes to achieve more student–teacher contact was successful. Also, the changes were well accepted and ran well. Janet does not, however, attribute the success of the initiatives to herself only. She recognizes that while it was she who had initiated dialogue on the matter, the staff embraced the changes enthusiastically and it was due to them that the transition was as smooth as it was.

With the new system of organizing pastoral care at the school level, Janet now sought to improve the quality of pastoral care provided by the co-ordinators of the different year levels in the school. Their role at the time of her arrival was to support the teaching staff and to take the initiative for discipline, absenteeism, enrolment, counselling in subject choice and career paths in some cases, and pastoral care. They used to suspend students whose behaviour in their opinion warranted it. On her arrival and with her full support, the deputy principal now made it very clear to the year co-ordinators that, legally, only the principal had the authority to suspend pupils. The deputy principal was also new to the school at the same time as Janet. He held a similar view to Janet's and was extremely supportive in the change of role. He was enthusiastic in taking back administrative tasks such as enrolment and subject choice. The year co-ordinators now became people to support students, to mediate in their disputes, to advocate their rights, to represent their views and to liaise with parents and staff.

Janet argues that the change which she promoted in the role of the year co-ordinators was a direct result of the memories of her experience at Eastern Suburbs SHS. She was reminded of the need to provide students with access to someone who would stand up for them – someone to whom they could turn if they were in trouble. By now her preferred method of pastoral care was in place and she felt confident enough to move on to the next stage in her reform agenda, namely, school development planning. This phase will be considered in detail later. However, it is important to stress that while she embraced school development planning wholeheartedly, she also continued to maintain and attempt to improve the school's system of pastoral care.

Another of Janet's initiatives to promote caring in her school was her encouragement of teachers to take 'ownership of rooms'. Up until this point the teachers moved about the school to various rooms for their different classes. Because classrooms had an atmosphere which was impersonal, student work was displayed. She agreed to spend money on maintenance of the classrooms, which she believed was necessary in order to promote an environment conducive to teaching and learning, as long as the teachers who would be given ownership of the classrooms within their department guaranteed that the rooms would be well kept. This innovation proved very successful. It helped to create a sense of pride in the teachers and students who worked in the classrooms. Janet noted that in the case of the teachers in one subject area who had opted not to have teacher ownership of rooms, the upkeep on the rooms was not on a par with those who had taken the idea on board. Slowly but surely staff came to see the difference. Now, five years later, room ownership is well accepted and Janet has gone a long way towards realizing her desire to create a homely atmosphere. This desire, of course, is not surprising in view of her background. In particular, her school experience with the Loreto nuns taught her that school should reflect the values of home and society and should be given respect by all members of the community; she, like the other students, had been responsible for the daily cleaning of classrooms.

Part of Janet's rationale behind her promotion of the notion of the ownership of rooms by teachers and students at Western Coast SHS may also be attributed to her great awareness of the sacrifices which her parents made in order to give herself and her brothers and sisters an education. It seems to have instilled in her a conviction that one must look after what one has in order to appreciate the privileges one has been given in this life. Teachers owning their rooms implies that they will demand respect for that room from those who enter it. Ownership also allows the teacher to personalize the room, thus sharing a little of oneself with the students. In this regard, and in the light of Janet's background, one is also reminded that presently it is common to describe the Catholic school as a Christian community sharing 'family values', in contrast to viewing it as a business or an institution.

It will be remembered that while Janet was taking initiatives which were building on the pastoral care structures she had put into place, she was now well into her second phase of her reform agenda, with the focus very clearly on 'school development planning' (SDP). In 1990, the year prior to Janet's move to Western Coast SHS, EDWA had instructed schools to initiate SDP policies. Because the previous principal had been placed at the school on a temporary basis only, he had not initiated any such policies, thus contributing to the sense of 'waiting' which Janet experienced when she visited the school in 1990. She was also most grateful for the situation in which she found herself because she did not have to step into a school which had already begun to engage in SDP. Had the situation been otherwise, she may have had problems in having to build up another plan. The staff, she felt, would also have been adversely affected by such a situation. Accordingly, she interpreted the decision by her predecessor not to put plans and policy structures into place as an act of consideration.

Janet approached school development planning with great enthusiasm:

> I confess that nobody, including myself, knew what to do at first, but there was a commitment to do something, and a commitment to make it a success. If the parameters of a task are restricting, I am the type of person who will find ways of working around them. The plan for 1991 was broad-based and concerned with working with parents to develop the school goals and performance indicators.

She took to school development planning 'like a duck to water'. It is reasonable to argue that this was because she is personally predisposed to adopting a planning approach to life. The influence of her five years of academic work at university, in which she learned the skill of problem solving and how to adopt a planned approach to work – both critical in scientific enquiry – came to the fore. Listening to her talk about her life and her initiatives, it becomes clear that Janet is a very goal-directed person. Words like 'focused', 'committed', 'forceful' and 'determined' come to mind readily when one seeks to describe her. Often, the connotations of these words are that the person to whom they relate is boring. Janet, however, belies the myth that because someone's lifestyle is ordered and predictable it must be dull and of little value, and that disorder and unpredictability make for a more fulfilling life. Indeed, in an apologetic manner, she occasionally describes herself as ordinary because of the routine of her lifestyle in her youth and now. Certainly, it is an ordered and relatively predictable life, but she is enthusiastic and others find her inspirational.

Janet's educational experiences, like her family life, have been very ordered. This is now reflected in her approach to her work. Not only that, but her 'total' life is very organized. She arrives at school daily at half-past seven, after dropping her daughter at the bus stop. She leaves school at four o'clock, collects her daughter from the bus stop and spends five minutes driving her home. This time she enjoys, as she and her daughter have a chance to talk to each other about their day before Janet goes to aerobics for one hour. She returns home to the evening meal which is prepared by her husband. Often, she then goes to a meeting or they all do their homework on the dining-room table together. Friday night is spent at home and is the time when the house is cleaned by the family. On Saturday morning the family, including her mother-in-law, goes shopping for the week and has breakfast at the local shopping centre. This is a pattern from which Janet derives much pleasure.

The structure and organization which surround Janet's present professional and personal lives reflect the routine which has always been part of her life, and which was reinforced at university by her induction into the scientific world. As a child, her family's commitment to their religious life was reflected in routine:

> Every night at about eight we said the rosary together, as a family, on our knees on the lounge room floor. Every Sunday we went to church and ate lunch together as a family afterwards. This was the way that it always was, for as long as I can remember, while I lived with my parents.

The family's commitment to its grandparents was responsible for another pattern, with Janet, her father and her youngest sister visiting the paternal grandparents every Friday night after tea.

Given this background, Janet's wholehearted adoption of school development planning is understandable. Indeed, it is arguable that the fact that EDWA was giving it a high profile legitimized her desire to move the management of the school in the direction in which she would have wished it to go anyway. At the time of her arrival, the 'school education council' at Western Coast SHS had been comprised of those staff in promotional positions only. Janet did not agree that this was necessarily the best approach if there was to continue to be an improvement in curriculum, teaching and learning within the school. As a consequence, one of the first things that she did on arrival was to alter structures so that all staff had an opportunity to take part in the decision-making process to decide the directions in which the school would move. She explained that everyone was in a position to contribute through participation in various decision-making committees if they had the expertise, had a 'stake' in the area which was the focus of the relevant committee and were in a position to implement the changes. Depending on the issues, different committees were formed.

Janet strongly rejects the argument that just because things have always been done in a certain way, that it is necessarily the correct way. Her approach to school development planning was a very participative one, with the aim of drawing in those with expertise as the plans developed, thus building up their sense of ownership. This view was nurtured by the experience with her staff at Pilbara SHS when, during her principalship there, they were required to implement Unit Curriculum. She took great pleasure from the ease with which Unit Curriculum was implemented in that school and attributes it to the sense of staff harmony there. She claims that the staff brought freshness to the school, as most were either new to teaching or new to their promotional positions. She says their strength lay in their preparedness to try things, share things and to remain unthreatened by change. She states that she gave them the freedom 'to do their own thing' and that she was supportive in guiding them.

It was not so easy to effect change at Western Coast SHS because many of the staff had been there for many years, were very secure and comfortable in their positions, and those in promotional positions had dominated the decision-making process. There was an atmosphere of expectation surrounding Janet's eventual arrival which came from a fear in some of the staff that changes might jeopardize their positions and, as a result, the authority that these positions carried within the school. The fact that there had been no attempt by the previous relieving principal to implement change no doubt added to the sense that things at Western Coast SHS would stay as they had always been. It was not long, however, before this was shattered by the manner in which Janet sought some changes.

Janet also promoted change based upon the importance that she attaches to students knowing what they will be taught, how they will be taught it and what assessments will occur, before they begin any programme of work. She came to an appreciation of this very early on in her career, when she was a new teacher in Northern SHS. Now, as an introductory step at Western Coast SHS, she committed herself to meeting all of the year eight students, visiting them whenever they were being taught in a core subject area, checking their files for organization in terms of having dividers, course outlines for the term, and assessment documents and marks. This strategy assists in identifying early those who are experiencing organizational problems and they can be referred to the reading resource teacher. She continues this practice in all year eight classes as she believes that if students are well organized and prepared the learning process will be made easier for them. Her hope is that the students, in turn, in seeing that she as the principal is concerned enough about this aspect of their work to visit them regularly, will reinforce the importance that their teacher is attempting to imbue while also providing an avenue of support for those who may need the assistance of the reading resource teacher.

Another initiative which Janet addressed through school development planning focused on the school's system of reporting to parents and students. On her arrival at the school she found that it was using a reporting style involving a range of descriptors, where staff ticked the appropriate box to indicate student achievement. Written comments could be added to this by each teacher. Staff indicated dissatisfaction with this method, particularly in relation to the time involved in the completion of each report, the work involved in the collation of each student report and the need for staff to fill out a report again if just one member made an error with an entry. It was also not acceptable to Janet, since she had to spend a lot of time with staff sorting out associated conflict. Also, as she saw it, the reporting system did not address students as individuals and gave little assistance to parents in interpreting their child's performance. She emphasized that the school needed to develop a reporting system which would provide 'appropriate and timely feedback to parents'.

The outcome of her initiative is a school reporting system to students and parents which provides written and oral information on students' performance and achievement. It was decided, through a consultative process, to change from the 'tick the box' descriptor method to a newer computer-style of reporting. The format involves the use of a database of comments, which was borrowed initially from another school to demonstrate its capacity to the staff. From this database staff can select the most appropriate comments to describe the performance of each student. There is space for 500 comments or items per department. Departments choose to add or modify comments to suit their subject-specific needs. Some departments do this on a regular basis while others do not. The teachers are also encouraged to use the comments generated by other departments if they think they will be useful.

The school now also has a number of other systems in place for reporting to parents. It holds an open reporting day for lower-school students and their parents. There is an upper-school report evening for students and their parents, although they can attend on the lower-school report day if they so wish. In the report day parents must pick up their child's report. They then have the opportunity to talk to the various teachers about their child's progress. No formal interview times are made but it provides the opportunity for parents to come to the school and to talk to the teachers.

Other methods of reporting include commendation letters of successful achievement which are posted to parents and 'at risk of failure' letters which are sent home during week six or seven to inform parents that their child is highly likely to fail a unit or units. Progress reports are also completed for students at risk. Teachers are encouraged to communicate with parents about students' achievement by telephone, letter and personal interviews and parents are encouraged to seek information on their child through any of these methods and through contact with the year co-ordinator.

In her first year at Western Coast SHS, Janet had made some significant and very visible changes to the school, with apparent ease. She had recognized what needed to be done and had succeeded in doing it through recognizing the worth both of her staff and of adopting a planning approach to her own work and that of the school. Janet comments on how she is regularly surprised by what others see as her achievements and her perception that she has simply done her best. She is a team player and believes in the worth of each team member and the contribution made by each person. As she puts it, 'without the individual effort there is no team and without a team, there is no outcome'. She had been reminded of this many times, in her own school life as a student, sports captain and prefect, throughout her university life and also during her teaching career.

As 1991 drew to a close, Janet had established the basis of a strong pastoral care system in the school and was starting to build on this with efforts to create a caring ethos amongst the pupils. In fact, four years later she is still taking initiatives in this direction. In particular, she is confronting the issue of school bullying. She encouraged others to pursue this and take a leadership role with the staff, and had stepped back and provided support and encouragement. The most shocking result of an in-school survey done on bullying in 1994 was that the students revealed that after the playground, the classroom is the next most likely place that they would encounter bullying. It made the teaching staff reassess what bullying actually is. It could not be assumed, they realized, that bullying is always an overt behaviour. It was also realized that bullying can interfere directly with the teaching process and that as a consequence of this, the effect of bullying on a student's ability to learn can be huge. The groundwork on how to address these issues is now being done and is linked into the learning programme across the whole school.

By the end of 1991, a school development policy was also firmly in place and provided an approach for systematically addressing areas to focus on in order to improve the quality of curriculum, teaching and learning in the school. Against such a background Janet entered a new phase in her initiatives. In this, she focused her efforts very much on the concept of 'accountability'. In 1992, 'accountability', along with school development planning, was very much what EDWA was emphasizing with its principals. This notion of accountability sat easily with Janet. It corresponds with her conviction that 'we all must account for what we do no matter what it is we're doing in life'. This attitude that you are responsible for your own actions is one that Janet had learned throughout her life from her family and from her single-sex Catholic schooling. Her father was a person who had been content with the choices that he made in his life, even if they meant that his own ambitions had been curtailed. He had sacrificed his chance of promotion by going back to the country in the banking sector in order to send his children to what he regarded as the best schools.

Janet introduced the concept of 'accountability' to her staff by inviting the District Education Officer to address them on the 'accountability of the teacher'. Shortly afterwards, she invited the Superintendent to address them on the associated theme of the 'accountability of the principal'. Janet invited these people into the school so that they would present an EDWA perspective and create an awareness that what was being promoted reflected international trends rather than her own whims. In bringing in EDWA personnel to inform and provide advice, Janet also once again displayed the characteristic of her father, namely, the importance of eliciting the advice of an expert when you are attempting to make critical decisions.

Janet's next step was to attend a leadership course on accountability and feed the information back to her senior staff by way of two pamphlets which she created on her return. One dealt with what accountability is and the other traced the links between the school, each subject department and each teacher. She sees the decision to attend the course as having been part of her personal and professional responsibility. Courses are other ways in which she seeks to expose herself to diverse views and to become informed. However, she is also quick to point out that she enjoys courses such as these, regarding them as treats of a kind. Also, 'accountability', which many see as a threatening and negative concept, was approached in a positive way by Janet. Instead of becoming a negative burden on the school, it became a positive force which emphasized that staff should be cared for, be given time by their superordinates for reflection, and be encouraged to constantly examine their practices and to strive for improvement.

Janet's first initiative was to meet with her HODs in three separate groups and recreate for each small group the workshop that she had attended. This workshop was aimed to inform heads of departments and teachers-in-charge about strategies that they might employ in accounting for the initiatives of the departments within their schools. The aim of Janet's workshops with her HODs was that they in turn would work with their teaching staff and ask them to account for the progress of each of their classes. Each HOD was asked to report back to Janet at their next meeting on each of the staff in their department. She impressed upon the HODs that they must approach the matter in a 'non-threatening' manner. She had anticipated that some HODs could be intimidating to their staff and she was anxious to avoid this.

The results of the interviews conducted between the teachers and the HODs were very positive, with only one HOD out of the eighteen who participated seeming deliberately to fail to cooperate. Of the staff, one teacher of fifteen years' experience confessed that it was really great and it had been the first time a HOD had spent time with her alone discussing each of her classes and her programme's aims. Janet says that it was 'the most rewarding thing that I have been part of so far'. The reward for her was in the fact that her expectation that the HODs would do this well had come to fruition. She had faith in them.

The 1993 school year began at Western Coast SHS with a school day which was ten minutes longer than previously, due to the changes made to the timetable and the Duties-other-than-Teaching (DOT) Time allocation. A major building programme was in place, which meant disruption to the staff and students in terms of classrooms and facilities. The staff room, for example, was relocated during the building programme. However, staff and students coped well. The school development programme was functioning effectively and the pastoral care system was proving to be very effective. Otherwise, the approach was one of consolidating what had been achieved rather than promoting further initiatives aimed at improving the quality of curriculum, teaching and learning.

In 1994, Janet set developments in train once more, again by facilitating her HODs in implementing an accountability model which they had developed to assist staff to examine their practices in the areas of curriculum, teaching and learning. Three questions which all HODs now put on an individual basis to their staff, for each of their classes, at the end of term one or at the beginning of term two were (1) How is the class going? (2) How do you account for the results that you are getting? (3) What strategies will you be putting into practice in order to improve these results or solve any problems that you are having? The HODs then met with Janet for about an hour and a half in term two to report their findings to her. They were then able to account to her in the same manner as their staff accounted to them. Furthermore, the process was followed up in terms three and four. The questions this time were (1) How did your plans go? (2) What would you do differently next time? Also, during the school staff-development days held in terms two and four, Janet requested that half of the day be spent by the staff in each subject area, discussing the plans that they had for their particular departments. The idea was that they would use the same set of questions which had been addressed to them by their department head in regard to their individual programming plans and aims. The purpose of this request of Janet's was that the staff of each department would work as a team to develop plans for the subject area, making the aims of the department unified ones which all the staff would understand. These procedures regarding individual and departmental accountability are now fixed as ongoing features of the school staff's professional development calendar in term four.

Over the 1994 Christmas break Janet reflected that she had not spent enough time helping her HODs to develop their roles as leaders. This comment is in keeping with her aim to nurture her staff and the school community. The time, she decided, was right, as other accountability structures were in place. She says that she could not do it alone so, with the deputy principals' help, she embarked on a programme to assist HODs to explore their roles as educational leaders. They were divided into three groups, one of which was led by herself and the other two by the deputy principals. They decided that they would meet every three weeks and that it would need to be an ongoing programme. The focus questions for the first term were: How do you ensure that all classes have a clear picture of the unit they are studying? Given that you have control of your own budget, what is your role in terms of financial accountability? Have you been in the classroom and supported teachers in any way? What is your goal as a HOD? During term two, a leadership workshop on managing people was conducted with the HODs and Janet described their response as 'terrific'. At their request, three further workshops have been held on 'understanding your personality' and 'planning'.

Janet has spent her entire life in education, as a student, a teacher and an educational administrator and manager, and she is very successful in her field. She is driven constantly to seek to improve the quality of curriculum, teaching and learning for her pupils and to do so by adopting a team approach. Her enjoyment of being part of a team is obvious in that much of what she strives to achieve is for the benefit of the team as well as for the individuals who comprise it. She places great emphasis on providing the very best support to her HODs and their staff in order that they in turn can give the very best support that they can to their students. She emphasizes the excellent work of her deputy principals without which such progress could not have been made.

In her five years at Western Coast SHS, Janet has guided the school through three distinct stages in her attempts to influence the quality of the curriculum, teaching and learning provided to students. In the first stage, the culture of the school was addressed through the pastoral care programme, and changes were made which ensured that it became a system providing for the welfare of the students of the school, not, as it had been, to discipline students. The second stage was concerned with the promotion of initiatives within a 'school development planning' framework. In the third stage, the emphasis moved from seeking to promote change through a 'whole-school' approach, to one based on individual teachers being facilitated in reflection on their classroom practices.

Janet's compulsion to constantly seek to improve the quality of curriculum, teaching and learning has been accounted for to some extent by religious, cultural, educational and family influences. However, she is adamant that much of it would not have been possible if it were not for the love and stability provided by Mike, her husband. He has been part of her life since 1969. He is a Catholic too, and Janet speaks of her life being easy in this regard, and of the fact that they have never had a crisis of faith. His support of Janet has enabled her to pursue her career.

Mike is fulfilled in being a classroom teacher and a major support to his wife. It has been Mike who has, she tells us, recognized her strengths and abilities and encouraged her to develop them. Of him she says: 'I got the best one. There is no one better.' She tells us that it is Mike who does the cooking and who is at home for Sharon when she herself goes to aerobics after school. They think that they are not alike, but in the big issues they seem to be in perfect harmony. These issues are their religion, their support for each other and their love for their daughter and their family.

Finally, in the light of Janet's gender and her rapid rise to the principalship, it is interesting that she claims she never encountered gender stereotyping until she returned to Perth to take up her position in 1980. Only then, she says, did she become aware of a culture where 'it was expected that men did well and women didn't'. In her Catholic family, with the father at the head, it had never been implied that, as a woman, less was expected of her than of her brothers and that she should refrain from setting high goals. Her favourite teacher during her school days, Sister Margaret, who taught her mathematics, made a huge impression on her. This Sister had studied history at university and communicated to her pupils that there was no reason why they should not do likewise. In addition, her Aunt Anne , her mother's sister, was also a Catholic nun of a different religious order. She also had a university degree, which was very rare for anyone of her generation. This impressed Janet greatly.

Janet proudly relates several stories, which illustrate aspects of her aunt's personality. At Anne's funeral one speaker told of her relishing the Vatican-led changes in the 1960s which modernized the clothing that nuns were required to wear because she 'did like to wear pretty things'. The influence of this aunt was great, as it served as an example to Janet that as a person you could make choices which would enable you to fulfil your ambitions without compromising your beliefs.

Earlier in Janet's life, gender was never represented to her as an issue which should influence the choices made. To her, one of the annoying aspects of the positions that she now holds on various education committees is that she is often invited onto them, she feels, in order to fulfil the obligation of gender representation. Nevertheless, she will continue to represent the education system over the next number of years, and will play her part in attempting to transform societal attitudes to women as leaders in education.

# 6

# SIMON JEFFREY

Cara Senior High School is a large government school, probably the second or third largest in WA, with 1,400 students. This number has declined from 1,530 last year. There are approximately 500 students in years eleven and twelve, and 900 in years eight to ten. The numbers will continue to decrease and we would expect a population of about 1,100 by the year 2000. This situation is being caused by the building of White SHS just to the north of us on the edge of the Perth metropolitan area. Presently 520–530 students are bussed down from the north each day. The government has finally fulfilled its promise of ten years to build White SHS. This has had the effect of having our year eight intake of students decrease from 340 to 200. That is the way it will be for the next five years, although we will be starting a publicity campaign which will increase our numbers slightly. The average age of staff members is twenty-six years. We have ninety-six teachers on staff and a non-teaching staff of about twenty. There is a significant number of staff who have been here a long time. The student population is very diverse. About 40 per cent will enter a university course while the number who will enter Technical and Further Education courses is very close to that. This is an extremely multicultural school. I sometimes jokingly say that we don't have any racial problems in this school. No one particular ethnic group can work out who is in the majority. We have a social justice co-ordinator. Cara SHS is a good example of cosmopolitan Australia. This is a typical government high school but we specialize to a significant degree. We have special aeronautics courses here. Then we have our special visual arts programme. We have a very vibrant Japanese programme. This is the only school in this area which offers Japanese. There has also been a big technology push in the school.

This is the matter-of-fact way in which Simon Jeffrey describes Cara SHS where he is the principal. Initially on talking to him one gets the impression that he has had little to do with the dynamism of the school and the interesting programmes which it has to offer. He is very modest about his achievements since becoming principal of the school seven years ago. However, there is little doubt that he has been a major driving force behind the elevation of this high school to its present prestigious status.

When Simon arrived at the school there were a number of discrete projects underway and a number of teachers who were anxious to promote innovations. However, they were impeded by an inertia associated with a lack of clear vision and direction in the school. Simon was to become the catalyst for change, the major driving force, harnessing the innovative ideas of others and motivating them to pursue their individual visions within the context of a school plan:

> This is my seventh year here so I think it would be true to say that in my first year I sat back and just had a very quiet look at what the school was actually doing. Then, together with a number of significant people in the school community, I designed a five-year plan. I describe the school as a sleeping giant when I first came here. The development of the technology programme in the school has been done with some very key people in the school. They were just waiting for somebody to give them the go-ahead and say 'let's go' and they would put their foot on the accelerator. The Japanese programme – there was one person here who was very keen to sort of say 'the Italian programme in the school is stagnating – and we need a modern Asian language.' I supported her efforts wholeheartedly. Then there is the aeronautics programme. We taught aeronautics in years eleven and twelve, but I could not understand why we were concentrating on it only in these years. So we extended it to years eight, nine and ten. Then there is the area of visual arts. We had four teachers who had formed a loose partnership but we gave them support so that they were able to offer planned programmes within the school's official plan.

Given this scenario, it is not surprising that the promotion of school development planning by EDWA in the late 1980s was welcomed by Simon:

> Just at this time, coincidentally, the whole idea of *Better Schools* and school development planning presented us with the opportunity to really have a look and say where is this school going? I support school development planning in terms of the model which is handed down from central office. I think in terms of having an improvement plan, call it a school development plan if you want to. I think if we all have some idea of at least what direction we are headed, then we can have a greater chance of getting there.

In this regard, it is interesting that his own education when he was growing up as a young Catholic boy in a strongly working-class area in Perth was one which was very goal directed. He recalls very clearly the nuns in primary school who, as he puts it, 'pushed us very hard to succeed in the examinations so that we could get out of our working-class environment of poverty'. This goal directedness was also something which permeated his secondary schooling, right down to the level of each individual lesson. Amongst his most vivid

74

memories in this regard are those relating to Brother Kelly, the school principal and his senior mathematics teacher:

> The guy could be called away on something because the place was burning down or something, walk out of the room and there was no difference. We knew what was expected and did it. He knew what we should have completed when he returned.

Simon now expects much the same approach from his teachers.

It was particularly fortunate for Simon that school development planning was being promoted at the time when he arrived at Cara SHS. He now had a higher authority legitimizing an approach he favoured in order to set his new school on the route he desired for it: 'The school was a tremendous school in what it had to offer, but I don't think it had come together as a school. It lacked the overall direction, it lacked the overall knowledge as to where it was going.' He also concedes that EDWA policy on its own would not have been sufficient to steer the school by means of school development planning. As he puts it, it also necessitated someone like himself 'grabbing the bull by the horns and actually doing things'. This is a matter which he returns to time and again:

> When I arrived here the school didn't seem to know where it was going. I wouldn't like you to think that I just walked in and said this is where we are going, but at the same time it was something I was very conscious of developing. I insisted that we should keep asking 'What are we on about here at this school?'

The outcome was a school statement on its overall philosophy and on the directions it was going to take. This was translated into a glossy brochure, a promotional campaign was undertaken and the student numbers, which had been on the decline due to the attraction of other schools, began to increase again.

At the same time, Simon is far from happy with all aspects of EDWA's policies on restructuring, devolution and school development planning:

> I'm sorry. I like to be positive but nobody will ever convince me that devolution isn't simply shifting the responsibility and the accountability from the centre to the local area. I know what EDWA's rationale is: get all the problems away from the centre out into the individual worksites. I wish if they were going to give me the responsibility they would give me the power, the real power.

He is also anxious to express his awareness that he can only be innovative within certain parameters and also to highlight that these parameters are set not just by EDWA:

> We work in a government system so I work within a certain regulatory framework, and like it or not there are those regulations. Although there

have been times in the past when I might have stepped outside them, in these days of increased accountability we are all just a little more careful. I remember 1989 when we just blasted away and did things. I was very naive but people were prepared to step more outside the regulations. So, from the employer there is the regulatory framework.

However, there is also the industrial framework from the union. This also cannot be ignored. Unfortunately, developments mean that I have to be a manager more than a leader. There are a lot of tasks that are deflecting me from being an educational leader and what I want to do in that regard. Sitting at my desk is the last place I want to be but it is also a place where I seem to be tied up more and more. Devolution has meant that a lot more tasks have come down to school administrators.

He also believes that much of the competition which is being promoted amongst schools is unhealthy. He illustrates this by putting forward his argument as to how his school should cooperate with the new White SHS which, it will be remembered, is in an area which previously sent students to Cara SHS:

Our school will have to have very close links with our neighbouring schools, particularly the new White SHS, instead of competing with it as to where pupils will do Italian and English literature for grade twelve final examination. If both schools compete for only a limited number of students in years to come, I think both schools will be the losers. School communities have to think rationally and develop a cooperative model as to how they will offer the best possible education to the students. That is a pretty sensitive issue here at the moment. It might mean that Cara SHS becomes a senior campus, surrounded by four or five middle schools catering for the years seven to ten age range. In the twenty-first century we may not have all these senior high schools with year eight to twelve students. Things are changing.

I chaired the steering committee for the establishment of the White SHS for three years and what became blatantly obvious is that we have not got a policy in WA for establishing new schools. We have a very good process for putting bricks and mortar together, but we think that schools are bricks and mortar rather than the people who are in them and the partnerships that exist between those people. I promoted the notion that White SHS would form a relationship with my school. However, the union became involved in industrial issues with staff selection and it just blew up.

Once again, Simon alerts us to the fact that it is not just the central management but also the teaching force and their union which have to make major leaps of imagination if flexible and improved schooling is to become a reality.

It will be noted that the notion of 'partnership' is very central to Simon's thinking. He contends that school development planning has no chance of success unless it is underpinned by healthy staff relationships where all work as partners to improve the educational experiences of the pupils. Regularly, he comments on this. He says that he 'would be very disappointed if any member of staff wouldn't be able to say to you that the whole ethos of the school is that there is a very big partnership here'. Again, he says:

> I was very supportive of the concept of partnership when it began to be promoted in EDWA policy. It's something I believe I share in common with a large number of staff. It is emphasized in our participative decision-making process here. We have got twenty-six committees in the school and that's the one thing they all have in common, the notion that education here is to be seen as a partnership.

Accordingly, it is not surprising that one of the first things he did on arrival was to introduce a school motto, 'Together We Achieve'.

Simon attributes the development of his commitment to this perspective to his responses to a variety of principals of schools where he worked in his earlier teaching days. One in particular, he argues, inspired him. He told Simon regularly that he was one of his 'valued members of staff', constantly encouraged him to try out new ideas in the classroom while insisting that 'if you stuff it up I want to know why', and enhanced his sense of professionalism by using first names in conversation. However, his negative feelings about other principals in schools in which he worked, he argues, have been an even greater influence. He became convinced that their authoritarian and legalistic approaches to staff and pupils were not favourable to the development of a positive teaching and learning environment. Accordingly, as principal of Cara SHS, he took a variety of steps aimed at raising teacher professionalism through encouraging partnerships and participative decision making. One example he gives is as follows:

> I handed over the whole $42,000 of school development funds to a staff school development finance committee. They have a list of criteria for professional development and know that every staff member has an entitlement to at least one day of professional development a year. Of course the staff have to justify how their professional development is fitting into the school priorities. They are comfortable with that. When I first came to the school the staff had no idea how much money was in the school budget. If you are going to say they've got to be actively involved in the planning of the school they have got to know how much money is on board. So the best thing to do with professional development funds is to say: 'Here is your money. Now, who's in charge of it and how are you going to do it?' They are very pleased with this situation.

He also led by example. In his first year at the school he visited all of the primary schools in the area to make himself known to the principals and to let them know that he was anxious to cooperate with them in any way and facilitate closer links between their schools and his. He has encouraged the school's parents' and citizens' association (P & C) to become more involved in the organization of a variety of extracurricular activities. Similarly, he has enlisted the support of the local Cara Rotary group:

> We now have close contact with the Cara Rotary group. They have been very very good to the school. They have been responsible for initiating and setting up a peer support programme in the school and they gave us tremendous assistance in doing that. They sponsor students to various conferences and promote public speaking. They are now heavily involved with the school's science camps over the vacation. We are about to turn to them to help us with our literacy programmes for next year.

The challenge now for Simon is to extend this level of partnership further so that a strong network of school–community links will be built up.

Simon has also adopted a number of approaches in his effort to raise the general morale of the school and create a sense of community. The most novel of these originated with a former temporary teacher named Paul:

> Paul had a vision. Because of the equipment we had in the school, he felt we had the capacity to show all of the students the excellence of each other's work. He proposed that we put network through the school and run a weekly television station. So, I said that we would find out what was involved. We were reticulated from the library to about four or five points, so there was nothing that we couldn't do from there. It was just a bit of an effort to do it. It was a matter of getting through the practical problems. It involved drawing a group of kids together from different areas to put together a TV programme which we could put out week by week as our success story. Just doing it would be seen as a great achievement. However, I was after the old school spirit, bring the whole school together. It is very important to let pupils and teachers see the excellence of what is happening in their own school. My maths staff did not know about the fantastic things which were happening in Japanese, in science or in design and technology, and some of the science teachers did not know the excellent things which were happening in mathematics.

Working closely with some of the state's TV channels, the idea of the weekly broadcast became a reality. For Simon, its real success is that it has survived the test of time; when the first group of pupils who started it left, it carried on with the next group. The overall result, as he sees it, is a much improved school spirit and sense of partnership amongst the stakeholders in the school.

Interestingly, the emphasis Simon places on partnerships goes to the heart of what he sees education as being all about. If there is one notion which is central to what he sees as being the aim of education it is that it should be concerned with the dynamics of interpersonal relationships. He bases his views on this very much upon his own school experiences. He vividly recalls being treated as an adult by Brother Seman on any occasion when, as a pupil, he met him out of school, while he remembers with affection that Brother Drake was, as he puts it, 'a man who made you realize that apart from being a teacher he was a human being. You could question him and you could talk with him at length.' Both of these Christian Brothers were, for him, 'highly inspirational sorts of guys and taskmasters and amazing operators'. He has similar memories of one of his university lecturers:

> Brian had very strong expectations and let you know that. Compared to some of the lecturers who were there, Brian would very quickly know your name. With some lecturers you would walk into their office and they would look at you and think: 'Are you in the wrong office? Do I teach this person?' That was the difference. Brian was the person you went to for help to solve your problems. Even if he didn't teach you it was well known about the place that he would be prepared to say: 'Have you a problem? Is there anything I can give you a hand with?' and if he had the time he would, while other lecturers at the university wouldn't want to know you.

Simon now encourages his teachers to adopt a similar perspective with their pupils and also with their peers, stating regularly that what schools need are 'people managers as well as subject managers'. Again on this, he also practises what he preaches:

> The important parts of my day are when I'm with the teachers or the kids. The most important part of the day is the forty-five minutes that I say are sacred. That is when I am out with the kids at lunchtime. It's the one thing that I won't give up. It is my opportunity to speak with the kids, to find out what concerns them, what they are thinking. If you do it every day they will engage, but if you only do it for a token once a term it won't work. The other sacred time is when I sit there and go through things like students' reports and actually communicate back to the kids. It is very simple but I'm very old fashioned that way. They are the important things.

In a similar vein, he states:

> For me, success is not measured in financial terms. Success is measured in terms of walking down the street and some kid you know you had a hell of a lot of problems with when you were at Hyco SHS when you were deputy principal in charge of discipline, still comes up and grabs you by the hand and says: 'G'day Sir, how are you?' I've often joked about having my phone number in the phone book for the past twenty-six years but I have

never had an abusive phone call. When I was at Hyco we lived right in the middle of the town and we had parents in tears with their kids at eight o'clock at night, but we never had rocks thrown on the roof or anything.

It is realizations like this which he sees as constituting the rewards which are important to him.

Simon's drawing of a certain amount of affirmation from the positive responses of his working-class students is also hardly surprising in view of his own working-class origins. Indeed, his commitment to trying to improve the lot of the less well-off led him in the early stages of his career from position to position in schools located largely in working-class areas. He also felt very comfortable working in these schools and found it easy to relate to the pupils. In his present position, he admits that if he has any bias then it is that he 'favours the underdog and giving something to the person who needs a bit of extra help and who everybody is not quite prepared to take on'. Indeed, it is this attitude which explains his allegiance to the state school system and which has prompted him not to apply for leadership positions within the WA private school system. He is also spurred on to work in a system which, as he puts it, 'opens its doors to all comers' by the memory of the financial sacrifices which his parents made by doing without the badly needed income which he would have brought into the family in his youth if they had not been anxious that he should attend a Catholic high school. He was, however, at least able to make some contribution to the household budget by working at labouring jobs every holiday period.

Now, as well as showing general interest in the welfare of the marginalized students in his school, Simon has been very instrumental in ensuring that they are provided with a compensatory programme:

> We have a 'Training for Employment' programme which we see as a crucial part of the school. We have it because we say 'Together We Achieve'. We are here for all of our students, not just the top flyers, the high flyers. These students are the students who for ten years have experienced nothing but failure, so they come into a one-year course. They do a survival course in English and mathematics, and there are also work studies and career awareness programmes. There's a lot of practical work and a lot of studies based in the workplace. They have two weeks of work experience a term. They go on camps, they build up that morale that has got to exist if they are to make it in society.

He is also insistent that, from the beginning of their high school education, there should be great stress on all pupils reaching high standards of literacy and numeracy, recognizing that these constitute the cognitional media through which all learning takes place. He argues that 'kids are not reading enough, they are just sitting back. Everything is so easy. It's just coming at them from the television screen'. Accordingly, he ensured that the school became involved in EDWA's special literacy 'Stepping Out' programme, which he describes as the first programme that he has been associated with professionally which has shown him how to tackle some of the pupils' language deficiencies. He concludes by stating: 'If I had been armed with that twenty-five years ago, some students who went through me might have been better citizens today.'

Simon is also very committed to the notion that pupils must be prepared to take control of their own learning. It is primarily for this reason that he has been promoting the use of technology throughout the school:

> In the twenty-first century our school community will be a different place, so our whole emphasis has been that students have access to modern technology. If students' learning is to be of a high quality then they must have access to good information and good information comes from technology. Twenty years ago good-quality information came from a set of encyclopaedias. Now we have twenty-one computers networked to a couple of CD-ROM players. Currently we have started a three-year plan as to how we will have students worked into the Internet.

He speaks of the importance of all of this as follows:

> I would hope that people would say that kids are at this school to learn how to learn. It's a trendy notion but it is true. In this, it is also important that kids make a few errors, appraise what they have done, and say 'OK, this is what I wanted to do. I tried to do it and this is the result.' Being prepared to fail and acknowledge there is nothing wrong with failure is vital. This stupid thing about people thinking that everything we do has to be perfect and that otherwise we are failures, that's not real learning.

He also argues strongly that pupils should be encouraged to help each other to learn. On this, he is very much influenced by a positive experience in his own youth:

> John was my next-door neighbour. He was my teenage academic mentor. He was two or three years older than I was. He was the one to whom I turned if I had any problems with homework or if I wanted to research anything. He was the one who would provide me with the facilities and the know-how. He was the one who kept the motivation high and always challenged me to go a bit further. He was able to give the knowledge to look a bit further ahead and steer me on the pathway.

He concludes by recognizing that while this was not a common experience, there is no reason why it need not be, particularly if the mentoring approach is one which is fostered by the school.

Simon is also quick to put forward his view that while it is vitally important that pupils be facilitated in taking responsibility for their own learning, teachers must also continue to improve their teaching skills. Once again, and taking his inspiration from Brother Kelly who taught classes while he was a principal, Simon leads by example, teaching a mathematics class in which he tried out a variety of alternative approaches to teaching the subject. Such experimentation, however, he reminds us, is not new to him:

> I remember at Kyle SHS, which is a very traditional school, I set up a mathematics workroom in an old cloakroom. I had a really old-time principal but I conned him into giving me a room and some furniture. I used to take kids into the room and it would be noisy and there would be nails and string and bits of plasticine, straws, you name it, around the place. The principal used to walk in and eventually he felt comfortable because he could talk to a few students quietly who would explain to him with some enthusiasm what they were doing.

At another school he recreated his own experience when he was a schoolboy and the Christian Brothers brought him and his high-achieving peers in to school for extra tuition on Saturdays:

> At Moola SHS there were some significant students right through the school. I worked with some of the other mathematics teachers, bringing these kids in to school on a Saturday morning. We prepared all week for three hours of this very different kind of mathematics where the pupils challenged us. It became quickly apparent to me that I didn't have all the answers. The kids would ask questions that I couldn't answer and I would tell them to come back next week to discuss them. But some of those kids would come back the next week and tell me ten times more than I had discovered myself.

He also stresses regularly for his teachers how important it is for them to work hard at being good at explanation. In order to illustrate what he means, he gives the example once again of Brian, his inspirational university lecturer:

> He was a teacher rather than a lecturer and he had the power to bring people along with him. His communication skills and his rapport were terrific. Unlike other people, he would ask 'Have you got that? Do you understand?' Then he would often say 'I don't think some of you have', and he would go back over it in two or three different ways. He was a person who really inspired me in mathematics. I hope that it would be said by my past students that one of the things about my teaching methodology would be that I did not just simply go through a problem one way, but tried to explain the thing from five or six different points of view because different people see things from different perspectives.

In stressing this approach, he also impresses on teachers that they have to set clear expectations for their students. He recalls that this is also a characteristic which distinguished those teachers who inspired him in his youth.

Simon's experiences of Saturday schooling and the positive outcomes associated with it may go some way towards explaining why he has introduced a flexible timetable in his present school. He speaks with great enthusiasm as follows:

> We have students in class between eight in the morning and half-past four in the evening. Keeping this school building and its plant available for an even greater number of hours of the day is what we plan for the future. I don't think it is beyond the realm of possibility that we will be running classes in a few years up to nine o'clock at night.

Introducing flexibility into the school's timetable also helps him to provide pupils with the 'balanced' education which he sees as a vital preparation for survival in modern society. For example, while he was a great supporter of the school's emphasis on the use of computer technology in the various curriculum areas, he ensured that 'a very well-planned outdoor education programme' was also provided for all pupils.

When Simon arrived at Cara SHS he found that the school had a property, Red Valley, in a rural area about three hours south of Perth which was used only about two or three times a year by one group of pupils as a very small part of their 'alternative upper-school' programme. He goes on:

> Again it was a question of asking the very obvious questions: 'Why have we got Red Valley? What are we doing with it? What is the purpose of it?' Well, Red Valley is a magnificent resource to have. We were pushing the school's technology side very heavily. The kids were getting lots of high tech. I felt that while this was important it had to be balanced by something else. I discovered we had 400 acres of the most beautiful jarrah forest. It provided us with the perfect balance to the high technological world; with the real world of nature to which we all belong. So, we decided to establish an off-campus programme. Now we have an outdoor education policy that all year eight pupils go down there for one week. The year nine pupils go down there in smaller groups and generally most year ten pupils go down there also. We also hold geography camps there. Outdoor education is now a separate subject in the school and the facility is used a lot by those pupils taking it.

In order to help develop the facility, Simon and some of the staff wrote to a variety of sources, explaining the importance of pupils having access to outdoor facilities for nature and environmental studies. As a result, they succeeded in getting a $50,000 grant from the state's lotteries commission and $25,000 from private industry. A local hardware company gave the school a gift of all the timber it needed to build a shower block.

Simon experienced some opposition from within the school's staff to pupils spending time away from the formal classroom; from teachers who argued that 'kids are in school to learn in the classroom and every time they lose a lesson in the classroom their education is suffering'. However, he succeeded in persuading them of the importance of the experience in reinforcing and extending classroom learning. He also offered another justification:

> It is very important to blend kids together, to bring them together as a school after they have come in from about eleven feeder primary schools. A great way to do it is to take them out of their environment, away from the television sets and the hairdryers. Take them into the bush, put them in canvas where they are all equal and say: 'Let's get to know the other people who are sleeping in the tent.' To me, that is a very good strategy to use. They grizzle and they complain, but they share an experience and that experience will be with them for the rest of their lives. It blends them together as Cara SHS students very quickly.

He suggests that his thinking in this regard was influenced by his own experiences in cadets and the comradeship which developed through cooperating in camps and group activities in the natural environment.

Simon ensured that the school's music programme, which had disappeared off the timetable, was reinstated. He also promoted enthusiastically the introduction of a Japanese programme:

> The school development committee had done a survey with parents about the needs of the school the year before I came in. The thing that appeared was that they wished for the teaching of an Asian language. In particular, they sought Japanese. The P & C committee was very ready to give resources for Japanese and the senior staff were prepared to give it a go. We were lucky on two fronts. Firstly, we were getting the vibes from the government that every student should study a second language. Also, we got a very good Japanese teacher. We introduced it as a compulsory subject for all year eight students. Now it has extended into year nine, and all pupils can study the subject up to year twelve level.

However, introducing it as a school subject was not sufficient for Simon. He also engaged the school in a twinning arrangement with a Japanese high school. Each year a group of Japanese students comes to Cara SHS for three weeks and they, in turn, send a group to Japan. Not surprisingly, Simon accompanies his pupils whenever he can.

From considerations so far, it is clear that Simon believes that pupils should be exposed to a broad and balanced range of school subjects. However, his vision extends beyond this. In particular, he urges teachers to teach in a manner such that they emphasize points of contact and similarity between their various subjects. Also, he encourages teachers to develop cross-disciplinary units: 'One of the greatest achievements in this school was getting the faculty of arts, manual arts, home economics, computing and business studies to come together to agree on four common technology units that all year eights would study.' He relates how this situation came about as follows:

The special visual arts programme happened before I came here. There were four teachers who got together because they believed they should not be going in separate directions in their work. They were the teachers of graphics technology, photography, art and media. They had a view on education which they shared, that what they offered was more than just a subject and more than just material. They saw that there were a lot of processes which were common to each of their areas and that they should be supporting each other and working cooperatively. When I got here after they had been working together for twelve months they were a bit lost and their excitement had died down. However, I was very excited about what I saw and heard. I decided to support them and pointed out that what was needed was a five-year plan so that their great seed of an idea could germinate. To help them sit back and see where they were going with it I managed to get a former colleague to come in to work with them. He is a great person to ask any difficult questions to help get a plan in place. I also like to think I gave them the confidence in themselves to forge ahead, try out their ideas, step a little outside the boundaries and take a few risks.

Simon also managed to enthuse both EDWA's Director General and its Director of Curriculum about what was going on. The outcome was the appointment of a technology development officer and a significant increase in the number of computers in the school:

The technology development officer did not teach but set the overall five-year plan as to how the visual arts would spread throughout the four areas from year eight up to year twelve. He also had the job of establishing links between the school and industry. Furthermore, he very quickly began to extend technology into the broader school spectrum. We didn't get a million dollars from industry but we now have very good industry links and we have people who come in and work in the classrooms and people who will sell us equipment at below cost price.

Simon now takes stock of the overall situation with regard to technology in the school as follows:

Lately we asked again: 'What do we want to do with technology?' We identified a list of competencies, we described those processes we wanted to be an integral part of education at Cara SHS. We put them all on paper. It was interesting because the people we were dealing with were cross-curricular – there was art, and design and technology. Business education wanted to come on board. We identified the common processes and competencies across curriculum areas and what we very quickly decided evolving was some shared experiences that we wanted to offer to all students in year eight. So, we set up four compulsory technology units for them. We had a common framework for a whole range of subject areas.

The greatest success was to have all of the teachers in manual arts, home economics, business education, computing, and art and design working together under one umbrella of technology. It was a great success. So now it is compulsory that all students do the four technology units in year eight, there is a compulsory technology unit in year nine and we have got technology very heavily embedded in year ten.

The outcome of all of this, Simon argues, is that there is a very strong technology flavour right through the school.

Simon's emphasis on cross-curricular activity is also reflected in his promotion of the school's aeronautics programme. Again, the original idea of having this programme was not his. Rather, he provided the necessary support for it to thrive:

When I arrived here I found an aeronautics programme which was struggling in years eleven and twelve and this was one of the subjects which was thought of as one of the high profile subjects in the school. It was seen as being helpful for those students who would go on to the Defence Academy and for those pupils who lived in the country and were flying a plane on mum or dad's farm. In order to give the programme a new lease of life we extended it to years eight, nine and ten. This was also to ensure that it would be a real integral part of the school and not just something tacked on at the upper-school end.

He gave the aeronautics teacher every assistance required to make the programme a success, encouraging him to take a few risks and developing his confidence by letting him know that the principal was there supporting him. He expresses his own enthusiasm for the programme as follows:

I think that the aeronautics programme is excellent. It is one of those subjects where you get your real high flyers of students who are taking double maths, physics and English literature, mixing with pupils who are studying the area as a non-tertiary education examination course. It is also an area in which you can take a risk in terms of what you teach and how you teach it. EDWA has no aeronautics section. There are no schools' superintendents who have aeronautics under their umbrella of responsibilities. So, you just have to say to yourself, 'Yes, the programme we have got is a good one. It is tremendous in terms of what we offer to kids. So, let's go for it.'

He ensured that an appropriate set of units was prepared and offered. He is particularly pleased that these act as integrative units for various academic work undertaken by pupils in mechanics, design and technology, business studies, home economics and graphics technology.

Given his commitment to cross-curricular work, it is not surprising that Simon does not like the HOD structure in schools, seeing it as reinforcing school subject territoriality and hindering the cross-disciplinary approach he sees as a necessary complement to good subject-based teaching. He is also anxious to highlight a number of other factors which he sees as constraining the improvements he is trying to promote. Neither EDWA nor the teachers' union, he argues, is really interested in radical change. In particular, he is frustrated by the fact that the rhetoric of central administrators is not matched by a change in regulations which would give himself and his staff much more freedom in the way in which they operate. At the same time, he is encouraged to carry on with the love and support of his wife and with his own love of his job:

> I am the sort of person who will never become a millionaire and I often feel sorry for my wife and family. Fortunately, I've got a wife who understood that right from the very start. I can come to school every day and enjoy it. Regardless of the hassles, and there are plenty of those, I still basically love what I am doing. I think that is the greatest reward in life you can get.

He has one last wish, which he expresses as follows:

> I would love to become principal of one of WA's so-called academic traditional schools and really question what they are doing and why they are doing it, and ask what else could they do. I would love to walk into a challenging situation. I would like just once more to start all over again. Probably the ideal would be to become principal of a brand new school, establish a complete new structure or redesign an existing one. I would love to have either opportunity and I think I will.

All of those interested in the development of education in WA can only hope that his wish will come true.

# 7

# DAVID SMITH

Greenfield Senior High School, established in 1974, is situated in the Perth metropolitan area, northeast of the city. David Smith was appointed principal of this 850-pupil school in 1992. He was initially attracted to the school because of its location in a challenging environment. Approximately 70 per cent of the area's population over the age of fifteen do not have an educational or skills qualification and there is a high level of unemployment which is consistently above the state average. These factors mean that the incomes of many families are very low. There are also many single-parent and second-marriage families. Because many families are often in rental accommodation, they have little financial commitment to the area. In a nine-month period in 1994, the transience rate was 31 per cent. This movement can be related to such factors as the seeking of other employment opportunities outside of the area, accommodation factors or a family breakdown.

Students come from diverse ethnic backgrounds: 8 per cent Aboriginal; 16 per cent Vietnamese/Asian; 8 per cent non-English speaking, European extraction; 68 per cent Anglo European/Australian. Some are recently arrived refugees who bring with them horror stories from their homeland. Many are also from a non-English speaking background. This means they need additional help to overcome the extra difficulties they face in their schooling. A large number of students commencing their schooling at Greenfield also have literacy and numeracy levels two or three years below what is normal for their chronological age. Meeting their needs is difficult because of the range of ability levels, so some of these students become disruptive and resistant learners. Truanting often results from a build up of pressure related to learning and behaviour. In 1994, for example, the average daily absentee rate was 17 per cent. The school sees the need for these students to be given individual attention after such absences so that they can engage in effective study. Without it, there is a likelihood of further truancy due to disaffection and alienation. As a priority school, Greenfield attracts Federal funding, which is designed to help it overcome the shortcomings which it experiences. The seventy-two staff and aides also implement strong programmes to help overcome some of these disadvantages.

DAVID SMITH

## A NEW PRINCIPAL, A NEW DIRECTION

David believes in schools having a student-centred focus. For him, this means that 'the decision-making processes focus on students rather than other peripherals' in order that good teaching and learning can take place. He also feels strongly that if students are to be successful, they need to know that people care. These factors were not given sufficient emphasis at Greenfield when David took up his principalship. To create a student-centred school, he has made, and continues to make, numerous changes to all facets of school life.

His first priority, making students feel safe and welcome at Greenfield, involved implementing deliberate systems and policies, linked clearly to actions and consequences. Once in place, and working effectively, David started developing qualities of pride, self-esteem and respect for others in his students, through enhancing the school's ethos and improving its image in the wider community. As these areas continued to be monitored and modified, students' support networks were expanded and enhanced, largely through structural changes to the school's organization and support sections. With all these strategies in place to make students feel valued, David has been able to turn attention to generating excellence in teaching and learning through curriculum changes which address the diverse needs of the students. However, before focusing in detail on David's restructuring efforts at Greenfield and looking at possible reasons for certain changes, it is necessary to stand back and take a look at some of the incidents that have shaped his life.

## DAVID SMITH'S LIFE HISTORY

David's life has been one of constant change and often adversity, but also one of success and achievements, especially in his teaching endeavours. He is attracted by challenges. He applied to Greenfield because he considered he could do something to improve the situation there. When he arrived, the school was ready for change. Throughout his life, David acknowledges, he has always felt the need to prove himself in new situations, and time and again he has shown himself capable of meeting the challenge, despite constant feelings of inadequacy which continue even today. He constantly asks himself: 'Am I up to this?'

Such feelings of inadequacy began to exist when David was very young. Following his first conscious memory, as a three-year-old, of a feeling of approaching terror as he was choking on a piece of cotton wool left in his mouth after his tonsils had been removed, are some other rather unpleasant memories of physical and sexual abuse by a family friend, memories which he has only recently shared with anyone. As he says, 'A three-year-old doesn't say much', but he feels that these experiences have had an impact on him as a person. Whilst there is evidence to show that many people who are abused as children in turn become abusers, David feels very strongly that children should be protected, not abused. This comes through clearly in his philosophy of education.

At age four, the child of a single parent and without understanding that his mother needed to work to earn money and couldn't look after him as well, David was placed in an orphanage for boys run by Catholic nuns, where, as he says, 'I coped for the next seven years. I recall not knowing what in the world was going on.' His memories of rigid days and of the nuns leading very strict lives and imposing the same strict structures on everyone are strong and vivid: 'It was not done maliciously or with scorn for kids. It was their life and you had to fit in to the order of their life.' Academically, David was clever enough to do all the work required of him and that, he feels, had its own rewards: he skipped a year and, he thinks, this made him feel okay about himself.

Physical punishment for numerous offences, many of them minor, was frequent. It was certainly not something David enjoyed, rather something he endured, because it was the done thing: 'It was the one thing I had been taught – to endure this.' He never questioned the justice of it. It was so much a part of his life and so much accepted that it wasn't even worthy of mention. He just thought that this was the way life was for everybody, so it was a real eye-opener to him to realize that alternatives existed.

He remembers running away from the orphanage because he disliked it and of being terrified over the way he was treated for regularly bed-wetting: 'I remember standing in the corner with the wet sheet over my head. I found that very hard and the memory is not good. I had to wash my sheets every day.' Here one is reminded of many of the child migrants who came to Australia in the 1940s. As many as one third of the arrivals had a bed-wetting problem. In his book, *Child Migration and the Western Australian Boys' Homes*, Coldrey (1991, p. 37) suggests that this problem was a result of the insecurity many of the youngsters suffered, having been placed in an institution by their parents at a young age. Distinct parallels exist between these boys and David's early life experiences.

David was expelled at age eleven for flicking a note in class on which he had written a vulgar remark he did not even understand. When he left, the door just shut on that part of his life. As his mother was working in the country, he was unable to take up a scholarship he had won to a city school, but instead spent the first three years of high school at a country high school, in a town close to where his mother worked and lived. He boarded in the town with a lady and several other students. His mother's chance meeting of an old boyfriend led to marriage and a vastly different life for David, aged fourteen at the time. For the first time he had his own room and bed. Unfortunately, his step-father died unexpectedly six months after he and his mother married. Prior to his death, he had been keen for David to take an exam for a job as a telecommunications technician. David scored in the top three in the state and soon after commenced work. He did not really enjoy the work, but his nature was to accept what happened, not to fight it. After his step-father's death, in consultation with his mother, he returned to school to complete his secondary education.

David admits to not making much of the opportunities presented to him at school and he certainly felt that he was not good enough for university. He started tertiary education at a teachers' college, and began a university degree in his second year, which he subsequently finished while teaching. He found himself drifting a bit academically. He did not have to push himself and did just enough to pass: 'So many courses at university were so good. I didn't know this until I opened a book two weeks before the exam.' On the other hand, he enjoyed sport to the full and was very competitive in this area, playing football, hockey, cricket and basketball. For him it was a means of acceptance: 'In the 50s, if you were okay at sport, you were accepted.' Indeed, many of the personalities who influenced David in his life were sports people. He admired the fact that they were good at something. His own feelings of inadequacy must have been lessened by the prospect of being good at sport, hence he drove himself to excel in this area. At the age of twenty-one, whilst in his first teaching position, he married. He and his wife had four children and a number of happy years of marriage, before divorcing when he was thirty-six. His teaching sustained him during this time and he remarried several years later. He and his second wife remain happily married and have one child. He has commented that he is enriched by this marriage.

David enjoyed his early teaching experiences and was quite surprised to find that his students liked him, were happy and responded to his teaching. He was also surprised by the amount of work he had to do, but was not deterred by it. During his teaching career, he has had a number of city and country postings. He taught general classroom subjects for nine years and was then made a head of department. During his eight years as a head of department he had a year's teaching exchange in England, which was followed by a year as acting principal of a suburban high school. He was then appointed superintendent of a curriculum area with EDWA, a position he held for fourteen years, during which time he was involved in curriculum development. He can be credited with much of the change that occurred in his field at that time and which impacted on developments within the state educational system. In 1987 he accepted a district superintendent's position, a position in which he was perfectly happy and comfortable.

In that same year, David accepted a redundancy package. This followed much discussion, looking at a range of possibilities for the future and examining what was best for the family. David did not resign in anger, dismay or despair. Rather, it was a family decision that suited at the time. For the next year he stayed at home to look after his young daughter while his wife returned to work. He became very close to his daughter during this time, but he did not like being at home at all. He found the experience both boring and exhausting.

His next work experience was as head of matriculation in an independently run institution for senior secondary students. This institution was plagued by financial difficulties. Six months into the position, the business became insolvent. Several key staff had departed and David was left to face the politicians, press and countless angry, frustrated and upset students. Hard work, perseverance, a strong network, determination and long hours – all unpaid – saw David place every student in another school and eventually receive some recompense from the receivers. This was followed by a two-year classroom teaching stint at a senior high school. David feels that this was one of the best things that could have happened. It proved not only an enjoyable time, but one which also helped him to sort out his values. It has been invaluable to him in his role as principal at Greenfield, his next position.

Having journeyed briefly through some of David's key life experiences, it is now interesting to look at them in light of Greenfield SHS and his principal-ship there. In particular, suggestions will be made as to how some of those life experiences might be shaping the restructuring that David is currently implementing. First, his creation of a safe and secure environment for the pupils in the school is outlined. Second, the pride, self-esteem and respect for others he develops in the students is considered. Third, the support networks he then created are examined. Fourth, his attempts to promote excellence in teaching and learning are discussed.

## CREATING A SAFE AND SECURE ENVIRONMENT

When David first visited Greenfield he perceived that he was in charge of a school which was at a very low ebb. He was left with many more negative impressions than positive ones. He wasn't thrilled or exhilarated by what he saw and felt that the staff had no great feeling of hope for the school. Its reputation was such that parents did not rush to send their children there. His big criticism was that he found policies focusing on management of behaviour but not too much on managing student learning. He found the emphasis to be on controlling, caging and confining. For David the emphasis was all wrong: he felt it should be on sensitizing, liberating and performing. Throughout his teaching career, valuing students and their strengths has been a priority. It has been important for David to have time for students and to develop relationships with them which enable him to see them in a different light and which give them the opportunity to show their true individuality. Not surprisingly, however, his early contacts with students at the school were very negative. He found many of them to be very bitter, tough, not at all welcoming and not visibly happy. In his first weeks in the school, there were many student fights and several students ended up in hospital with concussion. In particular, it became clear to him that this situation could be partly addressed by making a special effort to meet the needs of ethnic minorities in the school. He also became concerned about the fact that parents tended to visit the school only when they had complaints, of which there were many. No doubt, David's high levels of tolerance, his even-handedness in dealing with issues, his consistency and predictability were distinct advantages in dealing with these matters. These qualities of equanimity and resolve characterize much of his approach to school leadership. They are also qualities which he has admired in others from his childhood years through to his early teaching career, and on to more recent years in senior positions in education.

His approach was also appropriate in addressing the difficulties arising from variations in staff morale. Teachers offered a range of opinions to David, from 'Thank God you're coming' to 'Take your time – don't jump to conclusions. Don't do anything in the first year.' Others, on the other hand, regularly commented that 'Things are pretty well under control here.' David talks of the folklore associated with coming to a new school and of the perceived need to stand back, appraise, not judge too quickly and not make any major changes in the first year. That presupposes that a lot of things are going right, which in David's opinion was something he did not find. He clearly realized that there was a need for a strong statement of direction.

Much of David's philosophy is in agreement with the school's purpose statement:

> The Goal of Greenfield Senior High School is to ensure that all students develop the understandings, skills and attitudes relevant to individual needs thereby enabling them to fulfil their potential and contribute to the development of our society.

However, before success of the type sought in this statement can even begin to be possible, student welfare must be addressed. David saw that creating a safe environment so that students would feel welcome on campus was vital. He believes strongly that students should feel at home when at school and is very sensitive to their need for affection.

In order to provide a secure environment for the students at Greenfield, David had to ensure that efficient systems and policies were in place for dealing with students; systems and policies relating to attendance, discipline, pastoral care, assessment and general student procedures; systems and policies in which all players – principal, staff, students, parents and the community – had a clear understanding of actions and consequences. This order of things goes against the fact that David feels he is not the most organized of people. He says that he doesn't like rigid days and sharp organization. However, his common sense told him that the very nature of running a large organization requires order. His great experience in a variety of leadership positions over many years, coupled with his wide reading in educational management and pedagogy, provided him with a store of suggestions and ideas as to how to go about this process.

Initially, David acted alone in implementing his decisions about what was best for Greenfield. In the early weeks of the 1992 school year, he made some very definite statements to staff, students and parents and acted quickly on many fronts, although his own personal criticism is that he feels that he didn't jump quickly enough on about thirty different fronts. He paid a clerical assistant for a month to set up a new central filing system to increase the efficiency with which paperwork was dealt. High absenteeism was a concern. At one time it averaged 15–20 per cent. Since close monitoring of attendance has been introduced, this has dropped to below 10 per cent. This was brought about in several specific ways. Initially, he appointed a person whose brief was to ring families when students were absent and to look closely for patterns in the reasons given for absence. It was found, for example, that students from particular ethnic groups were enrolled at several places and spending several days at each. This enabled the parents to claim money for education expenses. It became important to educate parents about school expectations if this was to change. Comprehensive attendance procedures, which teachers are expected to follow, were very quickly clearly outlined in a staff handbook and a procedure was put in place so that all absences are noted, followed up with students and, if necessary, with parents. Students are expected to explain all absences and detailed records of attendance exist. Truancy is not tolerated.

David told teachers and students that he was at Greenfield 'for the long haul' and dispelled any notions that he might leave quickly if he was offered a promotional position elsewhere. He quickly established his position as principal, outlining clearly his expectations, so that an environment existed where students knew the boundaries and were able to feel safe. He made sure not only that students clearly understood the consequences of their actions, but also that they could expect there to be consistency when staff dealt with problems. He was trying to win, but not at any cost.

David instigated a lunch pass system, so that only students with express permission to go home for lunch could be out of the school grounds. When he first arrived, 200–300 students would go across the road to the shops every lunchtime. As well as being concerned about the students' health and safety, he felt that their absence from the school grounds during recess periods militated against the development of a strong sense of community. Experience also taught him that if he was to be successful in stopping this exodus, he had to provide alternatives that looked attractive, and not just lay down the law. These students had to want to stay at school.

By enlisting the help of the community, parents and police to enforce the lunch pass system and by developing a multiple strategy approach which included providing extra facilities, such as seating, organizing lunchtime activities, improving the food at the canteen, installing cold water drinking fountains and generally giving students a purpose for staying at school at lunchtime, within two weeks he had turned around what had previously been a major problem for the school and nearby shopping centre. Whilst he made stopping this major lunchtime exodus a personal project, he readily acknowledged that he was able to do so with community support and fairly generous student acquiescence. Tackling this problem immediately and head-on is also representative of much of the way David has handled his life experiences. One is also reminded of his comment about seeing a challenge and always having to prove himself. In this instance, he faced the challenge and, in the process, not only proved to himself that he can succeed, but won support and recognition from the staff and respect from the students; qualities essential to gain credibility early in a principalship if one is to successfully introduce and sustain change.

David sees himself very much as a team player; a view which developed to some extent from what he experienced during his early teaching years. Adopting such an approach, he argued that in creating an environment at Greenfield in which all students could feel safe, it was important for staff to deal with situations in a unified manner. As David himself stated to staff: 'In this challenging environment we can be effective only if we are unified. If we support each other. If we are working to achieve agreed goals on agreed time lines.' Writing a staff handbook in which major procedures and policies were outlined was a useful starting point for this unification and proved a valuable document for discussion on major issues as well as being informative reading for new staff. Its stimulus came from David's perception of a very run-down school, where the only information in existence about the school was a rough hand-drawn room plan.

Apart from having to deal with some staff who had an understandable resistance to change and were somewhat sceptical that he could actually make a difference to Greenfield, David also had to contend with much discontent over his appointment. There was a mix of personal and professional reactions cluttering the air. Many saw him as an intruder who would use the school as a stepping-stone to bigger and better things. But they had not reckoned on David's 'stickability', as he terms it; his ability to see things through to the end. Harnessed to this was his insight and understanding of the processes of school change and his knowledge of the importance of sustained leadership over long periods of time in order to maintain focus. He acknowledges that he owes many of these insights, understanding and knowledge to his detailed reading of the relevant academic literature, although his range of experience can also not be discounted in this regard.

There is a point of honour for David in seeing situations through. His own personal commitment to Greenfield has been for four to five years. His challenge to a hostile staff was that he wanted to work with them, not against them, and that his agenda was very much open for discussion and debate. The turning point was the delivery of a vision statement to staff six weeks into his first year. In it, he outlined a selection of issues and questions he wished to raise as agenda items to be dealt with in a time frame extending forward several years. Basically, David wants students to be successful and his statement discussed areas which needed to be looked at if that was to happen. Therefore, issues high on the agenda included student behaviour, a dress code, academic excellence, aspects of curriculum, parental involvement and support for the school, support for parents, the provision of additional facilities, student participation in school government and school administrative structures and systems.

Whilst acknowledging that his professional knowledge, views and working style would be significant factors contributing to the school's purpose, there is strong evidence of David's commitment to a consultative process, based on trust and collegiality, qualities fundamental to successful restructuring efforts. In his vision statement he acknowledged this most aptly:

A declared foundation for my agenda is the establishment of procedures that enable staff participation and involvement at appropriate points in policy formulation, strategic planning and decision making. I want to set up those processes that will make use of the talents that you already exhibit and that will release the creative potential that you all have. You are highly trained professionals and have an important voice in shaping your work environment.

This belief in the importance and value of collaborative work practices can be attributed to some extent to experience from his early teaching days, where several key teachers strongly influenced David, particularly as regards shared decision making.

The need to improve communication between all parties was clearly essential to the restructuring efforts at Greenfield. David set about achieving this in a number of ways. His expectations of staff and students had already been made clear. He complemented the staff handbook with administrative news sheets twice weekly in which he acknowledged the work and successes of staff; for students, a student information and homework diary, in which key information on student services, attendance, student behaviour, courses of study and general policy and procedure information are presented; for parents, a revamped newsletter twice a term and notes sent home for unexplained absences. By increasing the communication with parents and the local community he was also able to work on improving their attitudes to the school by highlighting positive aspects of the school and its students. This is done very well in the school newsletter, where information and positive highlights of the school are regularly addressed.

David's strong dislike of injustice appears to have a large impact on the way he sees students in schools and how he feels adults and students, and students and their peers should or should not relate to each other: 'I hate to see kids in schools forced to endure things they should not have to endure. I know it affects me.' This finds expression in school policy priorities. In particular, one policy priority was to strengthen the management of student behaviour. As David has put it, 'If we cannot do this effectively, our other goals for students will not be achieved.' Accordingly, 'Guidelines for Managing Student Behaviour' are clearly articulated in the staff handbook. The system used has evolved from the Glasser method of conflict resolution and conciliation at each point at which a rule is broken. The system aims to develop positive, cooperative relationships between teachers and students and concepts of self-worth, self-discipline and respect for others. The reduction in the incidence of weekly brawls suggests the policy is working. Also, the fact that Management of Student Behaviour (MSB) is regularly on the agenda at staff meetings suggests that the topic is at least being discussed because it is of concern. In summing up his strategy during his early days in the school, it is clear that he relied on a dual process of gaining control over student behaviour while at the same time focusing on the need to improve the quality of student learning. Indeed, in his own words, 'MSB and student learning are inextricably linked – the balance is what is important. MSB policy is predicated on the idea that all students have the right to learn and that the "rights" of an alienated or maladjusted minority should not usurp this.' In other words, misbehaviour by some should not be allowed to interfere with the rights of others to learn.

At the very least, the MSB policy ensures that all people know the path that is taken when a rule is broken. All classrooms display the school rules, which state that:

1  All students and staff have the right to work in a clean, safe environment.
2  Students and teachers have the right to work free from disruption.
3  Students have a responsibility towards their own learning.
4  Students are responsible for their own behaviour.
5  Students must follow the instructions of teachers.
6  All students and staff have the right to be treated respectfully and courteously.

Students have these rights, but they also have the responsibility of obeying the rules. The school policy on assessment is also clearly stated in the staff handbook, as are policies on movement within the school, bullying and fighting, smoking, student parking and homework. These policies provide the framework for student expectations and facilitate shared understandings by both staff and students for student actions and the consequences of such actions.

## IMPROVING SCHOOL ETHOS

It was only when specific systems and policies that were designed to give students a feeling of safety and security at school were in place that David was able to start to focus on the pastoral care of students in the way he wanted. He readily acknowledged that this would not have been possible in his first year at Greenfield: 'If I had done that first up, I would have been thought of as a soft touch and dismissed.' However, he also talks of spending much of his first year searching to see what he could do. Questionnaires to staff, students and parents towards the end of the year provided feedback on levels of satisfaction and discontent that assist with school development planning. His commitment to soliciting staff opinion underlines his knowledge of and belief in the importance of shared decision making. He expresses this in the following

97

way: 'Collaborative school culture is the central platform for educational reform.' This is a view that he has arrived at, not just from his wide and varied experiences in education, but from his close reading and understanding of the relevant research literature.

Given the particular school context within which David was working, he became convinced of the need to establish the appropriate foundations on which subsequent quality teaching and learning processes could be implemented. The 'appropriate foundations' in his conception included the establishment and institutionalization of school practices built on social justice, an 'inclusive' curriculum and equity for all members of the school community. These, he believes, provide a firm foundation on which to build a healthy school culture in the pursuit of effective teaching and learning.

One of the ways in which David set about building this 'foundation' was by highlighting the pastoral care of students and developing strategies to raise their self-esteem and pride in themselves and their school. In discussing this matter he clearly recalled his own teen years, when he thought that he was not worth much. It may be that this is one of the factors, as he puts it, 'in the tangled and broken threads linking many events and situations which, combined with reading, study, life and professional experience, contribute to the formation of personal and professional philosophies that are still evolving.'

The first of David's initiatives aimed at improving the school's ethos focused on the notion of rewarding excellence and effort. When he first arrived at Greenfield students seemed to have little incentive to achieve. Anyone who did well was, in his words, 'attacked'. Subsequently, activities have been designed and implemented so that students 'feel that it is okay to be successful'. Excellence and effort are acknowledged and rewarded in a number of ways. Gold commendation letters can be sent home to parents commending students for particular achievements. Twice-termly newsletters acknowledge student achievements in areas such as dance, music, sport and writing. These newsletters always aim to present a positive message to parents and the community about the school and its achievements. The principal's report, for example, always highlights good things which have been happening. At the end of one such report, David commented:

> It can be fairly said that the sum of these activities represents a vital school community where student achievement, success and pastoral care is being fostered and where the efforts of students and parents are doing much to promote a very positive image of Greenfield in the wider community.

Continued good behaviour and attitude are rewarded with end-of-term lunches, movies or social outings. An achievers' club, set up to recognize student academic achievement, undertakes special activities designed to be stimulating, motivating and enjoyable; to reward high achievers in the school; and to encourage more students to aspire to become members of the club. A house competition, in which students earn house points for things such as appropriate dress code, year competitions, school representation, teacher commendations and a Friday quiz, fosters friendly competition and highlights positive achievements of students. The instigation of an awards night and graduation ceremony allows year twelve students to celebrate their achievements with family and friends.

'Why so much positive reinforcement?' some might ask. Students such as these need a reason to make the most of the opportunities presented to them. Tangible extrinsic rewards seem to be the starting point for motivating them to expand effort to achieve something. Clearly, David's knowledge and awareness of the need to motivate students and teachers derives from his regular reading of 'best practice' research literature in the areas of teaching and learning. This gives him a good understanding of the need to strongly support and appropriately acknowledge students' and teachers' work, and to develop reward systems towards that end. At the same time, it would be remiss not to acknowledge that there were educators who influenced David and of whom he has strong, positive memories. He makes regular reference to the fact that he was left with positive impressions of the people who took the time to notice him and acknowledge him and his work. They were also very good at something and, as he puts it, 'quite decent people'. By way of example, a university professor took time to talk to David and challenged him to study. The result was a history prize for an essay written in two days as a direct result of this professor's influence. It was people like this who had an impact on David and helped him put his values into place. He also notes that 'names are very powerful. Kids like to be recognized', and remembers early in his teaching career the strong relationship of mutual trust and expectations that developed when he really got to know the personalities in a class because he taught them in more than one subject area.

David feels that having time to spend talking to students gives one a greater appreciation of the total person. This becomes evident from an examination of the ways he is improving Greenfield's ethos, through the ever-developing pastoral care system. Every year group is divided into several form classes and these are the main focus of the pastoral care programme. Form teachers have the primary responsibility for pastoral care of the class they see every day. Time spent daily in areas other than academic pursuits helps to establish rapport and respect between teachers and students. The whole programme is co-ordinated and integrated between each year group, which is facilitated by a year leader. Form teachers work with year leaders to plan and implement a programme of suitable activities to develop this care. Activities are diverse and might include Friday quizzes, an inter-form basketball tournament, yard clean-ups and the planting of trees. A 'house' system provides the infrastructure for the programme and other associated activities.

Sport has developed in the school, something which is not surprising given David's love of it. There is now much lunchtime sport, inter-house and year level competition, and teams compete against other schools. David feels that the current sporting programme is better than ever before because it is more to do with people. In his own school days, sport was the only area in which he really showed an interest. As he has stated, 'If you were good at sport in the 50s, you were accepted.' It seems that in the 1990s little has changed. Sporting people were role models for David and it is likely that he accepts the power of the sporting hero to be a positive influence today and uses that to advantage with Greenfield students. Well-known sports personalities visit from time to time to give motivational talks to students.

Implementing a dress code with broad appeal to students was another way of helping students to develop pride in themselves and their school, and therefore of changing the school's ethos. David felt that establishing high standards of dress was one way to break the tyranny of the negative peer pressures to which many students were exposed. A code, which has the overwhelming approval of staff, students and parents, was adopted in 1992 and refined in 1994, and aims to improve the image, safety and educational tone of the school. In a newsletter to parents, David addressed the issue as follows:

> Support for a dress code that is sensible, economical, reasonably fashionable and that has been developed in consultation with students and parents is a reasonable thing to request. It is not an attempt to force conformity or to discourage individuality. A sensible dress code takes students' attention away from the distractions of competitive dressing. It encourages students to focus on their prime reason for being at school, which is to study and develop the skills, knowledge and understandings that are necessary preparation for future life opportunities.

A new student-designed school crest adds to the sense of pride that students feel in their school. It forms part of the new T-shirt design and is on all newsletters and official school stationery.

## STRUCTURAL CHANGES

Making students feel safe and welcome at school and developing in them a sense of pride and self-esteem are necessary ingredients if they are to realize that they can succeed. David worked hard to establish this at Greenfield. With the necessary structures in place, it then became important that support networks were established to help maintain a sense of student security and facilitate this success. In his restructuring, David first established systems and policies in order to lay down some groundrules for staff, students and parents. Modification of these has been ongoing as the school's ethos and image within the community have been developed. Whilst these areas are continually modified and improved, it is useful to focus on some of the structural changes, together with the other changes which have facilitated the increasing success of the students.

A major change has occurred in the 'student support services' department which looks after students' needs outside the classroom. This area is the hub of school action. As its head has put it: 'We try to make school a more productive place and deal with crises as they arise.' The role of the head of this area, whom David feels is one of the most effective teachers in the state, is to oversee pastoral care, attendance, academic progress and social and behavioural problems of students within the school. The head's foresight has done a great deal of good. He is supported by a large team of people, which has been consolidated with the addition of three new specialists, and consists of a lower-school co-ordinator, Aboriginal education worker, Aboriginal education specialist teacher, school psychologist, social worker, youth education officer, chaplain, Vietnamese liaison officer, nurse, school-based community police officer and off-campus programme teacher. David readily acknowledges the tremendous work that these people do, adding that Greenfield is the only school in the state to have two full-time staff devoted to pastoral care. This suggests not only that the school has need of these services but also that he has recognized that in order to assist students to be successful, these services need to be available to all. It is also clear that he recognizes the value of others in putting his ideas and theirs into practice. He believes in giving credit where credit is due, in all areas; a belief which extends back to his commitment to ensuring that all students feel safe at school and know that people care.

Another big change at Greenfield has been the introduction of a 'student council', which meets with the head of student services on a regular basis to discuss issues of concern for the whole school. The main functions of the council are to present student views to staff and to promote a positive school image. David sees this as a very significant change in the structure of the school, clearly fitting in with his belief in the importance of a student-centred school. From having no say, the student council is now central to the student body and students have input into what happens in the school. This role of the students brings with it responsibility for self, others and the school; a responsibility which David never had the chance to experience during his own school days. Students let him know that certain things need to be done, he gives them permission where appropriate and they go ahead and do it.

The student council comprises representatives from each year level and is run by a president and a vice-president, who are elected independently by a vote involving all year twelve students and staff. Council members are chosen from form representatives that consist of students from each form of a year level. These students meet weekly with their year leaders to arrange activities for their particular year. Form representatives and student council members are trained in conducting meetings, public speaking, organizational skills and in developing interpersonal skills. Another very deliberate structure designed to provide a support network is the youth support system, which has been established to help year eight students adjust to senior high school. All year eight students are allocated to a small group with a trained year eleven youth leader. The groups meet once a week during terms one and two to discuss concerns and to get to know each other. These year eleven students attend various seminars, workshops and camps as part of their training.

Research conducted over many years consistently shows that the closer the parent is to the education of the child, the greater the impact on the child's development and educational achievement (Fullan, 1991, p. 227). At Greenfield, parent and community involvement in the school is encouraged. David's strong belief in parental involvement has developed over the years, a belief he attributes to a close understanding of the research literature. In fact, he introduced a policy to improve parent and community participation at Greenfield. It is also seen as providing positive communication to others of the way the school functions. Prior to David's arrival, there was little volunteer work undertaken. Because there was an element of distrust evident, parents tended to come to the school only when there was a problem. It was important for David to alter this perception. Parents are now quite active in the school and are invited to volunteer for such activities as canteen assistance, staffing the switchboard, library work, accompanying students on camps or becoming involved in policy committees. A group of parents, many of them unemployed, recently completed a water reticulation scheme for a large part of the school. Community groups, such as the local Rotary Club and Lions Club, help parents, students and staff on annual 'busy bee' days to clean up the school. Parents are invited to information evenings, can be members of the school council, and can be involved in the Parents and Community Association.

The WA 'council on the aging' runs a 'volunteers in schools' programme which has trained volunteers working with children who need special support and David has enlisted their support in the school. Although volunteers help students for one hour a week in their literacy programme, many believe it is really a self-esteem programme – for both the volunteers and the students. Trusting relationships are developed and when asked, 'Why do the programme?' its developer stated that it not only gave him a reason for getting out of bed, but that he cares about his students. The volunteers do not pretend to be teachers; merely adults with time to listen. It is felt that if this is all they do, that in itself is beneficial to these students. Any improvements in literacy learning are a bonus. David has thanked the volunteers for their valuable contribution to the education and welfare of students. One wonders how much the memories of his own school days and the lack of attention, let alone affection, that was shown to him, have contributed to his feelings of the value of this programme.

When David started at Greenfield the school day was divided into four seventy-minute periods. David identified this as a major problem area. He felt strongly that seventy minutes was too long for a lesson, and observed that students were bored stiff and simply did not have the attention span for this length of time, nor did a number of teachers have the skills to provide a variety of activities and stimuli to 'spark' the students. With all their disadvantages,

David felt that Greenfield students were not achieving in school largely because their time on task was simply not enough to equip them with the skills they needed; a view which is supported by the studies of Anderson (1990), which show that time on task is highly related to achievement. One teacher in the school proposed that by increasing the time on task in each subject by forty minutes a week, students would be given almost another full year of instruction over five years. After much discussion and lobbying, the structure of the school day was changed in 1993 to five sixty-minute periods, with a daily form period of twenty-five minutes, during which activities designed to extend the pastoral care programme are arranged, or students are encouraged to study or complete homework. David is conscious of his lack of involvement in his own schooling, despite the luxury of being academically able, and of how he found himself drifting academically. Clearly, this is not something he wishes for Greenfield students.

## CURRICULUM ISSUES

Creating an environment where good teaching and learning can take place is vital to David. As the students' needs have been increasingly addressed within the restructuring at Greenfield, it has become possible to focus on ensuring that the curriculum offered meets the diverse needs of the students. David's focus is on student-centred learning and, as such, decision-making processes centre on the students. At the same time, David is adamant that people who judge the effectiveness of schools by their performance when measured against explicit written curriculum outcomes are not looking deeply enough. He is convinced that there are other ways of assessing effectiveness.

David has been an innovator and a risk taker in teaching for a long time. Even in his first teaching position he did things 'a little differently'. In a classroom removed from the rest of the school, he felt like he was away from interference; he put curtains on the windows, planted a garden outside and developed a strong rapport with his charges – fifty-two year three students. He has had weather stations operating in country schools and has implemented different approaches to the teaching of social studies which at the time were thought of as quite radical. So, whilst changes he has implemented to curriculum areas since 1992 highlight his belief in the student-centred school, and may be thought of as innovative by many, they are to David simply what needs to be done to offer the best for students. He sees nothing radical about any of it. There is also evidence to suggest that several people with whom David worked in his early teaching days influenced him in their ability to be individual thinkers and rise above the norm. However, it appears that the predominant influence has been his commitment to his own professional development, particularly his commitment over the years to familiarizing himself and regularly up-dating his knowledge of research findings in the areas of school administration, human resource management, motivation, and curriculum, teaching and learning.

Literacy is one of the focus areas in the school development plan and is a school priority. David knew that this was a problem area. Testing revealed that for 68 per cent of the school's students their reading and writing abilities were below what they should be for their chronological age. He has committed Greenfield to using an EDWA professional development programme which develops strategies to promote literacy development. Involvement of large numbers of staff across faculty areas in this programme has had a profound impact on teaching strategies and on the development of students' literacy skills at the school. Various departments have incorporated ideas from the programme into their curriculum and homework programmes. The focus for improving literacy skills is as specific as ensuring 'that students can identify key words, the main ideas and supporting details and use appropriate note-making frameworks'. David has also shown that an aggressive programme can improve results. Children who were at risk and who would not normally remain at school after fifteen years of age were targeted. They were in one class with one teacher for the year. They really did improve and are now back in mainstream classes and achieving significantly above the level at which it was thought they could achieve.

David has also been instrumental in ensuring that the school has a number of special educational programmes designed to target the needs of students. For example, small-group classes in English and social studies are provided for students whose first language is not English. When students' reading, writing, listening and speaking skills are adequate, they are transferred to mainstream classes. The school offers a homework centre for Aboriginal students which is designed to give them the opportunity of assistance in core subjects. An off-campus programme operates which provides positive, individualized instruction and care to a small group of students who are experiencing difficulty assimilating into mainstream school for a variety of reasons. Education support units also exist to cater for students with special needs.

David also supports a school policy of a heavy investment in computer equipment for use not only in technology studies, but also in other curriculum areas. To ensure maximum benefit from this equipment, all year eight students have computer instruction for a minimum of one hour a day, four days a week for one term. The goal is to have all students proficient in the use of a word processing programme and to ensure that from then on they have ready access to computers so they can employ them for a significant proportion of their written work. The hope is that by employing technology the school will be able to bring about improvements in students' literacy.

As already discussed, David has addressed the creative and expressive areas of the curriculum, with resounding success. The school's expressive arts department continues to strengthen, increasing the opportunities students have to broaden their education by highlighting areas other than the academic. Drama is now a curriculum choice and a choir has been formed. David pushes this area whenever he can and it is expanding with the help of a young, vibrant and talented staff. A special dance course, with entrance by audition only, is offered to those students who show ability and promise in this area. Greenfield is one of only four schools in WA to offer this course. The dance group is in constant demand and performs regularly at school and public functions, such as dance festivals, charity functions and school concerts.

No foreign languages were taught at Greenfield when David arrived. Despite comments from teachers suggesting that children have enough trouble learning English, one other language, Vietnamese, has been introduced and Indonesian is set to follow. David wanted to be seen to offer something different to what is on offer in other schools. Vocational programmes are also developing every year. The school's food, hospitality and tourism unit, which includes a most successful catering department at year eleven, will expand into year twelve. Industrial studies is offered full time to year eleven students interested in acquiring practical skills with a view to pursuing a career in manufacturing industry. Vocational business training is a two year course. EDWA's Innovative Skills Training and Education Programme (INSTEP) is offered as a full-time course available to students in years eleven and twelve who are interested in the areas of retail, childcare, nursing, hospitality and tourism, hairdressing, soft furnishing, office administration, and the auto-mative and metal trades. It involves three days at school and two days out in a workplace of their chosen area.

David has a great interest in increasing teachers' skills to better equip them for addressing the needs of Greenfield students. On this he says:

> I have a great interest in improving pedagogy so we don't bore kids to death. Schools bore kids terribly. If their most memorable experience is being in a sporting team, in a school production or the school ball, then we are doing lots of things very badly.

He agrees that much of this belief has to do with being bored himself at school. School held no real interest for him – it was almost as if he did his time in the classroom, so that he could get outside and play sport, where he focused his energies. He is a strong advocate of all sorts of alternative structures for schools being considered and debated openly and honestly. He feels that many teachers are very conservative in their views on education. He wants schools to have teachers who are able to sensitize students to learning and help them develop the work habits he never had, so they are better able to succeed.

Teachers have taken up this challenge in the area of homework. An initial plan by the school's social studies department to help with independent study skills has expanded and the social studies and science staff took the initiative to extend that programme into a homework programme, which is now being developed in all curriculum areas. Subject staff prepare ten homework exercises across a ten-week span. David speaks with pride when he says that 'the science package is so good that it is being marketed throughout the state', adding several thousand dollars to the school account in recent months. Another significant project underway involves developing individual education plans for students considered at risk, determined in consultation with staff, parents and the students involved.

## CONCLUSION

The restructuring efforts at Greenfield have had a positive impact on all the players – staff, students, parents and local community. The greatest impact, though, has been on the students. It is here that David sees the biggest change he has made at Greenfield. He has put the students at the centre of everything that is done. While the school increasingly attracts recognition for its achievements from many quarters, David is humble about his own record at Greenfield. Like many well-respected principals, he tends to play down the amount and degree of successful change accomplished, despite the fact that the change which has taken place can, at the very least, be characterized as major. In his more reflective moments, he admits that even good schools have intensely distressing moments. The role of the principal has often been acknowledged to be a lonely one. At such times, David is prone to acknowledge the keystones which underpin his approach to leadership and innovation. In seeking support and affirmation for his innovatory policies, many of which represent considerable risk-taking and uncertainty, David pays particular tribute to 'long hours and hard work', 'great family support' and 'having a critical mass of like-minded professionals working with him at Greenfield SHS'. Along with acknowledging the fundamental importance of these factors, he also is at pains to highlight the major contributions made by his close friends and colleagues with whom he is able to discuss many contemporary educational issues, and his extensive professional reading, especially in regard to school administration, human resource management, motivation, curriculum theory and learning theory. He has put systems and policies in place, improved the school ethos, made structural changes and generated curriculum innovations. In doing so, the school community has developed to a point where all people have a sense of working together as a team and possess pride in their school and in themselves.

# 8

# ANNE JONES

## INTRODUCTION

This chapter centres on the work of Anne Jones, the principal of Sanderson SHS. First, a brief outline is given of her life history and of Sanderson SHS. Second, the innovative activities she promoted in the school aimed at improving the quality of curriculum, teaching and learning are detailed. Third, a set of theoretical findings related to her activities is presented.

## THE BACKGROUND

Born in Ireland, Anne, the eldest child of three, emigrated to WA with her family at the age of fifteen. Prior to coming to Australia, she attended three Catholic primary schools in Ireland. The nature of Catholic education at the time was such that single-sex education was the norm in Ireland at primary school level. Anne also had no experience of co-educational secondary schooling in Ireland, where she attended an all-girls, Catholic secondary school run by nuns in Dublin for the first three years of her high school education. She describes this as a 'classical' phase of her educational experience where her attraction to the arts became evident. This, of course, is not surprising, since the secondary school curriculum in Ireland at the time was very much orientated towards the humanities. For example, at junior high school level it was compulsory for all pupils to study a core curriculum consisting of Irish language and literature, English language and literature, mathematics, geography, history and one other subject of their choice, which was usually Latin or French. As well as being exposed to such a curriculum, Anne was involved in extracurricular activities, including choir and debating. Interestingly, she also recalls that her secondary school had a vocational strand as well as an academic strand and that it was clear that the academic strand had greater prestige attached to it.

A most significant aspect of Anne's life experience was her migration with her family to Perth, Western Australia. On arrival in Perth she entered year eleven in high school and progressed to complete year twelve the following year. During this time Anne held part-time jobs. She then spent three years at the University of Western Australia (UWA), completing an Arts degree in history, geography and English. She was a bonded student with the Education Department of Western Australia (EDWA) throughout her undergraduate studies and she completed her teacher training at UWA directly after completing her bachelors degree.

Anne spent her first two years teaching in the WA countryside in a small district high school in the wheatbelt. After this, she moved to Mansfield SHS to take up another teaching position. Mansfield is an outer suburb in the metropolitan area of Perth. It is located approximately ten kilometres northeast of Perth's city centre. The school catered for years eight to twelve and had a student population of approximately 700. It was during that period that she met her husband, Andrew. They married in 1977. Anne's first promotional appointment was as a deputy principal in a small rural senior high school in Korinda. She then took up a similar position at Folkestone SHS, a typical WA senior high school in the Perth metropolitan area . During this time Andrew continued teaching.

With the arrival of their second child, Anne took two years' leave. At the same time, she also enrolled in postgraduate studies, completing a diploma in educational policy and administration. She then returned to work in her previous role. It was at that time she seriously considered her career options. She recalls being dissatisfied with the thought of continuing in her 'old' role and was eager for a challenge. This influenced her decision to apply for a principal's position at Sanderson SHS. Her application was successful and she eagerly took up her position in a remote rural area in the northwest of WA. Anne was appointed as principal to Sanderson SHS by the EDWA merit selection process. The principal she replaced had been at the school for five years. In her opinion, he had made an enormous contribution to the school. However, some of the impact was diminished due to a prolonged absence during his final year at the school. Discussions with him supported her initial observations regarding the school and also encouraged her. This was important for her in coming to an understanding of the 'impediments to change' which existed.

Anne observed that the school had not operated according to an explicit plan. There appeared to her to be little integration of structures. School development days were used by the teachers to organize for classroom preparation. There was no management information system (MIS) and there was limited documented policy. The community played only a very small role in decision making in the school. She also perceived that there was a great sense of selective acknowledgement and appreciation within the school. As a result of her awareness of these circumstances, Anne endeavoured to create a school development process which explored possible ways of changing the school's work organization to improve student achievement.

ANNE JONES

# INITIATIVES AIMED AT IMPROVING CURRICULUM, TEACHING AND LEARNING

From the time she arrived at the school, Anne undertook a number of innovations in order to improve the quality of curriculum, teaching and learning for the pupils. These initiatives can be seen as consisting of four main types, namely, initiatives aimed at reforming planning structures, specific curriculum initiatives, initiatives aimed at strengthening external community links with the school, and initiatives aimed at improving the professionalism of the staff. These four types of initiatives were promoted concurrently. Each of them will now be discussed in turn and Anne's reasons as to what motivated her in her activities will be outlined.

## Initiatives aimed at reforming planning structures

Shortly after arriving at the school Anne began to attach great importance to the need to develop a school development planning process and an accompanying school action plan. Strategic management and collaborative team management have been her models for school development and she argues that these are models to which she is 'committed'. These approaches have been used by her to increase staff awareness and accountability in relation to curriculum, teaching and learning. A first step was to focus direction and reorganize the available staff development time so as to engage and motivate staff.

Anne created participative decision-making groups amongst the staff and she reallocated resources so that the heads of department (HODs) were given their own budgets. This was supported by training and development. In introducing school development planning, Anne did not immediately engage staff in the process. Rather, she recognized the lack of a culture of planning in the school and set about addressing it. She circulated material on a range of educational issues, including current policy guidelines and frameworks. She brought more formality into staff meetings. She sought to provide professional development on the activities which emphasized change and the importance of collegiality and 'whole-school' planning. In this way, she sought to make school development planning a more meaningful process for her school.

Anne seized every chance which presented itself to provide opportunities for her teaching staff to take responsibility. In this regard, delegation is a central strategy in her leadership style. She believes that the delegation of duties promotes responsibility, trust and open communication amongst her colleagues. She also argues that if teachers are able to capitalize on every opportunity presented to them to engage in decision making then it is inevitable that improvements will be made in the quality of curriculum, teaching and learning. She concludes: 'I perceive delegation as a learning opportunity for others. I work at developing the technique of letting go. Choosing the moment is sometimes a challenge.'

## Specific curriculum initiatives

Anne also proceeded to address specific curriculum issues. She felt that the traditional curriculum was inappropriate and inadequate for many of the students in her school. Accordingly, she undertook what she terms 'post-compulsory initiatives'. This involved the introduction of a curriculum which included vocational training for students in years eleven and twelve. The school offered EDWA vocational programmes entitled INSTEP and FAST TRACK. INSTEP (Innovative Skills, Training and Education Programme) is a structured work placement programme which encourages students to remain at school beyond the compulsory years. The programme requires students to undertake one or two days per week of structured work experience, during which they are instructed and assessed by the cooperating business. FAST TRACK is aimed at improving literacy at the post-compulsory school level. It specifically targets students with literacy disabilities.

Along with introducing the INSTEP and FAST TRACK programmes, Anne addressed low literacy rates in her school by introducing a curriculum package from EDWA known as Stepping Out. She also instituted extensive professional development, including workshops on collaborative planning, to improve the professional commitment of teachers to her curriculum initiatives. The workshops, which provided the staff with a sound understanding of the processes involved in these curriculum initiatives, were conducted in a friendly and non-threatening manner. As a result, the teachers were motivated to perform their duties to increasingly higher standards, thus improving the quality of the learning environment for the students. Anne argues that she herself also learned greatly about management and change from this experience.

Following the introduction of these specific curriculum initiatives, Anne implemented initiatives targeted at dealing with issues which she sees as being part of the 'hidden curriculum'. These initiatives were influenced by EDWA's Students at Risk Programme (STAR). This programme aimed to improve the participation and retention of students considered least likely to complete secondary schooling. In particular, she targeted what she saw as inappropriate student behaviour. She was especially concerned about behaviours such as bullying, racism, truancy and juvenile offending. Students with learning difficulties, and students with social, emotional and behavioural difficulties had also to be considered. Her concerns led to the creation of a revised management of student behaviour (MSB) policy. This policy directed a process which was organized by a specially appointed MSB consultant. Teachers were involved in this process. Data on behaviour management across the school were collected. These were later analysed and presented back to them for discussion. From this, further recommendations for the improvement to the MSB policy were made. In this way, the teachers were given a stake in the process, with Anne's guiding principle being that teacher ownership of innovations is necessary if they are to be successful. This is essential if there is to be an improvement in the quality of curriculum, teaching and learning offered to the students. Overall, the process also constituted a significant step towards the development of accountability awareness amongst the staff.

Anne also began exploring the possibility of introducing initiatives concerned with alternative classroom arrangements. In relation to this, she promoted an initiative which she termed 'Gender and the Learning Environment' and negotiated with staff for her school to participate in 'The Single Sex Classroom Pilot Programme'. This programme targeted girls' participation in science and mathematics and necessitated the professional development of teachers on issues such as gender-inclusive curriculum. Single-sex classes were run in year eight science and mathematics. It was generally agreed in the school that this initiative, at the trial stage, made significant contributions to the improvement of curriculum, teaching and learning in science and mathematics for both boys and girls. Also, it generated interest in the issue across learning areas.

Anne also promoted initiatives aimed at increasing the availability and use of technology and information systems in the school. The school developed what she termed a 'reticulated computer network policy'. The policy guided the school's investment plans aimed at upgrading and increasing the number of computers in the school. Computer technology was introduced to specific curriculum areas to assist the development of understanding of the general content of each learning area for the students. Information stored on the computers could be freely accessed by both students and teachers as a source of content for any curriculum area and computer information networks were developed between the departments in the school to improve communication and information storage between curriculum areas. This strategy also had a significant spin-off in that it promoted amongst some teachers a new way of working together.

## Initiatives aimed at strengthening external community links with the school

Anne also promoted initiatives aimed at strengthening community links with the school. She believes that having good relationships with the local community is most conducive to developing a positive approach to education. During her years at the school she redefined roles to focus on student needs. This was supported by the appointment of a school welfare officer and a community policing officer. Likewise, she increased the school's representation on local committees. She also worked on improving links with the feeder primary schools. Her aim was to create continuity between the schools, thus promoting a collaborative professional environment in which there would be excellent support available both for teachers and students.

Anne was also keen to increase parental involvement within the school. This was a complex issue and involved participation in a number of local committees, including the Sanderson Youth Committee and the Sanderson Community Committee. This participation built respect for the school amongst the community and strengthened local commitment to collaborative strategies. Anne is also quick to argue that some of the groundwork had already been laid by the previous principal and what she was doing was building on solid foundations.

## Initiatives aimed at improving the professionalism of the staff

Anne has also taken initiatives aimed at improving the professionalism of her staff. She was not long in the school when she became aware that many of the teachers were unsure of their roles. In this regard, it has already been noted that she engaged staff in activities aimed at improving collegiate interaction and communication and at encouraging them to accept the idea of shared accountability. Anne also shared her interest in professional development with the staff and sought to broaden their professional development opportunities by encouraging them to attend a wide variety of courses. The school became a member of the Australian Institute of Management. Reflection and discussion are also highly valued by Anne and she promoted the notion amongst her staff that they are essential for sound decision making. In order to promote it amongst her staff she encourages reflective writing.

Finally, it is noteworthy that the merit selection process is promoted by Anne in her school. This process ensures that teaching vacancies are filled according to the merit principle. This has been agreed upon by EDWA and the State School Teachers' Union for all promotional positions. She favours this process, not just because it is consistent with the importance she attaches to issues of equity and justice, but also because she believes that if the staff are promoted on the basis of their previous efforts and can demonstrate their own learning, then it is more likely that they will work to a high standard in the classroom and in their other duties. In this way, she argues, it is more likely that the quality of the curriculum, teaching and learning in the school will improve.

So far, considerations have centred largely on the changes which have taken place at Sanderson Senior High School since Anne's arrival. In particular, the initiatives which she promoted aimed at improving the quality of curriculum, teaching and learning have been outlined. However, the manner in which she dealt with these changes and the processes by which they took place are also interesting.

A number of constraints operated to restrict Anne in her efforts to improve the quality of curriculum, teaching and learning in her school. The geographic isolation of the area created difficulties, especially when trying to access resources, both human and material, for the hosting of professional development courses. Also, Anne indicated that previous circumstances had led to the development of a culture of complacency in the school. This, she argued, greatly affected the quality of the learning environment in the school. A number of the teachers, she argued, also had 'attitude problems'. On this she stated: 'Some teachers were paternalistic towards a few Aboriginal students and this made school difficult for some of the students.'

The situation was aggravated, Anne argued, by the existence of a group of teachers she labelled the 'social clique'. Their perceived ownership of the school was a central problem for her. This aspect of the school social structure made it difficult for her initially to engage in team building. She suggested that these teachers were unaware of the need for curriculum responsiveness and account-ability. In particular, she recalls how they failed to debate or challenge any of the pre-existing structures in the school. She attributes this to the lack of collaboration and to their general unawareness of the effectiveness, or ineffec-tiveness, of the school. She also argued that their discriminatory attitudes to both students and other staff members arose out of their inability to set boundaries on their roles. In other words, certain teachers showed favouritism towards their colleagues and towards students they knew in a social context.

At the same time, Anne possesses a number of qualities which allowed her to overcome these constraints. Her passion was the most enabling factor present in this equation. She states: 'I love and enjoy the role of school principal.' She considers her most enabling personal qualities to be, as she puts it, 'my willingness to question existing paradigms, my belief that learning must be fun, my commitment to my professional development and personal well-being, my holistic approach to the challenge of school leader-ship and my communication skills'. When Anne sets high expectations within the context of the school environment, she sees the need to be respected. She comments: 'I still want to be a real person, a high performer who meets her goals in a non-threatening way.' Finally, Anne mentions that staff changes were advantageous for her in promoting initiatives in the school. She recalls: 'Change provides opportunities for new dynamics. Timing can be critical.' The arrival of some new staff members assisted her in implementing structured changes to the school without the resistance of the teachers belonging to the 'social clique'. 'The support of a collaborative executive culture is especially important,' says Anne.

## THEORETICAL FINDINGS

In analysing Anne's promotion of initiatives aimed at improving the quality of the curriculum, teaching and learning offered to her pupils, three major propositions were developed. First, the existence of present educational restructuring trends in WA is critical in an understanding of Anne's innova-tions. Second, given the restructuring context, the nature of the school in which Anne finds herself goes a long way towards explaining her innovations. Third, Anne's life history is a significant factor in explaining her innovations at a time of restructuring and at a time when she is operating within her particular school. In other words, the restructuring and the nature of the school have presented Anne with an environment in which she can be innovative. It is within this environment that her life history has come to play a part in shaping the nature of the innovations which she has promoted, the way in which she has gone about promoting them, and her motivation for her actions. Each of these three propositions will now be considered in turn.

**Proposition 1: The existence of present educational restructuring trends in WA is critical in an understanding of Anne's innovations**   It is likely that if it were not for the current climate of restructuring Anne would not be as active as she is in promoting innovations in her school in curriculum, teaching and learning. In other words, she is greatly enabled by the presence of a framework for curriculum and work organization. The advent of educational restructuring, with its emphasis on flexibility and the devolution of power, balances harmoniously with her educational leadership ideas. On these ideas she states:

> I provide educational leadership aimed at effecting manageable organ-
> izational change within schools. To achieve this I pursue my own
> learning, tap into the special strengths of the staff within my school and
> access resources compatible to the needs of my school. Through the
> implementation of strategic management processes, I ensure that the
> resources necessary to support change and innovation are available.

In this regard there seems to be a fundamental compatibility between the nature of restructuring and the leadership style of Anne. This is to argue that it would be very difficult for her to expose and implement her leadership ideas in a more highly centralized system.

Anne goes on to argue that principals need to be given the opportunity to make major decisions and provide leadership. She expands on this in relation to the management of resources as follows:

> I have an understanding of the need to integrate resource allocation to
> strategic planning. I am diligent in the linking of resources to
> organizational effectiveness and improvement in outcomes. My con-
> ceptual framework for resource planning and management incorporates
> the integration of the human, fiscal and physical resource elements.

However, she also argues that staff need to be involved in decisions. She offers an example by way of illustration: 'Situational analysis revealed that the staff at my school had a limited understanding of the processes involved in financial management. The majority mindset was that financial management was guided by benevolent autocracy.' Combined with this there existed a myth that the school's financial resources were a bottomless pocket. These percep-tions were inappropriate to the objectives of school-based financial management and accountability within a devolved system. She was facilitated in attempting to change these perceptions by the fact that restructuring is designed to open the education system and make the schools become more accountable for their operations.

Anne also speaks of the importance of the school 'picking up and running on its own momentum'. By this she means that staff should be intrinsically motivated, constantly seeking ways to improve the quality of the educational experiences of their pupils and getting enjoyment from this task. She realizes that this necessitates the generation of initiatives within the school. To this end, she also welcomes opportunities to present her staff with educational ideas. She views this process both as a motivational strategy and a professional development activity aimed at encouraging the integration and collaboration of the staff and involving them in an open system of school development planning. Again, the present restructuring climate, with its emphasis on school development planning, provides her with an environment favourable to the pursuit of such an approach to the principalship.

Anne, however, is also clear that she cannot continue to provide appropriate leadership and encouragement without also committing herself to being a life-long learner in the field of education. On this, she elaborates as follows:

> I share ownership and accountability for the quality of the learning curriculum in my school. I am committed to the provision of a quality learning experience for the students in my school. To achieve this it is necessary for me to be cognizant of contemporary curriculum issues confronting schools and be prepared to measure the existing learning environment in my school against desired outcomes. As a school administrator, I have consistently accepted the challenge which this presents.

She concludes by arguing that the ultimate justification for this is improved educational experiences for the pupils in her school.

Anne then sees herself as a catalyst for change and as someone who supports and develops her staff in the change process. In this regard she argues that 'it is the duty of the principal to be creative and inspire others to work as a team towards a common goal.' She also argues that she 'develops skills in others through appropriate delegation'. 'Delegation is', she says, 'a crucial aspect of quality management.' Her ability to translate these ideas into practice is enabled by the fact that the restructuring policy of EDWA is also promoting similar ideas. Anne also argues that fundamental change is not possible unless teachers understand the change process and possess the skills to deal with it. She extends this to argue her belief in 'maintaining excellent professional relationships with colleagues, students, parents and the wider community'. However, she also argues that there is a need for a major change in the general societal view of schooling if restructuring is going to be successful. On this, she gives an example to illustrate her belief that there is a public misconception of where the power within the education system exists:

> I have been trying to obtain quotes to upgrade the computing lab in my school. When approached by the company that was covering the tender I found that they had followed the specifications that were standardized by the education department. When I explained to them that this is not what I had planned they failed to see the significance of my comment, believing that the education department held the final say.

It was only after much effort that she succeeded in getting what she wanted. As she sees it, while current restructuring policy in education, as promoted by EDWA, is creating an environment which supports and legitimizes the management approaches which she feels are conducive to improving the quality of the curriculum, teaching and learning experiences offered in schools, there also have to be changes in the wider societal view of education in order to allow the new approach to blossom.

**Proposition 2: Given the restructuring context, the nature of the school in which Anne finds herself goes a long way towards explaining her innovations** It is also likely that the nature of the school in which Anne finds herself goes a long way towards explaining her innovations. The school, it will be remembered, is in a remote town, and while telecommunications and computer networks are reducing the isolation of the area, it still has an influence on the school. Many teachers and principals use the school as a step in the ladder of promotion, coming for a while to get experience and then moving on to a more attractive school. One consequence of this situation is that the school has not had a tradition of innovation and change. Anne was attracted and challenged by this. She saw it as presenting 'possibilities for challenges to leadership, skills and reflection,' and wished to remove the constraints embedded in the school culture by building on the positive impact made by previous colleagues.

Before Anne's arrival, the school had operated under a linear accountability model. She favoured a collaborative approach to the operation of the school. She says that the school provided her with the opportunity to open up challenges for leadership, skills and reflection. It gave her 'the opportunity to do something different, something that pointed in a different direction'. It appears also that it was what she saw as the 'inappropriate behaviour in the school' that combined with the factors mentioned already, to jolt her into action: 'Some behaviours were unprofessional.' In particular, the existence of what she termed a 'social clique' and their perceived ownership of the school presented a challenge to her as principal. She was also driven by the attitude that a number of the teachers were not concerned about promoting a school culture which would help meet the needs of all students, including Aboriginal students. It is against this background that the contributions of her life history to her innovative activities can now be considered.

**Proposition 3: Anne's life history is a significant factor in explaining her innovations at a time of restructuring and at a time when she is operating within her particular school** It will be remembered that Anne is promoting a number of innovations aimed at improving the quality of curriculum, teaching and learning in her school. These innovations were outlined as four separate initiatives in the descriptive findings. A partial understanding of her promotion of these initiatives has been formulated in terms of the influence on her of the present climate of restructuring and the nature of the school within which she works. Within this context her innovations can now be considered in relation to her life history.

The relationship between Anne's life history and the promotion of innovations in her school can be illuminated through an examination of four themes. First, there is a set of life circumstances that goes some way towards explaining why she is an innovator. Second, her innovations are characterized by the importance she attaches to placing curriculum, teaching and learning at the centre of her activities. Third, her life history goes some way towards explaining the nature of some of the specific initiatives which she has undertaken in her school. Finally, her life history also goes some way towards explaining the way in which she has gone about promoting her initiatives.

## Anne's life circumstances which have influenced her as an innovator

There is a set of life circumstances that goes some way towards explaining why Anne is an innovator. It appears that her relationship with her family is one of the most important factors in this regard. In particular, the support of her husband and family provide her with an emotionally secure environment. She also speaks of various doubts and troubles she has had over the years and how her relationship with her husband provides comfort and reassurance. Within this secure environment he has supported her in her career: 'He has never put obstacles in my way.'

Anne has made choices which have allowed her to be free. She commented on how she has managed her circumstances in order to create a secure and supportive home environment. This has allowed her to focus much of her energy on her work without being distracted by financial issues. Her history of capitalizing on the circumstances in which she has found herself and turning them to her advantage is also significant. Her survival mentality can be traced to some extent to her experience of change, moving schools in her youth and, in particular, her migration to WA. This move was a critical incident in her life. She recalls the impact it had on her:

It was a very lonely time for me. My views of myself were coloured. I had a

117

lack of confidence and a lack of good reference points to nourish my self esteem, my internal stuff. On reflection, this, I'm sure, has helped me to meet and manage change in my life.

She also suggests that her family's promotion of the notion that 'things will work out for the best' has been significant. With regard to her early years in Perth, she made the best of the situation, drawing very much on her family for emotional and intellectual nourishment. An uncle who lived in her family's home was very influential in this regard. She remembers him as someone who encouraged her a lot and who challenged her regularly to think, and in various ways, to be adventurous: 'He was always there, a refuge. He always took an interest in me. He was a self-sufficient person.' Working in a predominantly male environment when she was a classroom teacher seems to have been significant in Anne's life. In particular, she argues that this stimulated her to seek promotion:

> I was the only woman teacher in a department of all men and I had the biggest teaching load. That was a significant time. Promotion for women stopped at deputy principal. I became aware of this. I noted that men were actively interested in and aware of promotional issues, structures and opportunities. I began to question this.

However, she also argues that she was not, in fact, reacting against individual males. Indeed, she recalls clearly that a number of men, both peers and superordinates, were significant in encouraging her to challenge the system and seek promotion in a male field. She was also fortunate in that she worked with women who held promotional positions. They provided excellent role models for her. One deputy principal was particularly supportive and encouraged her to develop her own career.

## Curriculum, teaching and learning are central to Anne's thinking on education

Anne's innovations are also characterized by the importance she attaches to placing curriculum, teaching and learning at the centre of her activities. There certainly seems to be a life history dimension to this central frame in her thinking. Her enthusiasm for education, and specifically curriculum, teaching and learning, is possibly a result of the influence of her parents. From them she acquired what she sees as a broad perception of the importance and purpose of schooling:

> Both of my parents are intellectual. However, they also hold a healthy disrespect for the conformity of schooling. I remember noting this even as a child. While the right to attend school was very important, my mother in particular questioned rules which seemed to have little relevance to learning and which impacted on her rights as a parent.

118

It also seems that central to Anne's notion that issues of curriculum, teaching and learning should drive all other school activities is that education is largely, as she puts it, 'about developing good relationships with students'. For her and her staff this, in turn, demands that students be given fair representation in school. The importance of such representation, she argues, is something she has learned.

Anne's ideas in this area are influenced, in particular, by her experiences as a newly recruited teacher during her first years in the country. She recalls: 'I remember the staff meetings being held and you weren't allowed to speak. You weren't allowed to say anything. There was this real climate of control.' She argues also that the pupils, in turn, had even less representation than the teaching staff. She compares this situation with her own experience of schooling, illustrating the similarity by offering a variety of examples like the following:

> I remembered in primary school getting in trouble. The teacher left the room and there was the usual movement in the classroom. I was pushed as I was getting an apple out of my bag. The apple shot across the room as the teacher came back in. My mother was called to the school and I was in a lot of trouble. There was no opportunity to explain. I didn't mean it and hadn't intended doing anything wrong.

Associated with this view is Anne's emphasis on honesty with pupils and parents and on making time available to demonstrate that honesty to them. She sums up the core of her position on this in relation to parents by saying:

> I believe in sharing information. I give the parents all of the information regarding what the school is doing, why it is doing it and what it aims to do for the future. I trust them with this information. When you have lots of influence you must be aware of the impact of it.

She concludes by saying that she hopes this will bring forward a more critical questioning approach on the part of parents, especially in the area of curriculum.

Another dimension to this view is Anne's belief that students should see the point to schooling. She develops this issue by recalling her own primary schooling in Ireland:

> I was predisposed to like school but there was little acknowledgement. At times I lost interest in schooling. I saw much of it as boring and irrelevant. I saw exams as a schooling hurdle. I am very cynical about them.

She recalls that much of what she did seemed aimless, since nobody took the time to explain the importance of it apart from the fact that what was being addressed was important to passing examinations. Certainly, one of the main aims of the Irish educational system was to prepare students for the Primary

Certificate Examination which was taken at the end of primary schooling, the Intermediate Certificate Examination which was taken at the end of the first three years of high schooling and the Leaving Certificate Examination which was taken at the end of two more years of high schooling. The system was not largely concerned with developing a questioning approach to life and with promoting critical thinking. Rather, it was based around an acceptance of knowledge as a 'closed system'. The focus was on 'busy work' and a clinical, disciplined approach (O'Donoghue, 1990). Anne has similar memories of university: 'I saw University as vague. I am unsure of what I took away.' In other words, her memories of much of her own educational experiences is that she perceived them at the time as being irrelevant: 'I didn't have any awareness of the realities of what I was doing. I was very unclear about the purpose of my learning. I was confused much of the time.'

Closely related to this view is Anne's belief that schooling should be connected with pupil interest and she continues to ensure that her initiatives are relevant to the interests of the pupils, as evident in those she has taken in the post-compulsory and gender domains. Likewise, giving pupils opportunities to experience a wide variety of experiences is another important issue for her. She believes that such opportunities should be available to everyone. In particular, she claims that she has been influenced in this regard by her own experiences as a pupil when she was denied access to certain subject areas in the secondary schools she attended in Perth:

> On enrolling at school in Perth I remember they wouldn't allow me to do English literature because they didn't know my background. The subjects I was channelled into were seen as being relatively 'low risk' — they were seen as being for anyone to do. This experience had a major impact on me. Actually, most of the subjects were fine and were what I wanted. The point I am making is that they did not seem to be valued by the school.

Equally, she argues that she finds it remarkable that in all of her years of formal education she was never taught how to learn and never encouraged to discover and capitalize on her own learning style.

Finally, Anne argues that school should not be fraught with anxiety. Again, she is quick to recall some of her own experiences in this regard:

> I often faced primary school with anxiety. One time I was embarrassed about my work in sewing class, so much that I flushed it down the toilet. It was never right. Others were always better. What was so important about sewing to create that much anxiety? Doing a button hole! I question the value of this.

By contrast, as a principal she is a great advocate that students should enjoy learning. She says that there needs to be a contribution towards creating a student-centred environment. This environment should be one which is concerned with student enjoyment, active learning and a positive framework. She concludes by arguing that this sometimes requires a shift in school culture. Her attempt to promote this shift is reflected in such initiatives as those aimed at increasing the professionalism of the staff, particularly through creating increased collegiate interaction and communication within the school.

## The relationship between Anne's life history and her specific initiatives

Anne's life history also goes some way towards explaining the nature of some of the initiatives which she has undertaken in an attempt to improve the quality of the curriculum, teaching and learning to which the pupils in her school are exposed. On this, it will be recalled that she has applied strategic and collaborative team management models to the school's development planning approach. At the same time, she argues that while such planning structures are necessary, schooling does not have to be inflexible. This approach is driven by her nature to be innovative and flexible. Here one is reminded of Hoff's (1982, p. 68) image of such an approach:

It is like that of water flowing over and around the rocks in its path – not the mechanical, straight-line approach that usually ends up short-circuiting natural laws, but one that evolves from an inner sensitivity to the natural rhythm of things.

From her own experience Anne has developed the notion that flexible schooling enables student achievement. In particular, she recalls her experience as a student in Ireland:

Some aspects of schooling were quite flexible there. For example, you could miss certain years in the merging stages into secondary school. I missed year seven. I went straight from year six to year eight. Acceleration on the basis of ability rather than insisting that one cover set content was what was considered. It could be arranged. It was favoured by teachers and parents alike. I question the age cohort model as being appropriate for all students.

She draws upon this memory in making the point that there is scope in WA for such flexibility and that it could be formalized with the adoption of a developmental learning model.

It will also be recalled that Anne initiated specific curriculum initiatives in her school. One such initiative reflected her interest in gender issues for girls. This interest developed over time and largely in response to the male-dominated authoritarian style of school governance which, it will be recalled, she experienced as a teacher. Similarly, she recalls that she observed a lack of support for women seeking promotion. On this, she contends, 'The perception was one of women having no right to promotion, especially to the principal's role. I went through a lot of that.' Interestingly, it would seem that it was this perception which spurred her on to succeed.

Other initiatives promoted by Anne, it will be recalled, were those she undertook to improve the quality of the curriculum, teaching and learning for those pupils in her school who were in the post-compulsory phase of their education. These were largely based on an approach which rejected the 'traditional' academic curriculum. In this, she was possibly influenced by the dissatisfaction which she experienced in her own education with the 'traditional' curriculum, especially at senior high school level in Australia. In this regard, she spoke as follows:

> I don't know why but you did maths 2 and 3, physics, chemistry and literature. What ever else you did didn't really matter. If you weren't one of those students, then what did you do? There is a disproportionate emphasis on this aspect of the curriculum. It's still rooted in our school culture. There is an assumption that they prepare you for everything. I always questioned what they were a pathway to during my own education. I still do. It seems to be a real block to the thinking of teachers and parents. Regardless of whether they realize it or not, the schools actually accept and promote that culture.

Similarly, the promotion of initiatives such as the integration of technology across learning areas, which has emerged out of Anne's philosophy of learning, also has a life history dimension. She also recalls being discouraged by her mother from doing domestic science in school. Her mother's argument was that the associated skills could be adequately learned by any intelligent person in extracurricular settings. What she stressed was that school should teach the skills which would allow one to guide one's own learning in the future, thus providing the tools, especially for girls, for seeking out opportunities and realizing their full potential. Now, as a principal, she argues that 'learning how to learn', which is facilitated by the availability of computer technology, is an important skill to develop in both teachers and students. She has come to appreciate that the introduction of technology provided opportunities for teachers and students to engage in new learning.

Anne's initiatives aimed at strengthening community links with her school are also interesting from a life history dimension. She recalls:

> In Ireland I lived in inner suburban neighbourhoods. As a child I liked solitary activities. I would often just go outside, walk around, and talk to people. I would go to the shop next door and read the magazines on the counter.

The sense of community which existed, she argues, taught her that good relationships and a healthy, productive working environment can be fostered simply through regularly talking and communicating with people. She says that she learned this from a young age, recalling in particular how she 'enjoyed the company of old people'. She now seeks to do that in relation to her school in order to create a healthy learning community for all connected with it. At the same time, she is a realist in the sense that only what seems possible is given her undivided attention. Equally, she is very patient, claiming that from her life experience she has developed a tolerance to most situations. This, however, is not to suggest that Anne does not fight for her goals. Quite the opposite is true. She was, as she puts it, 'determined as a child'. This quality appears to have continued into her adult life.

### The relationship between Anne's life history and the way she promotes initiatives

Anne's life history also goes some way towards explaining the particular way in which she has gone about promoting her initiatives aimed at improving the curriculum, teaching and learning in her school. She explained that as an innovative principal promoting reform in her school, she needs to be respected: 'I still want to be a leader and a team member, a high performer who meets her goals in a non-threatening way.' In this regard, Anne is very subtle when it comes to implementing change. Above all else, it can be said that she adopts a 'nurturing' approach.

In considering Anne's nurturing approach it is noteworthy that essentially she is a caring person. Care is an important aspect of the support she offers in developing personal relationships between her colleagues in an effort to produce a positive working environment for her staff. She adopts a similar attitude with regard to the students:

> All students are entitled to be there. They are entitled to a quality education and it is my responsibility to make sure they be given every opportunity. I must be there for them, provide for them, and ultimately provide for the teachers too.

This caring approach has been part of her life since, as a young child, she was treated as a mature person and as an equal by her parents.

A number of dimensions to Anne's nurturing style are also identifiable. Above all else, she needs to create a safe and secure environment for her students and her teachers. She argues that the influence of the Catholic social justice ethic and her own school experiences within the Catholic system of education seem to be a source of much of her own position in this regard. She states: 'Growing up in a Catholic school was a significant influence. Most significant is the Catholic ethos. In particular, I have been influenced by their stresses on social justice issues which is a core value of the system.' One implication for Anne is the need to develop an environment in which all can feel safe and secure in realizing their full potential. Associated with this is her belief that school should not be fraught with anxiety. She argues that she regularly looks back on her own schooling in this regard and is determined that the children under her care will not suffer the anxiety with school which she experienced as a child.

Another dimension of Anne's 'nurturing' style of leadership is the importance she places on developing trust amongst her staff. She believes strongly that her trust in others and the trust which others place in her are essential in the pursuit of her vision. She also argues that giving her staff responsibility is an important part of developing trust amongst them. She attributes some of her feelings in this regard to the fact that as a young teacher she was made to 'feel like one of the pupils' by the school authorities. The lesson she says she learned is that teachers must be treated as professionals who must model autonomy within a collaborative framework. Accordingly, she views line management as 'a primitive model' for running schools. She stresses the importance of principals understanding their functions in relation to other members of staff, and also of having a variety of approaches to decision making. She also believes that every teacher has a unique skill that can be harnessed and that teachers need to be made aware of this. From considerations so far, it is arguable that this is the position which she will continue to emphasize more and more and that the effective school which she has developed will continue to grow and develop under her guidance and leadership.

# 9

# JASON JOHNS

Bluehill SHS is a city school located in a low socioeconomic area. Indeed, in terms of income the area is one of the five poorest city council shires, with an average income of less than $18,000 per year. It is also an area where over 17 per cent of the adult working population is unemployed. What Jason found on arrival at the school was a situation where the social and emotional problems of the pupils were seriously affecting their performance. Since his arrival the school has undergone significant change. Certainly, there are still major problems. In particular, attempted suicide and self-harming continue to prevail amongst the student population of 650 and many are still not performing to their potential. Nevertheless, what one meets in the school yard are outgoing, open and fresh pupils, and the staff of sixty teachers is highly motivated, enthusiastic and energetic.

The school was selected as a NPQTL school on the inception of the project. Since then, a host of innovations have succeeded in raising morale and giving purpose and direction to the school. Last year it won a state award for its physical education programme which was designed and largely run by the pupils themselves. One of the school's teaching programmes for the hospitality industry, which is now used in other schools, won an award for educational innovation. The school also won an Education Department innovation award for its work in the promotion of teaching teams at the lower-school level. Students who worked on fashion design, returning to school at weekends, also won a major award. Currently, the staff are writing new courses to cater for the needs of those pupils in the bottom 10 per cent in the school in terms of overall performance and, in keeping with the general optimistic mood in the school, have termed it an 'access to success programme'. They are also developing an approach to school reporting where the pupils are involved in self-assessment and reporting to parents on their performance over a broad range of school activities. It is also a school which encourages drama productions, school sport and regular camps, and evening classes in technical and vocational education.

Overall, the school's turn-around can be attributed to the leadership of its principal, Jason Johns. Jason is a West Australian from a farming background who trained initially as a specialist physical education teacher. Throughout his career as a teacher and a principal, he has broadened his own education by studying for a variety of postgraduate qualifications in education. Between 1962 and 1977 he was a class teacher of physical education, social studies and English in four high schools throughout the state, as well as being a HOD in two of them, and since 1979 he has been a principal of four high schools, interrupted by a two-year period as a schools' superintendent. He is known throughout the educational world of WA as being a hard worker, a visionary, a positive thinker, a great motivator and a lover of sport. Since coming to Bluehill SHS in 1992 he has enthused the teaching staff, bombarded them with a host of ideas and initiated many of the school's innovations himself, as well as supporting those of others. However, what distinguishes his performance is the manner in which he has placed the concept of 'student-centred learning' (SCL) centre stage in the school's reformist agenda. This chapter discusses Jason, his life and his work largely through an exposition of this concept as it has assumed meaning in his school.

## STUDENT-CENTRED LEARNING

In 1991, the year prior to Jason's arrival, the school staff identified 'passivity' as a major problem affecting student performance. It was decided that the best way to deal with this was by encouraging students to take greater responsibility for their own learning, by increasing their motivation to learn, by encouraging them to see relevance in their learning, by engaging them actively in their learning and by improving learning outcomes. Accordingly, in that year student-centred workshops were held for all staff in school time. However, when he arrived in 1992 Jason increased the emphasis on the concept and voluntary workshops were held for two hours over twenty weeks for a 'core' group. The outcome was a school plan on SCL which has since been in operation throughout the school. The central notion underpinning the SCL approach adopted by the school is that students should be encouraged to participate fully in, and take responsibility for, their own learning and that this, in turn, involves them in the planning, organization and evaluation of their learning. This notion is one based largely on humanistic psychology principles, with a particular influence being Carl Rogers, who presented the argument that one cannot teach people anything, one can only provide the environment in which they can learn, with the ultimate goal being that of self-actualization; becoming the best person one is able to become. A student-centred approach, it is argued, will lead to greater ownership, commitment and enthusiasm for their learning on the part of students, will help them to achieve their full potential and move them towards self-fulfilment. Following the outline of this argument is a list of principles to govern practice. Particular emphasis is placed on teachers and pupils negotiating, planning, goal setting, choosing learning experiences, establishing classroom rules, engaging in reflection on performance, and evaluating.

The process is monitored with the aim of constant improvement. During senior staff meetings a 'round' is used to enable senior staff to explain the progress being made in their areas. Meetings also take place between HODs, learning-area co-ordinators and Jason to discuss the progress made in each learning area. Staff surveys are used to establish concerns and successes and the results are collated and published. Success stories are also presented in various forums and are disseminated in various written forms. Signs and posters in the staff room capture some of the key concepts. Jason has also encouraged staff to promote subject-specific programmes based on SCL approaches. He has given particular recognition to the physical education department's promotion of an innovative 'Sport Education' programme. This SCL approach embodies a number of characteristics: a formal schedule of competition; matched, mixed-ability teams to promote balanced competition and unpredictable outcomes; students are given responsibility and ownership within physical education; the teacher is cast in the role of learning facilitator; modifications are made to traditional games' rules and team sizes; students are involved in record keeping and the publication of results. Besides helping pupils learn to become good players, the programme encourages them to fulfil other roles necessary for sport, such as umpiring, team management, coaching, administration and publicity. A stated aim is that as students assume greater responsibility for learning, teachers will relinquish traditional 'up-front' direct teaching roles, after moving off stage to facilitate skill learning through a range of SCL strategies. Jason speaks highly of the success of this programme in the school and is delighted that the school is involved in a project run by a local university physical education department aimed at improving both the programme and teachers' skills in implementing it. This enthusiasm of his, of course, is understandable in light of his own involvement in and love of sport all of his life, and his own history of being a physical education teacher.

Another major development in the school is based on a concept developed at the Koln-Holwede school in Germany. This has involved the introduction of 'student–teacher teams' for years eight and nine. As in Germany, the teams are designed to allow for the development of stronger and longer-lasting relationships between teachers and students, and among students, thus increasing student and teacher morale with the aim of enhancing students' personal, social and academic growth. In 1995 students in years eight and nine were organized into two and three teams respectively with approximately sixty students in each team. As far as possible, the teams remain intact for the first two years of students' secondary schooling. Each team is divided into two classes and students in each class study all of their compulsory subjects together while mixing with others for optional subjects. Whole-team extracurricular-activities, excursions and camps are also promoted to assist the team-building process.

A teaching team comprises a minimum of four teachers. At least one teacher from each of the 'core' subject areas is assigned to each student team. These teachers are responsible for the personal, social and academic development of the students in their team for the two years. For this period they all teach both of the classes in their team at least in their own subject areas and occasionally in other subject areas as well. The teachers meet regularly to discuss the educational and pastoral care issues confronting their team and to develop whole-team plans for addressing these problems. The school's timetable allows for at least one team meeting a month, but some teams meet more often than this and most maintain frequent and regular informal contact. While all of a team's teachers take responsibility for the care of their students, the pivotal pastoral care role in each team is taken by the team leader. Each leader is allowed a certain amount of time free from teaching to co-ordinate the team's efforts concerning both pastoral care and curriculum issues. The leaders also maintain regular formal and informal contact with one another so that whole-year and lower-school problems can be discussed and addressed.

Evaluation of the student–teacher teams by means of surveys, questionnaires and interviews is ongoing. The indications are that teams are moving towards the goals which have been set for them. The teachers report that their regular and long-term contacts with the students in their teams allow them to get to know the students really well and thus to better tailor their teaching and learning programmes to meet the students' academic and social needs. Some have also commented that class time is being used more effectively as discipline problems have been reduced. The students also appear to be generally positive about being in teams. Some have argued that because they know each other and their teachers really well they are more inclined to take risks and to seek and receive help from their peers and teachers. The whole-team extracurricular activities are greatly appreciated by many year eight and year nine students.

While it is too soon to determine the long-term effects of SCL and student–teacher teams at Bluehill SHS, all of the indications are that these central initiatives are worth maintaining and developing. There is also consensus that while the staff had at least given some consideration to SCL prior to Jason's arrival, it is his leadership which has been mainly responsible for making the school the vibrant and innovation-minded place it is today. In examining his work and his life, four major themes emerged which facilitate an exposition on this situation. The themes are 'his enthusiasm for education', 'his enthusiasm for SCL', 'winning the confidence of his staff', and 'maintaining the change process'. Each of these themes will now be considered in turn.

## HIS ENTHUSIASM FOR EDUCATION

Jason is very clear that at least from the age of thirteen he knew that he wanted to be a teacher and to be involved in education. He has very positive memories of his own schooling: 'I liked school and learning generally. Whatever popped up I liked to take it on.' He also feels that he was influenced by the fact that there was something of a teaching tradition in the family. In particular, both his maternal grandfather and his maternal step-uncle, both teachers, were held up to him as role models of what he could become.

The most common recurring theme in discussions with Jason on education is that it should be aimed at producing responsible lifelong learners who possess the qualities of trust, respect and honesty. Underpinning such thinking, and his views on SCL and associated innovations in curriculum, teaching and learning in the school, is a notion that education has the potential to produce better citizens and a better world for all to live in. While he is not explicit on this when talking to his staff or in the many discussion documents which he has prepared, it is evident from his spiritual reflections and from the ethos of caring which permeates his proposals that he has such a view. Accordingly, the strong humanistic and caring approach which informs the principles governing SCL in the school is not surprising. Furthermore, this is underpinned by a spiritual dimension which, while not clearly formulated in his mind, is nevertheless strongly felt.

Jason is not generally known as being very religious. Indeed, he is not a regular churchgoer, although he has attended church in various places where he has worked. However, he reveals that he is very spiritual:

> I believe that I have a good relationship with God and I also believe that I have enormous faith and I am his vehicle. He is the real force behind all that I do. It is not me that is doing all of this work. I'm just a channel of some sort. I'm not hung up on any of my successes or losses. I enjoy the process as I go along. I see it as part of my spiritual belief.

Such a position can, to some extent, be attributed to his early socialization. The religious influence of his mother was particularly influential in this regard and she also made sure that he was a regular attender at Sunday school. However, the fact that he grew up on a farm outside a little wheat and sheep town also seems to have been influential. The very affectionate way in which he speaks about his relationship with the land, about how it is still in his bones, and about dealing with it and the complexity of the seasons suggests that he has developed a somewhat pantheistic outlook on life.

It is the land which also goes some way towards explaining the social conscience which seems to be related to his spiritual outlook. In particular, there is a very strong family memory of how both of his parents' fathers took up virgin land and worked very hard to clear it and make it productive. The associated informing notion seems to be that if people are given an opportunity and are motivated to work hard then there is the possibility that they can adopt a wholesome fulfilling life. However, his social conscience was also formed through growing up alongside an Aboriginal community:

> I used to live near a large tribe of about eighty people who lived in tin shanties near our farm. Their dogs used to jump on me as I rode my bike

through their settlement. As kids, we used to chase ducks together, climb hills, catch rabbits and build canoes on the lake nearby.

As well as recalling these pleasant memories, he speaks of how he came to appreciate the sensitivity of the Aboriginal population and later on, as a teacher, how he came to appreciate their deprivation:

> Mixing with Aboriginal kids in my youth has been a great influence on me. I have an affinity with them. I can relate to them. I understand them. I can handle them. I am determined to do something through the school to better their lot.

He argues also that the experiences in his youth of hard work, frugal living without electricity, running water or refrigeration, and associating with the marginalized, has given him a desire to work with the underdog in society. Accordingly, it is not surprising that not only is Jason comfortable being principal at Bluehill SHS, but that he also made a special request to be posted to that school.

Jason's experience back in the early 1980s as a young principal of a residential school which specialized in agricultural education also convinced him that not only were his educational ideals justified but also that they could be realized. He was given great freedom at this school in terms of who he could enrol. He recalls how he went out and 'pulled them in from everywhere, even kids who had been expelled from other schools'. The outcome, he argues, has convinced him that he could 'take any kids from any setting and in six months turn them around' once they could be exposed to 'the right combination of academic, practical and extracurricular experiences coupled with good supervision'. He still looks back to those days, and particularly the effect which he feels the practical experiences which were offered had on the pupils, and he tries to think about how he could translate some of them to his present situation.

Jason is also clear that education is very much about teachers establishing good relationships with their pupils and also about the pupils establishing good relationships with each other. In particular, he emphasizes the importance of everyone caring about each other. He captures very well his thinking on this in one of the many written reflections which he shares with his staff:

> There is some evidence to suggest that society at large is becoming more compassionate, that we are entering a therapeutic era. Qualities which were regarded as weak just ten years ago are now seen as desirable. Injustice in many areas is being tackled with fervour. We are, and must be, part of this great change.

He considers that his mother has been a great influence on him in this regard, particularly as she was a member of what many regard as the most noble of the caring professions, nursing. She herself was from a big family and as a mother she placed a great stress on family life, on all members helping one another and also helping others. He also recalls vividly those teachers in his youth who, as he puts it, 'were interested in us as people'. Unconsciously, it appears that he may to some extent be modelling himself on his primary school teacher, John Glynn, with whom he is still very good friends. John is important to him as 'the guy who cared about kids and loved teaching. He was keen on our welfare and remained keen. He was always enquiring about our progress. He just cared about us as people.' Also influential seem to be his memories of life on the farm with his two younger brothers and his final two years of high schooling in a hostel as a boarder at a high school. The memories are ones of harmonious living, where everybody treated each other as equals, looked out for each other and organized life to facilitate each other's enjoyment, learning and extra-curricular activities. These keep returning to him as ideals which could now be achieved at Bluehill SHS.

The argument to this point is that Jason is clearly motivated in his work by his educational philosophy. However, it is also clear that he is driven to succeed and to be seen to be successful in his chosen profession. This is something he readily admits and is also something he can account for. In particular, he realizes that he has enormous energy which has to be given an outlet and channelled into something worthwhile. He speaks of being like his parents in this regard: 'They were very hard workers who had enormous energy. I have too.' However, he also argues that being a 'workaholic' is something which also has other roots. In particular, he places great stress on the very high expectations which his mother had of him and his brothers:

> Mother had very high expectations of us. It still drives me. I often ask myself what in the past has made me put in very long hours as a teacher and later as a principal. I am now convinced that it was partly to meet her expectations although at the time I was not very conscious of it. Secretly, I think, I have been trying to meet those expectations which she had which have been part of my psyche from a very early age.

These expectations, he argues, used to come flooding back to him, particularly in the form of rules and sayings for governing life.

While Jason remembers his father with great affection as having been 'a man's man', as someone who was very popular and who was always laughing and making them happy, his mother clearly stands out as having been the dominant influence. However, he also argues that he was greatly affected when he failed his tertiary entrance examination. While this did not preclude him from attending teacher's training college, he was not able to attend university until he became twenty-one years of age and was classified as a mature student. This situation, he believes, has driven him to work very hard and to be a high achiever ever since. Finally, he places great emphasis on the healthy relationship which he has with his wife. She likes to work at home as an artist, is very tolerant of the long hours he works and is not very time-conscious herself, as she likes her own company. He talks freely about him and his wife being 'great mates' and considers the long chats which they have about all sorts of things as being a vital steadying influence in his life. She likes to question what he does and encourages him to be himself when it comes to making decisions. He gains comfort and relaxation from her creative life as an artist, from her 'laid back' approach to life and from the kindly way she can tell him to 'lighten up' when he becomes too intense.

Jason, then, clearly has a personal philosophy of education which stresses the importance of facilitating human growth and displays a commitment to caring. He also has committed himself to implementing his ideals amongst the marginalized in society due to his attraction, as he puts it, 'to helping the underdog get on in life'. However, his particular commitment to realizing his vision through an approach centred largely on SCL is in need of further exploration, particularly since, like his personal philosophy of education, it can be attributed to some extent to his life experiences.

## HIS SPECIFIC ENTHUSIASM FOR SCL

Unprompted, Jason argues that growing up on a farm may have had a lot to do with his enthusiasm for SCL, and particularly for his emphasis on pupils setting their own learning goals, although he feels that the influence is unconscious since he does not deliberately cast his mind back to those early days in search of direction and inspiration. Farming was, he says, 'our total way of life'. It was at the centre of the family's life, and thinking about it was constant and all-consuming. Because of its seasonal and precarious nature it required a lot of planning, including the development of alternative plans for various eventualities. Furthermore, the associated goal setting had to be both long term and short term. As he puts it, 'farming requires one to be in there for the long haul. It often takes years before it yields any results.'

Jason feels very strongly that this mode of thinking in his youth and teenage years became ingrained and made him a goal setter and a planner who is able to see complexity in situations and accept and respond to diversity. Furthermore, he feels that he acquired it largely because he was placed in situations where he was given responsibility:

> Life on the farm was one where you were dependent on yourself. There was so much to be done. You had to clarify what the job was from time to time. Also, you realized you had to do it yourself if it was to be done. After a while you also realized that you could do it.

It was not just on the farm that he found himself in positions of responsibility. He vividly recalls that as a fifteen year old, when he was head boy of the local district high school, he was regularly involved in 'helping organize events, coaching, umpiring, running school sports. The teachers just drove up to see that I had everything under control and then they left again.' Such activity was not seen as unusual at home since his parents were actively involved in community organizations and activities: 'My mother was always secretary of this and that and the other.' His level of responsibility and planning reached even greater heights when he attended boarding school. As head boy, he put a lot of energy into 'running the place as it should be run'. He is still proud of the fact that he took initiatives which got rid of bullying and a range of initiation rites in the school hostel.

Jason also clearly recalls that not only did he take initiatives aimed at improving life in the hostel but that 'others let you do it'. Again, he expresses a belief that this influenced his enthusiasm for SCL. Equally, he argues, the learning style he adopted when studying for a graduate diploma in educational administration was very influential in this regard. As external university students, he and his friend decided to work together to attempt to overcome the loneliness and isolation of studying at a distance. He speaks with great clarity about how their system evolved. They used to read the set texts and then meet at one or the other's house to discuss their readings, share questions and ideas and write drafts of essays before swapping them for critiquing. He describes this as having been 'a very exciting method of learning and of teaching each other'. After a while, he argues, the process began to make them feel more confident about their courses. He also relates that the approach of the dean of studies at the university proved influential in allowing him to value the importance of flexibility in learning. He found one of the curriculum units particularly boring and, on raising the matter with the dean of studies, to his pleasant surprise he was able to design his own course on 'integration' in the social studies curriculum, operationalize his ideas with his own class and submit his findings to the university as one of his projects for assessment. Accordingly, he argues that when he was introduced to notions of SCL and particularly to the concept of students setting their own learning goals, he became very enthusiastic largely because what was being promulgated was in accord with his own experience.

At the same time, it is significant that Jason does not see teacher implementation of the process of SCL as being sufficient on its own for the realization of his educational ideals. Rather, he is adamant that it needs to be matched by an enthusiasm for learning on the part of his staff, believing that this enthusiasm is infectious:

> Enthusiasm stands out for me in what I want from my teachers. I consider
> it to be the most important characteristic in a teacher. It drives my
> thinking on the way I want to organize a school.

He goes on to argue that he 'wants the kids to love learning' and that if this is to come about then 'the teachers must love what they are doing'. There are a number of dimensions to his belief in this regard. First, he stresses the importance of teachers loving their subject. He speaks of the destructive effect of unenthusiastic and uninspiring teachers, pointing as evidence of this to his experience of being a disappointed BA and diploma-in-education student because of 'boring lecturers presenting lectures in a boring way'. By contrast, he recalls with great admiration the teachers of his boarding school days and how their love of their subject was so evident that it 'rubbed off' on him and many of his peers. However, loving one's subject for Jason also means that one's relationship with one's subject-matter should be such that one should be constantly questioning it. In other words, one should be a lifelong learner and one should try to encourage this approach amongst one's students. He recalls that one of the greatest experiences in his own life was when he was studying geography part-time for his BA and teaching it at the same time in school: 'I was learning while I was teaching. It was great to be learning with the kids.' He is quite clear that this experience has had an effect on his present practice whereby he encourages his teachers, as he puts it, 'to be always making their subject-matter problematic for themselves and their pupils'. 'In this way,' he goes on, 'teaching becomes more than just a matter of getting the lesson plans correct.'

Jason also stresses the importance of teachers being enthusiastic in their teaching. Again, he recalls his boarding school days, and his mathematics teacher in particular, who held everyone's attention 'by the way he stood in front of the class, by the way he explained things and by the way he wielded the chalk to conjure up yet another example if he thought you didn't understand'. Coupled with this is the stress he places on teachers making themselves available outside of classroom hours to give extra tuition when it is needed, either by the slower learners or the students who want to accelerate their progress. This is also a memory he carries from his boarding days as to what characterizes an effective teacher.

Finally, Jason believes that teachers need to be involved in extracurricular activities: 'I have a very strong commitment to the importance of extracurricular activities. They are important if the pupil is to develop as a well-rounded person.' Certainly, his own education was one of great involvement in sport. As a teacher and HOD in four schools and as principal in four others, including his present position, he has promoted this principle and led by example. At various times while holding these positions he has coached school teams, organized and led school camps, gone with the pupils on various trips, directed dramatic productions and produced school newspapers. Furthermore, he has had similar involvement in the wider community. Also, when recalling those teachers who influenced him more than others during his teaching career before becoming a principal, a recurring theme regarding their behaviour is their wholehearted participation in extracurricular activities. His memory is not just of teachers organizing activities but also of them partaking in them with the pupils. Such participation is something which he encourages amongst his staff. This is consistent with his humanistic approach to education and with views that human growth largely takes place through the intimacy of interpersonal relationships.

JASON JOHNS

## WINNING THE CONFIDENCE OF STAFF

While Jason's commitment to a particular philosophy of education and to SCL are significant in arriving at an understanding of the direction which his school has taken in terms of curriculum, teaching and learning, this direction would not have been possible if he had not won the confidence of his staff. This was not an easy task. It was certainly facilitated to some extent by the fact that the staff had not only recognized many of the problems in the school prior to his arrival but had also been engaged to some extent by the previous principal in clarifying them. However, teachers were 'reluctant to change' and there was 'a bankruptcy of trust'. Above all else, there was great suspicion about, and opposition to, anything he wanted to do. He goes on:

> This situation manifested itself in amazing ways. For example, to even arrive at a decision as to when we were going to have a parents' night we had to negotiate a host of things. I remember thinking, 'Gees, how far back do we have to go before we can accept some groundrules?'

However, he stuck to the task and after a while the tide began to turn. A number of factors were influential in this regard. Certainly, his own capacity for hard work put in over long hours won the respect of many. Jason gets up most mornings at 4.30 a.m. and does school work at home for two hours before going to school. He usually arrives at school at 7.30 a.m. and chats with the deputies before settling down to work, usually without leaving the premises and without taking a break, and eating his lunch while working or while walking around the yard meeting pupils. At about 4.30 p.m. he leaves for home and has a meal with his wife and three children from 6.00–6.30 p.m. Then, he watches TV or takes a nap for about twenty minutes before going on to do about two hours of school work. He is usually in bed by about 10.30 p.m. As staff became aware that he kept this strict and arduous timetable and listened to his professions of desire to bring about improvement in the school, they became convinced that he was committed to them, to the school and to the pupils. In short, they realized he was there 'for the long haul'. He also gave them some breathing space by promising that he would not try to initiate any major changes in his first year.

Jason also involved the staff in a lot of debate, clarifying the issues which troubled them and also the direction in which he wanted to take the school. Initially, he found a great deal of hostility. This was not directed at himself or at the process. Rather, staff were demanding that they be consulted on issues as they arose. When the school was formally accepted for the NPQTL project he was delighted and immediately set up a steering committee of staff members to oversee the entry of the school into the project. When he announced this decision, his staff retorted angrily, 'We were not involved in the decision' and 'We were not consulted'. He was, in his own words, 'flabbergasted'. However, he tackled the issue immediately, setting aside a half-day for an open discussion and a sharing of felt grievances. This was followed by a disbanding of the committee. The staff then, on being asked, decided that they should be involved in the project, proceeded to elect a steering committee and became involved wholeheartedly. Jason considers this first occasion on which staff took ownership for their activities to have been a major turning point in their attitude and a significant event influencing their positive disposal to innovations which would present themselves in the future.

## MAINTAINING THE CHANGE PROCESS

While winning the confidence of his staff early on was vital for Jason in order to implement his reformist agenda it was equally necessary for him to maintain it and to keep staff interested and committed in pursuit of the school's educational vision. Focusing much of their thinking around SCL was certainly influential in this regard. However, he has also utilized a variety of other strategies. His high work rate has already been noted. What is significant in the present context is that much of this has been related not just to administrative aspects of school life but also to curriculum and pedagogical aspects. He partakes in committee work, holds regular meetings with his HODs, visits classrooms and disseminates research material amongst the staff. He expresses his views on this participation as follows:

> I like to be in a situation where I can influence things which annoy me, which I want to do something about. I don't want to do it all by myself but I am prepared to do an enormous amount by myself. I do whatever has to be done to get the job done. I'll double my work load if necessary.

While he has been a hard worker for most of his life, his commitment to hard work was reinforced greatly when he took up his first principalship:

> I went to the school prior to the beginning of the school year, prepared the timetable and got everything organized. I really didn't know what the principalship was all about and I regularly worked twelve to fifteen hours a day. I was also very naive. I took everything as gospel. The regulation was that principals should teach half-time so I taught nineteen periods a week. I also helped teachers to prepare lessons.

He argues that while it was physically and emotionally exhausting, it set the pattern which was to characterize his behaviour for at least the next ten years.

It is clear, however, that the last number of years has brought about a change in approach for Jason as he has developed from being a principal who was always mainly in control to being a delegator and someone who now places great emphasis on being an appreciator, a congratulator and an applauder. This change appears to have taken place in the school where he was principal prior to taking up his present position. Up to this point he had always worked with a young staff. Here, however, he had a much older and much more experienced staff and he quickly realized that he could only involve them in change if he gave them responsibility. His belief in this regard was reinforced by the readings he was undertaking for his postgraduate studies at the time and particularly the body of theory which, as he puts it, indicates that 'to make things work you have got to get people inspired'. A further factor was that for the first time he was dealing with a staff of seventy teachers rather than thirty and he realized that it was not physically possible for him to do everything himself and take responsibility for all that was taking place in the school. He recognizes that the associated changes were not easy for him:

> I am slightly saddened by all of this. Every time there is a release of responsibility to other people there is a slight leakage in me. I do enjoy seeing other people get a lot of satisfaction from their work. That's terrific. But there is an enormous satisfaction from doing it yourself. Even as a superintendent, when I used to talk to teachers about how to improve, I used to walk away with enormous frustration. I wanted to get in there and do the teaching myself.

However, he also recognizes that there is no going back for him now and that he must do as much as possible to continue to empower his staff.

Jason has maintained the confidence of his staff and kept them focused by also constantly reminding them how important it is to be always thinking about ways 'to make things better for kids'. He puts in a lot of time and energy to promote this thinking amongst them. He spends time each year going around to every teacher saying, 'Tell me, what ways have you involved kids in the planning of their work?' He also spends time in each classroom observing what is going on in terms of SCL and writing up a one-page report by way of feedback, emphasizing the positive aspects of the lesson. Also, he has made it his business to investigate the particular problems, stresses and requirements of teachers arising out of the nature of the subjects they teach and such associated issues as the numbers of pupils in class, the available equipment, the necessary resources and the particular atmosphere created by the mode of teaching. This, in turn, has presented him with an understanding which has assisted him in engaging in discussion with staff and trying to distribute resources more equitably. He also places great emphasis on staff sharing experiences at staff meetings by regularly asking them 'How are things going?', 'How do you feel?' and 'What have you learned about your teaching lately?' His closeness to the pupils in the school also maintains his credibility both amongst them and amongst his staff. Just as John Glynn, his district high school teacher with whom he still meets regularly, did in his time, Jason makes a point of regularly moving around the school during lunch break, 'talking to the kids in their own little territory'. His affection for them is clear: 'They wear their hearts on their sleeves. They are good to be with. I really enjoy them. I'd love to spend more time teaching them.' Accordingly, it is not surprising that he is a regular attender at school camps and at school functions.

Jason also maintains the impetus of his reformist agenda by constantly stressing the importance of teachers informing their work with the findings of educational research. He has established a close relationship between the school and the local university education faculties. The school is readily available for educational research and university lecturers run workshops and professional development sessions for the staff. This commitment by Jason is, of course, understandable in light of the great amount of time he has spent on his own postgraduate education; since graduation as a secondary school teacher from teachers' college in 1962 he has successfully studied as a part-time student for a BA, a university postgraduate diploma in education, a postgraduate diploma in educational administration and an M.Ed. degree. However, while he encourages any of his staff who are interested to follow a similar path, he argues that all of them should have enquiring minds as to what is going on in the school and be generators of data to bring clarity to problems experienced in the school. The availability of such data, he argues, 'empowers the quiet majority' and does not allow those who are vociferous to push a particular agenda if it is based on conjecture and a perception which might not be generally shared.

In maintaining staff morale and enthusiasm and in continuing to promote change it is important to Jason that he maintains an overview on what is happening and how it relates to the school vision and to the SCL strategies emanating from it. He certainly has a capacity to stand back and see the whole picture and the benefits for everybody. This capacity, he feels, unfolded in him when he was a head boy in the hostel at boarding school: 'I could accept all the kids there and organize things to include everybody. I could certainly handle complexity. I liked doing lots of different things.' However, the wide variety of experiences which he has had during his career in education has also been very formative. Not only has he taught in four schools and been principal in four others, but he has also taught a range of subjects, from physical education, to social studies, to English. Also, each of the schools has been in a different geographical, climatic and social environment. Accordingly, his life has been one of regular change and adaptation. Furthermore, on each occasion he has made the transition smoothly. The consequence of this, as he sees it, is articulated by him as follows:

All that moving and having to adapt to so many situations has been valuable in allowing me to develop my ability to maintain an overview on situations. I have been helped by the fact that all of the situations have been very different.

He has also benefited from the fact that he has, throughout his career in education, become friendly with colleagues who have been anxious to spend time discussing professional matters and enable pupils to 'make a shift and have some personal growth'.

The final major question which arises is 'Where to from here with Jason?' What stands out more than anything else in this regard is that he has no desire to retire in the immediate future. In fact, far from entertaining any notion of 'slowly winding down', Jason speaks of constantly seeking new challenges, if not at Bluehill then somewhere else. He is quick to remind one that to entertain a thought of retirement would be contrary to family tradition. Just as his family viewed farming, not as a job, but as 'a total way of life', so he views teaching and his involvement in education. His father 'never gave up farming' and his step-uncle, a teacher, simply went and taught in another state after he retired in WA.

Throughout his life Jason has been very energetic. His early life was punctuated with the excitement of playing on the farm, weekly trips to town to shop, playing 'footy' and cricket, and jumping on the back of a moving train to get to school, while his outstanding memory of boarding school is that 'there was never a dull moment'. Since then he has channelled much of his energy into cultivating within himself a love of learning and seeking personal development through change and continuing to take on new challenges as an educationalist. He goes on:

> I am now in my early 50s and into my fourth principalship. I just want to keep it going. I am getting more enthusiasm. I believe that I can handle more things more capably than I have before. I don't know what the next step will be, as has been the case elsewhere.

He speaks with great passion about the work which still needs to be done in the school, about his plans to bring about structural changes which will result in big blocks of time being made available so that pupils will have the opportunity to learn not only in subject areas but also through investigating cross-curricular themes, problems and issues. He also has notions about how individual education programmes and individualized timetables could be produced and he is keen to do more to resist current trends towards the development of productivity measures for education, arguing that it is vital to continue to emphasize that education has multiple outcomes: 'You provide a service to facilitate the growth of all young people. Education is about providing an environment for kids to learn and, of course, because they are all different they all learn in different ways.' However, he concludes that once it becomes a case of decreasing returns for him in terms of satisfaction in his present position, he will seek a new challenge.

Throughout his working life Jason has been conscious of becoming worried when the excitement has started to wane. Accordingly, he developed the strategy of trying to have options available at all times. As he puts it, 'I was always doing things to create opportunities for the future.' Presently, he is developing the notion that maybe he will soon want to move away from adolescent education and is investigating the prospect of working in the field of pre-retirement education. He has just begun running short courses on 'preparing for retirement' for academic and general staff at a local university. The fact that he is thinking along such lines is also interesting in the context of current restructuring in the state. He clearly favours the rhetoric of the reform, particularly the notions of the self-managing school and the devolution of responsibility from the centre. He also considers that a variety of the Education Department initiatives have been very worthwhile, including the promotion of school development planning and a student outcomes-based approach to teaching and learning. However, he considers that what lies on the horizon is a situation where 'principals are going to be tied up more and more with an administrative load'. This, he argues, is a trend which is discernible at present and will continue as the devolution of responsibility will be accompanied not only by a requirement that schools be more accountable to government, and thus to the general public, but also that they be shown to be accountable. Demonstrating accountability is a bureaucratic exercise involving much form filling and report writing on the part of the principal. Accompanying this situation is the need for principals to be constantly alert and take whatever action is necessary to give legal protection to themselves and the school in general because of the responsibilities which have been devolved onto them. As he sees it, this will mean that less and less time will be available for what he sees as the major role that a principal should be playing in a school, namely, as an educational and transformative leader.

From these considerations it would be wrong to give the impression that matters have been all plain sailing for Jason and that he has not experienced knock-backs in his initiatives. One in particular stands out. It stemmed from his enthusiasm for research and his belief in the capacity of research findings to improve practice. This led him to engage in a research project with a university academic. The project was concerned with the impact of devolution policy on educational practice. Amongst the main findings of the project was that district superintendents were not fulfilling a function of great importance and that they constituted another level in the bureaucratic chain whose existence was not necessarily consistent with the principles of devolution. Jason had a sense of pride and satisfaction when the report was published and made available for public perusal. He also looked forward to what he considered would be a healthy debate ensuing from the report which would, in turn, contribute to the improvement of the state education system, whatever the outcome. He also expected that senior officials would be pleased that a school principal would be working actively to bridge the theory–practice nexus and contribute to the broader educational debate: 'I honestly thought in my naive way that it would be well regarded.' However, it appears that in challenging the status quo and being constructively critical of some aspects of current policy he was seen as being disloyal to the system. He became particularly upset when, shortly afterwards, his school suffered when funding ceased to be available for a very successful education programme.

Initially, Jason was very subdued about the situation and tried to highlight the issues involved through both political channels and the media. Eventually, however, with the support of his staff, he put it behind him. He continues to conduct research projects into contemporary educational issues with his academic friend. He also contends that he does not feel hateful about what happened or vindictive towards anybody and is very quick to express his loyalty to the Education Department, which he keeps reminding himself is responsible for the many opportunities which he has been given during his career. During his period as a superintendent he was very impressed by the caring and very supportive approach of the institution towards young beginning teachers and also towards teachers with various problems. And so he continues his work at Bluehill SHS, clarifying issues, informing debates with data, cultivating teamwork amongst the staff, utilizing as wide a variety of strategies as possible with them to promote divergent thinking and dealing with different points of view, encouraging them to reflect upon and write about their classroom experiences and experiments, and all the time emphasizing SCL in order to promote in students the confidence and enthusiasm to be problem solvers and ongoing independent learners.

# 10

# DISCUSSION OF CASE STUDIES

Studying the lives and professional careers of principals inevitably yields a rich abundance of data. In adopting a topical life history approach in the study of individual principals, one is concerned in making sense of the data, with looking for links and connections which help explain their current beliefs and practices, and the ways in which they understand the professional world in terms of significant past events and experiences. When engaging in the study of a variety of individual cases to produce a cross-case analysis along the lines presented in this chapter, it is helpful to identify, where possible, relevant typologies, key themes, and relationships between, and patterns of, themes. In adopting such a structure one is mindful of the need to clarify meanings and create understandings for the reader, who is thereby encouraged to relate his or her own experiences to those emanating from the cross-case themes. In this sense, the themes which emerge from the cross-case analysis presented in this chapter serve as touchstones against which readers can play off their own reflections, realities and experiences. We believe such a process to be an integral and invaluable part of professional learning.

Our analysis starts by presenting a typology of innovative principals based on those studied in our cases. It then moves to recognize the importance to their professional lives of those past and current experiences and responsibilities upon which they draw in order to promote, manage and lead innovation. This is followed by an analysis, first, of the broad general approach adopted by these principals in meeting the challenges of innovation within a restructuring context, and second, of how they go about the business of changing and restructuring their schools in terms of specific strategies, actions and behaviours. A diagrammatic representation of the general and specific strategies adopted by the principals then summarizes this macro- and micro-analysis. Our thematic approach is completed by recording the principals' deep-seated views and cherished notions concerning change, innovation and learning. By way of conclusion, a cognitive framework for conceptualizing the influences of life history on the principal is outlined and is summarized in diagrammatic form.

# A TYPOLOGY OF INNOVATIVE PRINCIPALS

Our reflections on the analyses of the six innovative principals in this study lead us towards the recognition of a three-fold typology. We formed this conclusion when it became clear to us that the manner in which the principals' life histories intersected with their particular work environments was quite different in each case. After studying closely the six principals and the relevant parts of their life histories, it occurred to us that they could be placed in one of three categories with respect to their orientation towards innovation and school restructuring. In one category are principals like David and Jason, who would probably be professionally innovative no matter what their work context or the particular environmental conditions in which they operated. Regardless of whether or not the policy context was one of reform and restructuring, and whether or not the local school context favoured change, it is likely that these principals would be promoting innovations. Such principals seem to have a predisposition and predilection towards innovation. It is their natural response to managing and leading their school communities. They have always been innovators throughout their teaching careers and their principalship.

In a second category are principals like Simon and Janet, for whom the restructuring context is very necessary in order that they realize their innovative potential. While it is the restructuring environment which galvanizes their innovative activity, the nature of the school does not seem to be crucial in this regard. These principals are taking a major leadership role in the promotion of innovations for the first time in their careers as principals. This may be so for at least two reasons. First, while they may have had a predisposition for innovation in the past, it is only since a favourable and supportive environment for reform has been created, through restructuring policy, that they feel comfortable in exercising innovative leadership. Second, for some who had previously given innovation little thought, the restructuring environment may act as a catalyst, a rich source of opportunities for experimenting and breaking out of established moulds. It is when this contextual condition is present that a favourable climate exists such that their life history experiences can be given free reign, allowing them to realize their potential as innovators.

A third group of principals are those like Bronwyn, who require both the restructuring context and favourable conditions in the school and its community in order for them to be innovative. In one sense, and when compared with the other groups, these principals are prepared to take the least risk with regard to innovation. It is only when both the restructuring context exists and the school context is favourable that their life history experiences can come into play in activating their innovatory potential. They are prompted to innovate only when both the macro- and micro-environments are conducive.

The three groups of innovative principals can be construed as 'ideal types'. Viewed in this way, the orientation of a particular innovative principal may fall neatly into one of these three types, or somewhere between them. However, it is accepted that this is unlikely to be a rigid framework. Rather, it is presented as a generalized outline to aid our understanding of innovative principals. Accepting such a position, however, it seems reasonable to argue that life history has an influential part to play in their orientation towards innovation.

## EXPERIENCES AND RESPONSIBILITIES

A comparison of all six principals reveals that they have had significant and varied experiences in positions of responsibility and that they frequently draw upon them in their working lives. All have previous experience of being principals in other schools. All are aged in their forties or fifties. All enjoy considerable support for their professional endeavours from their families and homes. While four of them do not have formal qualifications in educational management at masters' or doctoral degree level, all are convinced advocates of the need to inform school reform and restructuring according to best practice as presented at principals' conferences, in research literature and professional journals and in books by well-known scholars.

It is also significant that they seek such knowledge not just for its immediate relevance. Rather, it assists them in overcoming feelings of insecurity and uncertainty when they arise. Even the most innovative and successful principals admit that they experience times of adversity, stress, loneliness and isolation. At such times they seek support and affirmation for their innovatory policies, many of which represent considerable risk-taking. They also acknowledge other ways in which they gain support and reassurance for their continuing efforts, even during times of adversity. These include working long and hard, drawing on family support, relying on a critical mass of like-minded professionals, valuing the major contributions made by close friends and colleagues with whom they are able to discuss many contemporary educational issues, and reading extensively across the professional literature, especially in the areas of school administration, human resource management, motivation, curriculum theory and learning theory.

What, one may ask, is the message in this for those who argue that our schools need more 'young blood' and principals with management or educational management qualifications? One implication arising from these life history studies is that we should not undervalue the enormous benefit of experience which can be gained through occupying many and varied positions of responsibility. At the same time, this is not to argue against the accelerated promotion through the ranks of talented younger people. Neither is it to oppose the case for an all-graduate or all-certificated profession of educational administrators. However, it should be recognized that youth without experience and professional and personal support is unlikely to yield the quality of innovative school leadership required for successful restructuring. In the same vein, formal qualifications unaccompanied by practical common sense and hard-headed 'on-the-job' experience is unlikely to be sufficient to meet successfully the challenges of whole-school reform. It is also worth drawing attention to the fact that while the four innovative principals without higher degree-level qualifications stress the importance of practical experience, they recognize that their performance could be enhanced if they had the opportunity to obtain such qualifications. They have come to realize this partly through participation in diploma and short non-award bearing courses in educational management.

The foregoing deductions raise further interesting life history questions with regard to the principalship. One such question concerns the stages or phases of principalship and whether it is possible to identify a stage or phase in which principals are most innovative. Another concerns whether principals are more innovative at certain stages of their careers than at others. A further question relates to whether age is more or less important than the stage or phase of principalship. One might also ask whether there is a relationship between the age of principals and the principalship stage or phase in which they are located. And what are the relative effects of, on the one hand, accruing experience of principalship by remaining in one school for a long time, and on the other, gaining experience by spending shorter periods in a number of different schools?

Relatively little research to date has addressed these questions in regard to principals and the principalship. The work of Day and Bakioglu (1995) is an exception. These authors recognize four 'phases' of principal development in their research on secondary school principals in the Midlands of England. Principals of between zero and four years were deemed to be in an 'initiation' phase; those of between four and eight years of principalship were said to be in the 'development' phase; principals with more than eight years of experience were identified as being in an 'autonomy' phase; and a small number, who overlapped in experience with the 'autonomous' principals, but who displayed cynicism and negativity, were seen to be in a phase of 'disenchantment'. The latter principals were all over fifty years of age. Principals in every phase of development, except disenchantment, displayed the following characteristics: confidence (measure of self-belief); effectiveness (quality of their work and results); ambition (to change, to succeed); enthusiasm (willingness to be actively involved); management style (as defined by the heads); reaction to external demands (as they influence school culture); and development of professional expertise (strengths and weaknesses).

A more extensive body of research exists on teachers. Huberman (1989) and Leithwood (1990), for example, both argue that there are five stages of development in a teacher's career: (1) career entry; (2) stabilization; (3) experimentation/activism (new challenges and concerns); (4) serenity/disenchantment (reaching a professional plateau); and (5) disengagement (preparing for retirement). There are also those who, in harnessing this type of research in the study of the principalship, have assumed that what is true for teachers might also pertain to principals' ways of proceeding. This, however, may be problematic. Furthermore, while it is interesting to explore the possibilities of career phases or stages for principals, the resultant categories which emerge tend to reflect the characteristics of mainstream rank-and-file principals. If the focus is shifted to principals who are in some way different or exceptional, then the taxonomy of phases or stages may be called into question. Just as there are different types of teachers, so there are different types of principals. Huberman (1993, p. 4) draws attention to the former as follows:

> The fact that typical factors can be found should not hide the fact that there are some people who never stop exploring, who never stabilize or who destabilize for psychological reasons; a sudden awareness, a change of interest or values.

It is reasonable to argue that the same claim can be made in respect of principals. For example, Jason, as has been demonstrated in this book, is very innovative, yet if he was classified according to Day and Bakioglu's stages, he would be in the 'autonomy' phase. The argument is that during this phase, headteachers perceive that they have less energy, increasing prudence, nostalgia for the past, dissatisfaction with new external initiatives, a greater personal resistance to change, and, in some cases, a desire for an autocratic management style (Day and Bakioglu, 1995, p. 23). In fact, however, with the exception of increasing prudence, Jason, as with each of the other five innovative principals in our study, displays the opposite characteristics.

The project reported in this book also suggests that not all principals follow the same career path. The typical linear career progression through successive stages does not apply in the case of the six innovative principals studied. Their commitment, enthusiasm and boundless energy for change and improvement, far from waning with experience and age, show every sign of growing. This suggests that proactivity, which has amongst its characteristics enthusiasm, adventure and orientation towards innovation, is the property which, more than any other, distinguishes the innovative from the less innovative principal. The challenge for the life history researcher is to seek the genesis of this property in past experiences and significant others, events and opportunities.

Particularly significant in the life stories of the six principals studied is the support they have gained from family and home throughout the period of their present innovative activities in their schools. All are currently married and the support, understanding and tolerance derived from their spouses continues to be a source of strength, enabling them to maintain persistent and focused effort over long periods of time. It would be worthwhile to engage in a further, more focused and specialized life history study aimed at probing the values, experiences and events in their life histories which may have enabled them to cement positive relationships with their spouses, while at the same time coping successfully with a demanding professional environment. There is a clear need to improve our understanding of the relationship between personal life and professional life, especially given trends such as increasing rates of family break-up and ever-greater commitment to, and pressure at, work in order to succeed. The gender dimension is also in need of further investigation, particularly since three of our principals are females whose husbands are most supportive of their careers. In order to investigate this matter further, it is arguable that not only would it be helpful to study a greater number of innovative female principals who are married but also to study the life histories of their husbands.

## THE BROAD, GENERAL APPROACH IN MEETING THE CHALLENGES OF INNOVATION

All six principals possess at least three characteristics with respect to their general approach to managing the change and innovation process endemic to restructuring. First, they believe in a 'whole-school reform' approach. Second, they understand the importance of establishing the preconditions for change and innovation; an understanding which makes them strong advocates of preparing the groundwork, cultivating the culture and building a positive climate for change. Third, they approach the management of change and innovation in a noticeably 'structured' way. Furthermore, their life histories go a long way towards explaining their possession of these characteristics.

Adopting a whole-school approach to change rather than an incremental, piecemeal one is important since the nature of restructuring is such as to require change in many aspects of the school, including its structures, processes, culture and climate. Many of these aspects are interdependent, others are independent. The principals possess an understanding of restructuring which conceptualizes its multifaceted nature. They believe in change happening on a number of fronts at the same time, while being mindful of the dangers of overload on their staff. Also, they are able to handle, cope with and manage the extraordinary pressures which emanate from simultaneous multiple change. Indeed, in some cases they appear to thrive on the dynamic, challenge and excitement of being involved in change and innovation on a number of fronts at the same time.

The principals' whole-school or 'gestalt' approach to restructuring, in which the interdependencies, intricacies and connections implicit to the process are visualized, is distinguished by a number of significant characteristics. In particular, they realize the necessity of investing resources and effort in soundly preparing the groundwork, preconditions, culture and climate ready for change and successful innovation. They resist the temptation to race too quickly into implementing the innovation, preferring a more studied and patient approach to ensure successful take-up. It is arguable that the evidence provided in each of the six individual cases already presented suggests that there may well be grounds for believing that these qualities of patience, astute planning and careful, considered strategy have been developed and rewarded in their past experiences.

To dwell only on the capacity to handle change on a number of fronts simultaneously would, however, be an oversimplification of the approach adopted by the principals. As already indicated, they also understand the importance of establishing the conditions for change and innovation. Their whole-school reform approach is facilitated through a realization that there are priorities and that these change with time; that some innovations are required before others; that the sequence of events and the order in which innovations are tackled are therefore important; and that the push for whole-school reform needs momentum and focus. Furthermore, they realize that this momentum can be achieved by focusing on one reform initiative and using it as a 'conduit' through which effort and resources can be combined and focused in a synergistic way. As such, they have the capability of affecting many aspects of the school's operation. In the case of Simon, for example, he has emphasized the embedding of computer technology in the school curriculum as the driving force giving impetus to a host of other innovations. Similarly, Jason has placed student-centred learning strategies and the reconfiguration of teacher and student groupings at the centre of his reform agenda, recognizing their potential to generate other initiatives.

The principals' tendency to focus on a small number of initiatives so that they can act as 'conduits' is not something which characterized their approach during the early stages of their careers. Rather, it seems to be the natural outcome of great experience obtained over quite a number of years holding a variety of positions in varied geographical and social environments. Such experience, arguably, has led to an understanding of the complex, stressful and intense nature of classroom life and a realization that energy has to be focused on one or two initiatives containing a powerful set of concepts which can give meaning and direction to teachers' work.

Finally, it is clear that while each of the principals in the six case studies has undertaken whole-school reform in a distinctively different and unique way, they all share in common a 'structured' approach to change. Anne, Simon and Jason, for example, have placed more emphasis in their approach to multiple change on strategies which are concurrent, while David and Janet have placed more stress on a consecutive or sequential model. However, regardless of the model favoured, it appears that the emphasis on careful, conscious and deliberate 'structure', or strategy, is a key attribute of their approaches to innovation.

From a life history perspective, it is interesting that the case studies indicated that there are past experiences and significant events which seem to have contributed to their current abilities and beliefs on whole-school reform and multiple change. Their stories from childhood depict them as bright, energetic, responsive and ambitious; the sort of individuals who would easily be dissatisfied with the status quo if it were not to their liking. For the most part, their early childhood experiences taught them to be independent, self-reliant and to cope with the machinations of moving from place to place. By no means did they all have 'easy beginnings' nor were they all brought up in an environment of material comfort. Subsequently, their early and extensive experience as teachers and principals in the WA government education system, where movement every two or three years to and from schools greatly different in terms of type and location is a normal expectation before being located in the city, also appears to have contributed to their degree of comfort with change as an integral part of their lives.

## SPECIFIC STRATEGIES, ACTIONS AND BEHAVIOURS IN MEETING THE CHALLENGES OF INNOVATION

Along with the three characteristics which the principals possess with regard to their general approach to managing change, the case studies also reveal a variety of more specific strategies and techniques used in managing and leading innovations in curriculum, teaching and learning. These can appropriately be labelled 'micro-level' strategies since they characterize everyday events and interactions at teacher, classroom, department and internal-school levels rather than at levels external to the school. In one sense, our case studies reveal relatively little which is new, or which has not already been made explicit in existing research literature. What is different, however, is the demonstration that the life histories of the principals go a long way toward explaining their personal characteristics and, thereby, the approaches and strategies they adopt to school restructuring. A sum of these strategies is now presented under four headings.

### Vision-driven approaches

All six principals are driven by a desire to improve curriculum, teaching and learning for all students. Towards this end, they are believers in student-centred methods of learning and student outcomes-oriented learning. They believe that too many students are allowed to leave school without experiencing success in learning. They are proactive in believing that their schools, through restructuring at the school level in particular, can do much to address the causes of this lack of success. They accept, on behalf of their schools, responsibility for the failure of some pupils to learn rather than pass this responsibility on to others. A focus on improving the quality of teaching and learning through the adoption of a broader range of instructional techniques, more flexibly delivered to engage more students, is an essential part of their vision.

However, the vision-driven emphasis placed by the principals on the quality of curriculum, teaching and learning is coupled with a strong concern for the care and well-being of the students. Indeed, it is the twin focus on learning and care and the balance struck appropriately between them which more accurately

149

captures the visions held by the principals. The emphasis on the care dimension, it is arguable, is clearly attributable to their life histories, and particularly to experiences, both positive and negative, in the early part of their lives which sensitized them to being concerned about the physical and emotional welfare of others. In the case of Janet, for example, the still vivid memory of the deprivation suffered by some of her pupils during her early career, coupled with her socialization into the 'caring' philosophy of her Catholicism, are still major influences on her work as a principal. Each of the other principals have visions with regard to their work which are strongly impregnated by memories of this nature.

While possession of a vision, particularly one causing them to place an emphasis on curriculum, teaching and learning and on care, appears crucial in the innovatory strategy of the principals, it is significant that it is underpinned by an even wider vision; one which provides consistency, strength and coherence. In other words, the nature of their innovations and the ways in which they go about promoting them can be attributed to their particular philosophies of life. These, in turn, provide them with a powerful set of values which inform their work. Consequently, Jason and Simon 'champion the underdog', David is driven by the worthiness of developing 'healthy people' through appropriate schooling, Janet possesses a strong awareness of Christian values, Bronwyn views education as the 'passport to life', and for Anne, education is a means through which justice, equity and fairness can be expressed. Indeed, this latter set of values is shared by all six principals.

The implication of the six principals harnessing their educational visions to their philosophies of life and attempting to bring them to fruition is that expectations are placed on all students because it is believed that this will help realize the vision of a 'better life' for them. By the same token, high expectations are also placed on teachers since the fulfilment of the vision is also dependent on them. For this reason, the principals emphasize the importance of teacher development. They espouse the importance of teachers as learners; they strongly promote teacher professionalism; and they encourage open communication between teachers, students, administrators and all who make up the school community.

## Goal setting and goal achieving

Covey (1989, p. 137) refers to effective people having clear missions (visions), which are given structure and organised direction through expression in roles and goals. These principals recognize that for each of the many roles they play, there is a set of goals. Covey (ibid.) goes on to argue that effective goals focus primarily on results rather than activities. In these respects the innovative principals demonstrate the habits of effective people identified by Covey: they form visions, they operationalize these through identification of their roles, and for each role, they express and specify goals in terms of results they intend to see achieved. In highlighting this, it is recognized that Covey's contribution is one which identifies the characteristics of highly effective people. The project reported in this book, it will be remembered, did not seek to identify such characteristics in the case of the six principals studied; rather, the focus was on the fact that they are adventurous and innovative. Nevertheless, they are illuminative within the present context.

All of the six innovative principals in the case studies reported in this book possess an ability not only to form values-based visions but to apply sustained pressure towards their realization. Goal-setting and goal-achieving strategies are fundamental to their approach. All six attach importance to operationalizing their visions through setting specific goals, making them explicit and setting about their achievement. While they certainly have undergone various professional development programmes as principals which have introduced them to the efficacy of such an approach, the case studies demonstrate that largely what they succeeded in doing is heightening their awareness that they possess and utilize a skill which they have acquired through their life experience. Furthermore, they are not just characterized by the possession of this goal-setting skill. Rather, they all demonstrate the resourcefulness, determination and tough-mindedness needed to sustain pressure to achieve their goals and realize their vision. In respect of their will to succeed, their accounts impress with their sheer mental and physical energy, their degree of organization and their ability to manage heavy workloads as well as to handle stress. They are organized and disciplined and expect the same of others. Again, however, we have to look to their life experiences to come to an understanding of how they acquired these qualities. Certainly, their experiences indicate their survival qualities, with Anne, for example, overcoming her difficulties as an immigrant and, like Janet and Bronwyn, surmounting the barriers to success in the educational world which have arisen out of its male dominance. Similarly, we noted the case of Jason bouncing back from his early academic failure and acquiring a range of postgraduate qualifications while holding down a full-time job, and the cases of Simon and David overcoming the impediments which they had to overcome because of their humble origins.

The principals' life experiences also go a long way toward explaining another dimension to their goal-setting and goal-achieving characteristic, namely, their awareness of the need to seek and to seize opportunities, wherever and whenever they occur, to achieve their visions of school restructuring. This was well illustrated in the case of Bronwyn, who attributes her ability to 'seize the opportunity' when it presents itself to her adventurous childhood and the responsibilities she was given, along with the encouragement and support provided by her husband throughout her career. She, like the other principals, is now someone who is opportunity-aware rather than simply opportunistic; someone who is keen to capitalize on any event or situation which is likely to enable the achievement of her goals and the realization of her vision. Being opportunity-aware means that opportunities are sought and taken only in so far as they further the vision and goals set for the school. Opportunists, by contrast, could be thought of as simply responding and reacting spontaneously to particular situations or events, rather than framing or conceiving such events within longer term-plans.

Finally, Sergiovanni (1994, p. 192), noting Susanne Langer's contention that symbols and meaning make our world far more than sensations, reminds us of the powerful effects symbolic leadership can have in building a community of learners and leaders. He also notes that Thomas Carlyle recognized that it is in and through symbols that we consciously or unconsciously live, work and create meaning and significance in our lives. He goes on to argue that 'both meaning and significance are at the heart of community building' (ibid.). And he is unequivocal about the importance of community building being 'at the heart of any school improvement effort' (ibid., p. xi). Indeed, he regards it as the foundation on which improvement in teaching, curriculum, governance, assessment and professionalism rest.

The six principals realize the powerful effect of symbolic leadership in building a sense of school community; a community with shared ideals and values around which stakeholders can bond and unite. Many different types of symbols are consciously used to strengthen commitment to a school improvement ethos focusing on the notion of a community of learners. Sometimes, principals emphasize dress code or the school crest and motto; on other occasions, subjects such as the expressive arts are seen as helpful in promoting a sense of school community.

## Inclusiveness and collaboration

Discussion on the innovativeness of the principals thus far might well misleadingly over-emphasize their individual and personal accomplishments at the expense of their ability to engage in collaboration. The accounts rendered in the case studies testify that the principals not only realize the importance of interdependence, but possess an ability to include all stakeholders in decision making, both of which help to create and sustain a sense of community. In this regard, one is reminded of the position of scholars such as Sergiovanni (1994) and Starratt (1996), which emphasizes the crucial importance of building community in restructuring schools. Equally, one is reminded that family life and being part of a community is something to which the case study principals have attached importance throughout their lives and is also something which they recall as being vital in their development. It will be recalled that Jason, for example, emphasized the formative influence of having to grow up in an environment where survival on the farm, both physically and emotionally, was dependent on all members cooperating, and that he also attaches great importance both to the experience of boarding school life, where all had to 'pull together' to create a wholesome vibrant environment, and to significant individuals in his early career who reinforced in him his realization of the importance of cooperation.

It is arguable that the principals' present collegiate approach to decision making can, to a large extent, be attributed to the exposure to experiences of this nature. Furthermore, regarding this approach, they clearly demonstrate a realization that community is promoted through collegiality and collaboration. They are particularly convinced of the need to involve teachers, parents and community in the restructuring process. Open and continuous communication between all stakeholders is considered imperative in achieving this high level of involvement. In gaining the commitment of all parties, legalistic and bureaucratic approaches are eschewed for more flexible and responsive strategies.

Significantly, the principals build the sense of community around the core business of schools – curriculum, teaching and learning. As Starratt (1996) has lucidly argued, the notion of community is both a means of improving schooling and an end in itself. In both senses of the term, he is quite unequivocal in stating that a school as a learning community is primarily organized 'for the production and performance of learning and knowledge' (ibid., pp. 88–89). A lively, vibrant, healthy school community focuses on collaboration among its stakeholder groups in resolving key issues to do with the nature of knowledge, the balance and relevance of the curriculum, the desired approach to teaching and learning, the type of person it regards as 'educated' and the values it wishes to be imparted to its students. It is on these essentially educational issues that the innovative principals noticeably strive to focus their attempts to build community.

Yet, the ability to involve and work with stakeholders and to promote their ownership of the restructuring process is only part of the benefit flowing from the inclusive, collaborative approach taken by the principals. Their strategy extends beyond the simple involvement of key stakeholders. They realize that the prime objective is not only to get the best effort from each individual and group in the school community, but to get each to pull in the same direction. They also express and demonstrate a belief that this is best accomplished by broad agreement between stakeholders on visions and goals. In this, they are at one with Covey (1989), who argues that when collaboration is inspired by 'creative cooperation', fuelled by empathic communication and a win/win strategy, the result enables the attainment of the most prized state of all, namely, synergy (ibid., p. 262). This he defines as the essence of 'principle-centred leadership'; a state where the energy unleashed and results obtained by the whole come to more than the sum of the parts. It 'catalyzes, unifies, and unleashes the greatest powers within people' (ibid., pp.262–263). Synergistic ways of cooperating, communicating and decision making usually result in creative and previously unscripted methods of working and higher goal achievements.

While a formidable body of existing research has recorded the importance of collaboration and interdependence in the part played by principals in managing change, much of it has failed to capture and expose the more subtle elements. The case studies reported here suggest that the process which is at work is more complex than that recognized in many previous studies. It appears an oversimplification to claim that innovative principals are collaborative and inclusive in their approach without detailing what may be a crucial and all-important element in their collaborative qualities. Our analysis leads us to conclude that the approach of the six case study principals is frequently characterized by a tension or a dialectic. For example, while they are collaborative and inclusive, they possess a strong individual sense of vision and direction which they want their schools to take. They are decisive, but at the same time show tolerance in working well with people in a democratic rather than dictatorial way. They collaborate with and know how to bring the best out of others, but at the same time they have clear individual expectations. They are empowered professionals themselves, but they also empower others around them. This dialectic may not have been given sufficient emphasis in previous accounts of the principalship, particularly within innovatory contexts.

In all cases, the six principals feel comfortable and secure in including other stakeholders in, and sharing, the decision-making process. Evidence from their life histories suggests that this may be due to the positive experiences they have had when involved in collaborative situations in previous episodes of their lives. All found cooperation and a 'give-and-take' mentality to be necessary in order to maintain harmonious relationships in their early lives. All were lucky in their early careers in that they were involved in collaborative activities in teaching and management in the schools where they worked. Also, they all have a strong history of being involved in team situations and committees, particularly in the sporting domain, in their out-of-school lives. Indeed, both Janet and Jason are still active team-sport participants.

## Organizational analysis and re-creation

The ability of the principals to take a gestalt view while balancing it with a critical eye for detail has already been noted as a characteristic of their general approach to innovation. This is well illustrated by their capacity to decide purposefully on particular aspects of whole-school change for emphasis and priority at different times, as circumstances allow or dictate. This seems particularly important given the ubiquitous nature of restructuring and the multiple-strategy approach apparently necessary to resolve problems associated with restructuring. The capacity to keep the pressure for change going on a number of fronts simultaneously, while maintaining a critical awareness for fine detail, undoubtedly constitutes an important aspect of their leadership. Some commentators have labelled this the 'helicopter trait', that is, the ability to elevate oneself periodically above a situation to gain an overview, and then to lower oneself back into it.

Related to this are characteristics of a more particular nature. What is especially noteworthy is their willingness, when deemed appropriate, to confront problems head-on, rather than allow such problems to go unattended and invariably to magnify. They also possess distinctive ways of seeing their schools as organizations with structures capable of being moulded to suit and serve particular values and purposes at given periods in time. Rather than seeing structures as the enduring, stable elements of school around which the curriculum, teaching and learning activities must necessarily revolve, the reverse is the case. They are not fearful of challenging the well-established and traditional paradigms and characteristics of schools. The status quo in respect to school organization, which others might regard as inviolable, is questioned in terms of its efficacy. However, for all of them, current dysfunctional aspects of schools may need dismantling while at the same time new forms and structures may need creating. Schools may, therefore, need redesigning in order that structures and processes support rather than dictate changing aims and values built around more explicit policies espousing the enhancement of student learning outcomes.

In sum, these innovative principals realize the importance of flexible organizational structures and practices if their schools are to meet the increasingly diverse and demanding needs and expectations of their clientele. They are truly students of organizations; they undertake analysis of and reflection on their own school organizations with a view to restructuring their form and *modus operandi* in order to improve the service to all students. In this regard, they lead by example, encouraging other stakeholders to examine their contributions to school success.

Values and vision are not the only source of principles guiding the innovative practices of these principals. Their work is also informed by relevant professional and research literature, as well as knowledge gained from conferences and in-service training experiences. Ideas, techniques and strategies adopted in the daily leadership and management of the restructuring process frequently represent a symbiosis of all of these. Thus, new ideas emanating from research literature may be filtered and distilled through a 'screen' of values and vision and are only adopted after having been through such a process. Moreover, exposure to new ideas is always eagerly sought. Regardless of how well restructuring is conceived by those championing and promoting it, learning opportunities are constantly sought by the principals in order to embellish and support both current and future restructuring initiatives.

# A DIAGRAMMATIC REPRESENTATION OF THE GENERAL AND SPECIFIC STRATEGIES ADOPTED BY THE INNOVATIVE PRINCIPALS

Case studies yield 'thick' or detailed descriptions. An edited topical life history approach, such as that adopted in this book, can be expected to generate a wealth of data. Analysis of such case studies built around life history accounts will inevitably create a multitude of themes and a complex web of relationships between these themes. The foregoing account in this chapter illustrates well the complexity and difficulty presented in trying to make sense of the profusion of themes. Accordingly, it is helpful to construct a visual map, or cluster diagram, of key themes and the connections between them, such as is presented in Figure 1.

In this cluster diagram of the themes to emerge from analysis of the accounts of the six innovative principals, the central importance of values, vision, goal setting and goal achievement is emphasized. Built around these core themes are stakeholder input, research input, questioning of existing paradigms, seizing of opportunities, use of symbolism and maintenance of pressure. All of these themes interrelate within certain frameworks, including the ability to take an overview, to adopt a structured approach, and above all, to assume a whole-school approach to restructuring.

# PRINCIPALS' NOTIONS CONCERNING CHANGE, INNOVATION AND LEARNING

Our theme-based analysis is brought to a conclusion by highlighting that the six innovative principals are, above all, advocates for change. This common category which describes the fundamental approach of the principals has three aspects. First, the principals welcome change; second, they believe in lifelong learning; and third, they intend to continue as innovators.

Our analysis so far of all six principals has revealed their capacity to be comfortable with and in turn to welcome, change. The situation, however, is somewhat more complex. In particular, not only do they welcome change, within certain parameters, but they do so even if it is imposed by others. In the schools in question, restructuring is being imposed principally by the government of WA. Even when change is imposed, these principals, rather than respond negatively, feel able both to mediate and distil those aspects of change which appeal to them and to capitalize on the opportunities provided for the benefit of their school communities.

In this regard, it is difficult to escape the conclusion that life experiences have undoubtedly played a significant part in shaping how principals react to major challenges such as restructuring. They contribute to our understanding of why restructuring policies, which can be expected to evoke some negative reactions from many principals, can, in the case of some, result in them

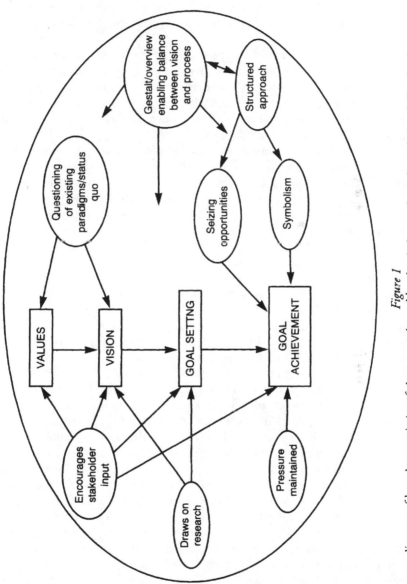

*Figure 1*

Cluster diagram of key characteristics of the approach used by the six innovative principals in whole-school restructuring

adopting a mindset which perceives opportunities and conceives advantageous courses of action, even in circumstances which ostensibly appear to be unfavourable. By contrast, the less innovative prefer to remain inactive, adopting a critical frame of mind, often preferring the status quo or some past state of affairs, playing for time and hoping that the press for change initiative will pass them by.

It is increasingly being accepted in certain sectors of the academic community that the way in which individuals react to situations is dependent on their 'mindset', 'frame of mind' or their 'cognition' at the time. This point is convincingly argued by Covey (1989) when he claims that 'the way we see the problem *is* the problem' (ibid., p. 40). In describing the habits of highly effective people, he recognizes above all their proactivity, which comes about through a propensity – when faced with difficult situations – to enlarge the areas of their lives over which they are able to exert influence and control and to downplay the corresponding parts of their lives which lie beyond their control. Proactive people, he argues, seek imaginative, creative ways to convert apparently negative, adverse situations into positive, advantageous circumstances. In guiding their responses, effective people 'begin with the end in mind' (ibid., p. 97). This is to say that they establish clear sets of values and principles which act as touchstones and frameworks within which their actions and behaviours can be shaped and determined. It is this, coupled with a sense of mission and purpose, as well as the capacity to follow through, which often distinguishes the innovative and effective from the rest. A contribution of the case studies presented in the earlier part of this book is the demonstration that individuals' life histories can go a long way towards explaining why they possess this sense of mission and purpose.

A second aspect of the innovative principals which characterizes them as advocates of change is their belief in lifelong learning and their capacity for engaging in reflection on past, present and future events and scenarios. As lifelong learners they exhibit the intrinsic values and characteristics upon which their schools are founded. They not only believe in continuous learning for themselves, as professionals, but believe that continuous learning is the foundation of the leadership of their school communities. The high value placed on learning can, in most instances, be traced back to childhood, to the inculcation of family values and to past successful experiences in learning. All of them now realize the need to enrich their thinking by exposure to new ideas. In Bronwyn's case, she learns through attending many short courses, including the principals' leadership course at Harvard. Jason, on the other hand, has recently completed a masters degree and intends to continue with more formal award-bearing courses of study. Others declare themselves as avid readers of the professional and research literature on school leadership and change, and regular attenders at staff development sessions. Associated with this is the emphasis which they all place on reflection. This is the capacity to think about experiences, to make sense and meaning of, and to draw connections between, phenomena, and to place such phenomena in context and perspective. Reflection maximizes learning and the processes of learning. Taken together, there is little doubt that learning and reflection constitute a sound base for innovation.

The third aspect of the innovative principals which characterizes them as advocates of change is that they seek new challenges for the future. Confounding theories of principalship based on career stages, which predict an eventual stage of maturity where innovation is displaced by consolidation and even disillusionment, these principals seem to reaffirm their enthusiasm, keenness and motivation for innovation the more their careers progress. Many motivation appear relevant as explanations for this disposition, including fear of failure, hope for success, dissatisfaction with the status quo, the excitement of undertaking a new challenge, and the desire to be well thought of by one's peers and associates. These, in turn, as the various cases have indicated, seem traceable to upbringing and past experience. Janet was influenced by her father very much in her ambition to succeed; Jason was equally motivated to make something of himself by his mother and an early experience of failure in school-leaving examinations; both David and Simon, like Jason, were profoundly influenced by their mothers to be ambitious and to set high goals to achieve from an early age. Since all were starting from a relatively modest background, this meant breaking out of the mould cast by their immediate environment and establishing new parameters, setting new goals and adapting to unfamiliar contexts. Their comfort with risk taking, a sense of self-belief and confidence, and native ability, enabled them to cope with these challenges.

## CONCLUSION: CONCEPTUALIZING THE INFLUENCES OF LIFE HISTORY

An analysis of the six cases in this book identifies a number of key factors or themes which, taken together, form the influences and experiences which constitute life history. These are conceptualized and summarized in Figure 2.

Three parts to this conceptual framework can be recognized. First, key sources of change in a person's life may be distinguished. Second, processes and effects characterizing the life history experience may be identified. Third, it may be helpful to break life history into phases or stages.

With regard to key sources of change in a person's life, these may be attributed to people, including significant individuals and groups; important events, activities and happenings; important norms, values and ideas. In reality, these all tend to interrelate to give the full life experience. Thus, it may be the particular combination of people, events and norms at a given moment in time which provides the life experience.

With regard to the processes and effects characterizing the life history experience, at least four sets or pairs of antithetical reactions and responses appear to exist: a particular life experience may either reinforce, or alternatively, provoke a counter-reaction to, an existing behaviour, belief or norm; a life

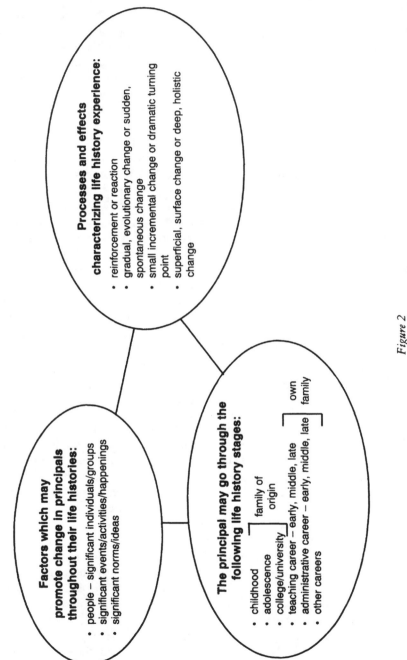

**Factors which may promote change in principals throughout their life histories:**

- people — significant individuals/groups
- significant events/activities/happenings
- significant norms/ideas

**Processes and effects characterizing life history experience:**

- reinforcement or reaction
- gradual, evolutionary change or sudden, spontaneous change
- small incremental change or dramatic turning point
- superficial, surface change or deep, holistic change

**The principal may go through the following life history stages:**

- childhood
- adolescence
- college/university — family of origin
- teaching career — early, middle, late
- administrative career — early, middle, late — own family
- other careers

*Figure 2*

A life history conceptual framework for school principals

experience may lead to a gradual, evolutionary change in a person or it might promote a sudden, spontaneous change; a life experience may feasibly lead to a small incremental change, or alternatively, it might constitute a dramatic turning point; a life experience might prompt a superficial, surface change or alternatively, a more substantive, deep change in behaviour, beliefs and norms.

With regard to breaking life history into phases or stages, accounts such as those pertaining to the six innovative principals may reveal phases or stages relating to childhood, adolescence, college/university, teaching (early, middle and late phases) and administration (early, middle and late phases). Occasionally, a school principal may have had an earlier career outside of education. If so, this needs to be taken into account.

We do not claim that this framework is necessarily definitive in enabling a complete understanding to be gained of such complex sets of processes constituting a person's life history. However, it seems to us that such a conceptualization, derived as it is from empirical study of six innovative principals involved in restructuring, may help in the future to elucidate and inform studies similar to that presented here.

# 11

# CONCLUSION AND
# IMPLICATIONS

Educational restructuring, as this book has indicated, is widespread in many countries of the world and is associated with moves to deregulate and decentralize the running of schools. The situation in WA illustrates that restructuring can also assume a form which aims to improve the quality of the curriculum, teaching and learning through making changes in work organization. Here, as in the rest of Australia, particular emphasis is placed on the role of the school principal in the translation of policy initiatives into practice. However, our stance in this book is that while advice to principals is plentiful, research on the principalship has not kept pace with the changing context within which contemporary school principals are expected to operate.

Our argument is that we need to know much more about how schools and school principals are responding to the demands made upon them by restructuring. Elaboration of the argument is as follows. Principals, along with others in school communities, are expected to respond to restructuring policies and initiatives. They do so in different ways. While it is important to study the different ways in which principals in general react to restructuring, we have been motivated in this book to focus on a small number of those who have been singularly adventurous.

It has also been argued that the challenge for researchers is to adopt a variety of research approaches in studying school leadership and restructuring and also to apply these in a range of contexts. The research approach adopted in this book is that of the edited topical life history, while the context is the WA state high school system. We have sought to develop accounts of schools, and the role of the principals within them, which integrate the perspectives of both the principals and the researchers, and also to provide accounts of these roles by examining the socializing influences relevant to the formation of each principal over the full life experience. This is to accept Butt *et al.*'s (1988, p. 68) argument that 'teachers' knowledge ... is grounded in, and shaped by, the stream of experiences that arise out of person/context interactions and existential responses to those experiences.' This knowledge and predisposition to act in certain ways in the present moment, they argue, 'is grounded as much, if not more so, in life history than just current contexts and action: it is autobiographic in character'. Starratt (1996, p. xxiv) lends further support to this proposition:

> Educational administration is, like teaching, autobiographical. That is, we work as we live and have lived: we are the primary tool in the crafting of our administrative work. . . . We may adopt, for example, a particular strategy in resolving conflict. . . . That strategy, however, will be colored by our personality, by our personal history of dealing with conflict, by our cultural roots, by our feelings towards the people involved in the conflict, by our class, gender, and ethnic biases, and so on. Although we strive to be objective in our dealings with others, each of us nonetheless brings his or her own interpretive frameworks to bear on his or her experience.

It has been the central argument throughout this book that a major contributor to the development of such interpretive frameworks is the individual's life history.

The particular approach to life history study adopted in the project reported here is one based on symbolic interaction. Accordingly, the perspective offered on restructuring is a holistic one where principals are seen in relation to both the internal and external contexts of their particular schools and also in relation to key events and influences in their own life histories. The individual case studies were developed to illustrate this perspective rather than to seek generalizations for the WA and other contexts. At the same time, it is recognized that they contribute to the pool of qualitative studies of individual principals and teachers in particular groups from which, as Butt and Raymond (1989, p. 404) put it, 'commonalities related to their lives and careers can be drawn'.

In arguing that one did not set out to seek generalizability one, of course, is not rejecting Stake's (1978) argument that case studies may be in harmony with the reader's experience and thus a natural basis for generalization. As Kennedy (1979), in the same vein, puts it, generalizability is ultimately related to what the reader is trying to learn from the case studies. Lancy (1993, p. 165) provides a different angle on this yet again when he states that such an approach 'is comparable to the law where the applicability of a particular precedent case must be argued in each subsequent case. The reader must decide whether the findings apply or not.'

The case studies can also be seen as having generalizability in the sense outlined by Uhrmacher (1993, pp. 89–90). Building his ideas on those of Eisner (1985), he argues for the production of cases which describe school life, interpret that life by exploring the meanings and consequences of educational events, and assess the educational significance of events described and interpreted. This 'thematics' approach, Uhrmacher (1993) states, is related to generalizing in social science research. He goes on to argue that rather than make formal generalizations, one can provide the reader with an understanding of the major themes that run through the cases under study. In turn, these themes provide the reader with theories or guides for anticipating what may be found in other situations; 'these theories provide guidance, not prediction' (ibid., p. 90). It is in this sense that the themes outlined in the previous chapter should be viewed. Most of these are neither surprising nor original. Some have been well reported in the research literature on effective principals and school effectiveness. However, the contention is that, when read in conjunction with the case studies, readers will be encouraged to reflect on their own personal positions, life histories and professional situations, and may derive new insights, understandings and meanings.

It is also noteworthy that as the project reported in this book progressed, it became clear to both the researchers and the participants that the individual cases could be useful in facilitating the professional development of others. This is not to contest a fundamental premise of the methodology underlying the research project, namely, that it is the meanings which have emerged from their life experiences which are likely to influence people's actions. Neither is it to contend that simply reading cases will automatically spur other principals into promoting innovations in curriculum, teaching and learning. Rather, it is to reiterate and extend the argument that if there is to be any hope of promoting educational change, teachers need interpretive knowledge every bit as much as they need prescriptions for sound practice.

The importance of 'interpretive knowledge' was argued strongly in the educational literature in the late 1960s and early 1970s, and the arguments hold just as strongly today. Stanley (1968, p. 235) defined such knowledge as that which gives us a cognitive map so that we can locate a problem within a set of meanings and allows us to gain a perspective on educational problems. According to Broudy (1967, p. 1), a case can be made for the interpretive use of knowledge; a use that enables one to conceptualize and understand an existential problem without necessarily enabling one to solve it. Traditionally, such knowledge has been promoted through the 'foundation subjects' of education, especially history, philosophy and sociology of education and, to a lesser extent, comparative education. Particularly in relation to history of education, the type of arguments advanced have been along the lines of those of Lévi-Strauss, who stated that those who ignore history condemn themselves to not knowing the present, because historical development alone permits us to weigh and evaluate in their respective relations the elements of the present (Marwick, 1970, p. 13). The same argument is made by Strayer when he states that the historian's learning is useful, not because it provides a basis for prediction but because 'a full understanding of the past makes it possible to find familiar elements in present problems and thus makes it possible to solve them more intelligently' (ibid., p. 18). Presenting individual edited topical life histories, particularly those of the type offered in this book, can add a further, personal dimension to this process. As Sultana (1991) puts it in relation to case studies in general, they can expose teachers involved in similar circumstances to material which could help them in clarifying and sharpening their own perceptions. In the language of Stenhouse (1975), they can aid in the development of the capacity to understand relationships and make judgements by constituting frameworks for others within which they can think.

There is also a strong argument that central-level bureaucrats who are trying to promote change could benefit from reflecting on cases like those reported in this book since, as Fullan (1982) has so strongly argued, to effect improvement, that is, to introduce change that promises more success and less failure, the world of the people most closely involved in implementation must be understood. In the same vein, Davies (1992, p. 212) argues:

> Because they are often called upon formally or informally to advise others about career choices, decisions and problems of dealing with inappropriate jobs and roles, those involved in the process of training, developing and educating others have a particular need to understand their own career pattern and the biographical narration around it.

She concludes that an outcome of such understanding is a greater depth and clarity of perception into our own approaches and limitations 'which enables us to perceive and empathise with others in their own career and development issues' (ibid.).

The possibility that the case studies may have the potential to promote change is also not discounted. It may be that, in Mandelbaum's (1973, p. 180) term, they will act as 'turnings' for some principals, leading to changes in meanings which will result in innovative actions in curriculum, teaching and learning. By 'speaking' to others who operate in similar and related contexts, who share some of the same concerns and who are on the threshold of promoting change, the case studies could provide a framework for developing enlightenment and guiding activity. In this way, it may be that they constitute a source of power to promote professional growth and to lead to transformative action.

To use case studies in this way would be to address Lieberman's (1995, p. 593) point that 'because direct teaching currently dominates much of what the public and many districts consider to be staff development, it is important that teachers, administrators, and policymakers become aware of new and broader conceptions of professional development'. In this regard, the contention of Darling-Hammond and McLaughlin (1995, p. 597) is also noteworthy:

> Professional development in this era of reform extends beyond mere support for teachers' acquisition of new skills or knowledge . . . it also means providing occasions for teachers to reflect critically on their practice and to fashion new knowledge and beliefs about content, pedagogy, and learners.

Case studies of the sort reported in this book may constitute one source to assist us in breaking away from a notion of in-service education as being concerned only with instrumental ends achievable through 'the recipes of tried and true practices legitimated by unexamined experiences or uncritically accepted research findings' and towards one of 'developing reflective practitioners who are able to understand, challenge and transform' (Sachs and Logan, 1990, p. 479).

Sachs and Logan (ibid.) go on to develop the latter argument by pointing in particular to the existence of system-initiated, centrally conducted courses to prepare teachers for specialist roles, such as administrators. These courses, as they see it, have been typically based on experience with practical imperatives for outcomes. The concern has been to provide teachers and administrators with practical, technical and personal support in classroom and school matters in order to achieve relevance and immediacy. While they see a place for such courses, they argue that an obsessive concern with them can lead to, or reinforce, an instrumental ideology or technical rationality which sees simple and universalistic solutions to particularized problems in unique contexts, irrespective of whether or not they are based on research or reflective practice. In short, principals' roles become inexorably restricted to those of technicians whose worth is judged in terms of how well they can efficiently and effectively meet the requirements set by central management. One way in which this approach can be counterbalanced is through encouraging principals to reflect on cases like those reported in this book. As Wolk and Rodman (1994, p. x) have put it, principals around the country and elsewhere may, through the reading of cases, 'identify in some ways with the individuals portrayed' and come to see that 'the status quo is not immutable, that change is possible, and that risk taking is worthwhile'.

Recently, English (1995) has added a further justification for the development and dissemination of cases in his argument for a reconsideration of biography and other forms of life writing as a focus for teaching educational administration. The main reasons for the neglect of such sources in teaching to date, as he sees it, can be traced to the field of educational administration favouring a positivistic definition of science, and research methods that marginalized anything not considered 'objective' (ibid., p. 203). However, change, he argues, has been fostered by a concern for the absence of morality in preparing educational leaders, a continuing confusion between management and leadership, and emerging concerns for preparing the 'reflective' practitioner. He then goes on to present criteria by which instructors can select forms of life writing for use in graduate curricula, and methodological examples are discussed as to how they may be used in the process of instruction. Arguably, the cases presented in this book have the potential to be used in the manner proposed by English.

Finally, this research project has convinced the researchers of the value of engaging principals in developing edited topical life histories of the type reported here. Sikes and Troyna (1991, p. 6) have argued that educationalists should engage in writing their life histories to expose and make explicit their 'taken for granted assumptions about education, schools, teachers and teaching in order that they should be able to examine them from a more critical perspective'. Similarly, Butt and Raymond (1989) have argued that the experience of researcher and participant working on a life history project has an 'emancipatory interest' in that the collaborative research process is designed to raise the participant's consciousness with respect to the institutional conditions of teachers' work. Of course, there is nothing new about this. In the early 1720s, for example, Count Giovanni di Porcia invited a number of Italian intellectuals to tell the story of their lives, partly for pedagogic reasons (Verne, 1991). In the 1970s, Abbs (1976) was arguing for the incorporation of autobiography as a linchpin of any teacher training programme: 'The act of writing an autobiography which reflects on the students' experiences of education will', he contended, 'reveal the intimate relationship between being and knowing, between existence and education, between self and culture' (ibid., p. 148). He claimed that inviting both student teachers and teachers to reflect in writing upon their own personal and educational experiences enables them to gain a deeper knowledge of the kinds of influences likely to affect their present and future abilities as teachers.

Woods (1985b) also has argued that possible outcomes of participation in life history studies are 'greater understanding of self and career, and an aid to morale' (ibid., p. 15). This, he states, 'may derive from knowledge of varieties of career and career planning, and the general contextualizing of one's own, which touch on feelings of success and failure, and general job satisfaction' (ibid.). He goes on: 'At the very least, the exercise will have encouraged reflexivity on their part, and caused them to examine their personal development in possibly a more holistic, integrated, systematic, scientific and detailed way than ever before' (ibid., p. 25).

Certainly, the researchers in the present study were struck by the participants' constant references to how useful they found their engagement in the research. They spoke of it as enabling them 'to take stock', of giving them the 'opportunity to clarify the big picture', of giving them some notion of where they have come from, thus making clear where they are at and indicating where they might go from there. In this regard, Aspinwall (1992) speaks of a teacher welcoming the opportunity to do some reflection on her present, past and possible futures, and of the engagement in this process helping her 'to reframe a present problem and feel that she was able to see a more productive way ahead' (ibid., p. 250). Similarly, Farrell (1992) reports her discovery that people find the telling of their stories to be a 'cathartic and healing process as well as a developmental experience' (ibid., p. 220). She contends that consciousness-raising is about 'telling life stories, listening to and swapping experiences, discovering the reality of each other's lives' (ibid.). Equally, Ditisheim (1984) reports that in her work with teachers she found that the life history approach has cathartic, structural, cognitive and energizing functions.

In highlighting this matter one is cognizant of the need not to give the impression that principal participation in life history studies may constitute the new panacea in professional development courses for principals. Indeed, in this regard one is chastened by Kelchtermans and Vandenberghe's (1993) study of how ten experienced teachers in four different Flemish schools experienced their careers, focusing on the personal perceptions and subjective meaning of these experiences. While the study showed the usefulness of the biographical perspective for a better understanding of why teachers act in the way they do, it also demonstrated that teachers' stimulated reflection on their career and personal development did not automatically change or improve their teaching practice. Equally, however, there are sufficient indications that participation in life history studies can lay the foundations for an ongoing critical appraisal of customary practices and beliefs in one's educational role. Such appraisal, as Woods and Sikes (1987, p. 161) point out, is necessary at the present time more than ever, given the 'massive individual adjustments that have to be made if the radical changes that are currently affecting the profession are to be successfully negotiated'.

Researchers and policymakers alike have, over the course of many decades, exhorted and advised principals and teachers to adopt prescribed practices in the cause of effectiveness and efficiency. Textbooks, manuals and handbooks have been written to this end. Likewise, countless numbers of principals have experienced professional development programmes based on prescriptive principles and practices. The underpinning assumptions to this approach are first, that performance improvement can be achieved by advocating and adopting generalized formulae and prescriptions; second, that it is appropriate to recommend these for all; and third, that these generalized recommended principles and practices are not problematic in terms of the meanings and understandings which they, in turn, generate for practitioners. In view of these assumptions having been drawn, it seems hardly surprising to us that both the existing literature on effective principalship and schools and the considerable investment in professional development have so far yielded relatively undramatic results in terms of improving practice.

The argument expounded in this book is that given the aim of improved practice, it is insufficient simply to extol a set of principles or procedures. This is not to deny the validity or importance of generalized principles or themes of best practice, the more so where such principles are derived from rigorous and robust research. It is, however, to argue that given the objective of encouraging every principal to formulate, adopt, internalize, and implement improved practice, it is imperative that individuals' current state of knowledge, skills and attitudes, as well as the significant and relevant events in their life histories and past experiences, be acknowledged as key filters and lenses through which meanings of best practices and principles are distilled. Put simply, if we want to create adventurous principals who are comfortable handling change and who in turn succeed as change agents, we cannot afford to ignore the person as well as the person's life history in the critical equation which unlocks the door to restructuring. We need to realize that each principal's leadership is a unique phenomenon. It is unique in the sense that how each principal responds to, and behaves towards, restructuring is a symbiosis of policy frameworks and associated expectations, principles and theories underlying best practices, individual abilities, and meanings imparted to all of these derived from both current and life history experiences. It is through adopting such a holistic, dialectic and symbolic interactionist perspective that policymakers, professional developers and writers and researchers are most likely to promote the genuine restructuring of schools through innovative principalship.

# REFERENCES

Abbs, P. (1974) *Autobiography in Education*, London: Heinemann Educational.
—— (1976) *Root and Blossom*, London: Heinemann.
Abrahamson, M. (1967) *The Professional in the Organisation*, Chicago, Ill.: Rand McNally.
Allport, G.W. (1942) *The Use of Personal Documents in Psychological Research*, New York: Social Science Research Council.
Anderson, L.W. (1990) *Time and School Learning*, Beckenham, UK: Croom Helm.
Angus, L.B. (1992) 'Quality schooling, conservative education policy and educational change in Australia', *Journal of Education Policy* 7, 4: 389.
Aspinwall, K. (1992) 'Biographical research: searching for meaning', *Management Education and Development* 23, 3: 248–257.
Beare, H. (1983) 'The structural reform movement in Australian education in the 1980s and its effect on schools', *Journal of Educational Administration* 22: 149–168.
—— (1992) 'What does it mean to be professional? A commentary about teacher professionalism', *Unicorn* 18, 4: 65–73.
Belenky, M.F., Clinchy, B.M., Goldberger, N.R. and Tarule, J.M. (1986) *Women's Ways of Knowing: The Development of Self-Voice and Mind*, New York: Basic Books.
Bennis, W. and Nanus, B. (1985) *Leaders: The Strategies for Taking Charge*, New York: Harper & Row.
Blackledge, D. and Hunt, B. (1991) *Sociological Interpretations of Education*, London: Routledge.
Blake, R.R. and Mouton, J.S. (1985) *The Management Grid*, Houston, Tex.: Gulf Publishing.
Blau, P.M. and Scott, W.R. (1963) *Formal Organisations*, London: Routledge & Kegan Paul.
Blumer, H. (1962) 'Society as symbolic interaction', in A.M. Rose (ed.) *Human Behavior and Social Processes*, Boston, Mass.: Houghton Mifflin.
—— (1969) *Symbolic Interactionism*, Englewood Cliffs, NJ: Prentice-Hall.
Bogdan, R. (1974) *Being Different: The Autobiography of Jane Fry*, New York: John Wiley.
Broudy, H.S. (1967) *Philosophy of Education: An Organisation of Topics and Selected Sources*, Chicago, Ill.: University of Illinois Press.
Brown, D.J. (1990) *Decentralization and School-Based Management*, London: The Falmer Press.
Burgess, R.G. (1982) 'The unstructured interview as a conversation', in R.G. Burgess (ed.) *Field Research: A Sourcebook and Field Manual*, London: Allen and Unwin.
—— (1984) *In the Field: An Introduction to Field Research*, London: Allen and Unwin.
Butt, R.L. and Raymond, D. (1989) 'Studying the nature and development of teachers'

knowledge using collaborative autobiography', *International Journal of Educational Research* 13, 4: 403–449.

Butt, R.L., Raymond, D. and Yamagishi, J. (1988) 'Autobiographic praxis: studying the formation of teachers' knowledge', *Journal of Curriculum Theorizing* 7, 4: 87–164.

Butt, R.L., Raymond, D., McCue, G. and Yamagishi, L. (1992) 'Collaborative autobiography and the teacher's voice', in I.F. Goodson (ed.) *Studying Teachers' Lives*, London: Routledge.

Butts, R.F. (1955) *Assumptions Underlying Australian Education*, Melbourne: Australian Council for Education Research.

Caldwell, B.J. and Spinks, J.M. (1988) *The Self-Managing School*, London: The Falmer Press.

Campbell-Evans, G. (1993) 'A values perspective on school-based management', in C. Dimmock (ed.) *School-Based Management and School Effectiveness*, London: Routledge.

Carnegie Forum on Education and the Economy (1986) *A Nation Prepared: Teachers for the 21st Century*, New York.

Chadbourne, R. and Clarke, R. (1994) *Devolution: The Next Phase. Western Australian Secondary Principals Association: A Response*, Perth: Secondary Principals Association.

Chubb, J.E. (1988) 'Why the current wave of school reform will fail', *The Public Interest* 90: 28–49.

Cistone, P. (1989) 'School-based management/shared decision making: perestroika in educational governance', *Education and Urban Society* 21, 2: 363–365.

Cohen, D.K. (1988) *Teaching Practice: Plus ça change*, East Lancing, Mich.: Michigan State University, The National Center for Research on Teacher Education.

Coldrey, B. (1991) *Child Migration and the Western Australian Boys' Homes*, Moonee Ponds: Tamanaraik Publishing.

Coleman, P. and LaRocque, L. (1989) 'Loose coupling revisited'. Paper presented at the Annual Meeting of the American Educational Research Association, San Francisco.

Cooley, C.H. (1956) *Human Nature and the Social Order*, Glencoe, Ill.: The Free Press.

Covey, S. (1989) *The 7 Habits of Highly Effective People*, New York: Simon & Schuster.

Cuban, L. (1989) 'The "at risk" principal and the problem of urban school reform', *Phi Delta Kappan* 70, 10: 780–784, 799–801.

——(1993) Foreword, in P. Hallinger, K. Leithwood and J. Murphy (eds) *Cognitive Perspectives on Educational Leadership*, New York: Teachers' College, Columbia University.

Darling-Hammond, L. and McLaughlin, M. (1995) 'Policies that support professional development in an era of reform', *Phi Delta Kappan* 76 1995, 597–599.

Davies, J. (1992) 'Careers: biography in action, the narrative dimension', *Management Education and Development* 23, 3: 207–214.

Day, C. and Bakioglu, A. (1995) 'Development and disenchantment in the professional lives of headteachers'. Unpublished paper: University of Nottingham.

Denzin, N.K. (1989) *The Research Act*, Chicago, Ill.: Aldine.

Department of Education, Queensland (1990) *Focus on Schools: The Future Organisation of Educational Services for Students* Brisbane, Queensland: Department of Education.

Derouet, J.L. (1991) 'Lower secondary education in France: from uniformity to institutional autonomy', *European Journal of Education* 26, 2: 119–132.

De Waele, J.P. and Harré, R. (1970) 'Autobiography as a psychological method', in G.P. Ginsburg (ed.) *Emerging Strategies in Social Psychological Research*, London: John Wiley.

Dimmock, C.J. (1990) 'Managing for quality and accountability in Western Australian education', *Education Review* 42, 2: 197–206.

——(ed.) (1993) *School-Based Management and School Effectiveness*, London: Routledge.

## REFERENCES

—— (1995) 'School leadership: securing quality', in C. Evers and J. Chapman (eds) *Educational Administration: An Australian Perspective*, Sydney, NSW: Allen and Unwin.

Ditisheim, M. (1984) 'Le travail de l'histoire de vie comme instrument de formation et education', *Education Permanente* 72–73: 199–210.

Dollard, J. (1935) *Criteria for the Life History*, New York: Libraries Press.

Duignan, P. (1990) 'School-based decision-making and management: retrospect and prospect', in J. Chapman (ed.) *School-Based Decision Making and Management*, London: The Falmer Press.

Eisner, E. (1985) *The Educational Imagination* 2nd edn, New York: Macmillan Publishing.

Elbaz, F. (1992) 'Hope, attentiveness and caring for difference: the moral voice in teaching', *Teaching and Teacher Education* 8, 5/6: 421–432.

Elmore, R.F. and Associates (1990) *The Next Generation of Educational Reform*, San Francisco, Cal.: Jossey-Bass.

English, F.W. (1995) 'Towards a reconsideration of biography and other forms of life writing as a focus for teaching educational administration', *Educational Administration Quarterly* 31, 2: 203–223.

Etzioni, A. (1964) *Modern Organisations*, Englewood Cliffs, NJ: Prentice-Hall.

Evetts, J. (1989), 'Married women and career: career history accounts of primary headteachers', *Qualitative Studies in Education* 2, 2: 89–105.

Farrell, P. (1992) 'Biography work and women's development: the promotion of equality issues', *Management Education and Development* 23, 2: 215–224.

Fiedler, F. (1973) 'The contingency model and the dynamics of the leadership process', *Advances in Experimental Social Psychology* 11: 60–112.

Fullan, M. (1982) *The Meaning of Educational Change*, New York: Teachers' College Press.

—— (1991) *The New Meaning of Educational Change*, London: Cassell.

Garms, W.I., Guthrie, J.W. and Pierce, L.C. (1978) *School Finance: The Economics and Finance of Public Education*, Englewood Cliffs, NJ: Prentice-Hall.

Gilligan, C. (1988) 'Remapping the moral domain: new images of self in relationships', in J. Ward, J. Taylor and B. Bardige (eds) *Mapping the Moral Domain: A Contribution of Women's Thinking to Psychological Theory*, Cambridge, Mass.: Harvard University Press.

Glaser, B. and Strauss, A. ( 1967) *The Discovery of Grounded Theory*, Chicago, Ill.: Aldine.

Goetz, M.D. and Le Compte, J.P. (1982) 'Problems of reliability and validity in ethnographic research', *Review of Educational Research* 52, 1: 31–60.

Goodlad, J.I. (1984) *A Place Called School*, New York: McGraw Hill.

Goodson, I.F. (1977) 'Evaluation and evolution', in N. Norris (ed.) *Theory in Practice: Centre for Applied Research in Education*, Norwich: University of East Anglia.

—— (1980–81) 'Life histories and the study of schooling', *Interchange* 12, 4: 62–76.

—— (1988) 'History, context and qualitative methods in the study of curriculum', in R.G. Burgess (ed.) *Strategies of Educational Research*, London: The Falmer Press.

—— (1991) 'Teachers' lives and educational research', in I.F. Goodson and R. Walker (eds) *Biography, Identity and Schooling: Episodes in Educational Research*, London: The Falmer Press.

—— (ed.) (1992) *Studying Teachers' Lives*, London: Routledge.

Goodson, I.F. and Walker, R. (eds) (1991) *Biography, Identity and Schooling: Episodes in Educational Research*, London: The Falmer Press.

Guthrie, J.W. (1986) 'School-based management: the next needed education reform', *Phi Delta Kappan*, 68: 305–309.

Hallinger, P. and Murphy, J. (1987) 'Instructional leadership in the school context', in

## REFERENCES

W. Greenfield (ed.) *Instructional Leadership: Concepts, Issues and Controversies*, Boston, Mass.: Allyn & Bacon.

Hallinger, P., Leithwood, K. and Murphy, J. (eds) (1993) *Cognitive Perspectives on Educational Leadership*, New York: Teachers' College Press.

Halpin, A.W. and Winer, B.J. (1952) *The Leadership Behavior of the Airplane Commander*, Washington, DC: Human Resources Research Laboratories, Department of the Air Force.

Handy, C.B. (1985) *Understanding Organizations*, Harmondsworth: Penguin.

Hemphill, J.K. and Coons, A.E. (1950) *Leader Behavior Description*, Columbus, Ohio: Personnel Research Board, Ohio State University.

Hersey, P. and Blanchard, K.H. (1977) *Management of Organizational Behavior: Utilizing Human Resources*, Englewood Cliffs, NJ: Prentice-Hall.

Hess, G.A. (1991) 'Chicago and Britain: experiments in empowering parents'. Paper presented at the Annual Meeting of the American Educational Research Association, Chicago.

Hoff, B. (1982) *The Tao of Pooh: In Which Way is Revealed by the Bear of Little Brain*, London: Reed.

Holly, P. (1990) 'Catching the wave of the future: moving beyond school effectiveness by re-designing schools', *School Organisation* 10, 2–3: 195–212.

Holmes Group (1986) *Tomorrow's Teachers: A Report of the Holmes Group*, East Lancing, Mich. MT.

Holt, J. (1970) *How Children Fail*, New York: Dell.

Hoy, W.K. and Miskel, C.G. (1987) *Educational Administration: Theory, Research and Practice*, New York: Random House.

Huberman, M. (1989). 'The professional life cycle of teachers', *Teachers College Record* 91, 1: 31–57.

—— (1993) *The Lives of Teachers*, London: Cassell.

Hughes, M.G. (1976). 'The professional as administrator: the case of the secondary school head', in R.S. Peters (ed.) *The Role of the Head*, London: Routledge & Kegan Paul.

Hunter, E. (1989) 'The role of teachers in educational reform', *National Association of Secondary Schools' Bulletin* September: 61–63.

Iannaccone, L. and Lutz, F. (eds) (1978) *Public Participation in School Decision Making*, Lexington, Mass.: Lexington Press.

Interim Committee for the Australian Schools Commission (P.H. Karmel, Chair) (1973) *Schools in Australia: Report*, Canberra: Australian Government Printing Service.

Kandel, J.L. (1938) *Types of Administration*, Melbourne, Victoria: Australian Council for Education Research.

Kelchtermans, G. and Vandenberghe, R. (1993) 'A teacher is a teacher is a teacher is a . . . : teacher professional development from a biographical perspective'. Paper presented at the Annual Meeting of the American Educational Research Association, Atlanta, Georgia.

Kennedy, M.M. (1979) 'Generalizing from single case studies', *Evaluation Quarterly* 3, 4: 661–679.

Knight, P. (1984) 'The practice of school-based curriculum development', *Journal of Curriculum Studies* 1: 37–48.

Kohl, H. (1984) *Growing Minds: On Becoming a Teacher*, New York: Harper and Row.

Kohn, A. (1991) 'Caring kids: the role of the schools,' *Phi Delta Kappan* 72: 495–496.

Kowalski, T.J. (1980) 'Attitudes of school principals towards decentralized budgeting', *Journal of Educational Finance* 6: 68–76.

## REFERENCES

Kozol, J. ( 1975) *The Night is Dark and I am Far from Home*, Boston, Mass.: Houghton Mifflin.

Kunz, D. and Hoy, W.K. (1976) 'Leader behavior of principals and the professional zone of acceptance of teachers', *Educational Administration Quarterly* 12: 49–64.

Lancy, D. (1993) *Quality Research in Education: An Introduction to the Major Traditions*, New York: Longman.

Langer, S.K. (1978) *Philosophy in a New Key: A Study of Symbolism in Reason, Rite and Art*, Cambridge, Mass.: Harvard University Press.

Langness, L.L. and Frank, G. (1981) *Lives: An Anthropological Approach to Biography*, Novato, Cal.: Chandler & Sharp Publishers.

Lawton, S.B. (1992) 'Why restructure? An international survey of the roots of reform', *Journal of Education Policy* 7, 2: 139–154.

Leithwood, K.A. (1990) 'The principal's role in teacher development', in J. Bruce (ed.) *Changing School Culture through Staff Development*, Alexandria, Virginia: Yearbook of the Association for Supervision and Curriculum Development.

Leithwood, K.A., Begley, P.T. and Bradley Cousins, J. (1994) *Developing Expert Leadership for Future Schools*, London: The Falmer Press.

Lemert, E.A. (1951) *Social Pathology*, New York: McGraw-Hill.

Levin, H.M. (1987) 'Accelerated schools for disadvantaged students', *Educational Leadership* 44, 6: 19–21.

Lieberman, A. (1995) 'Practices that support teacher development', *Phi Delta Kappa*

Lincoln, Y.S. and Guba, E.G. (1984) *Naturalistic Inquiry*, London: Sage.

Lortie, D. (1975) *Schoolteacher*, Chicago, Ill.: University of Chicago Press.

Malen, B., Ogawa, R.T. and Kranz, J. (1990) 'What do we know about school-based management? A case study of the literature – a call for research', in W.H. Clune and J.F. Witte (eds) *Choice and Control in American Education. Vol. 2: The Practice of Choice, Decentralization and School Restructuring*, Basingstoke: The Falmer Press.

Mandelbaum, D.G. (1973) 'The study of life history: Gandhi', *Current Anthropology*, 14, 3: 177–206.

Marsh, C. and Stafford, K. (1988) *Curriculum: Practices and Issues*, Sydney: McGraw-Hill.

Marton, F. (1988) 'Phenomenography: a research approach to investigating different understandings of reality', in R.R. Sherman and R.B. Webb (eds) *Qualitative Research in Education: Focus and Methods*, London: The Falmer Press.

Marwick, A. (1970) *The Nature of History*, London: The Macmillan Press.

Measor, L. (1985) 'Interviewing: a strategy in qualitative research', in G.R. Burgess (ed.) *Strategies of Educational Research: Qualitative Methods*, London: The Falmer Press.

Meltzer, B.B., Petras, J.W. and Reynolds, L.T. (1975) *Symbolic Interaction: Genesis, Varieties and Criticism*, London: Routledge & Kegan Paul.

Miles, M.B. and Huberman, A.M. (1984) *Qualitative Data Analysis: A Sourcebook of New Methods*, London: Sage.

Minichiello, V., Aroni, R., Timewell, E. and Alexander, L. (1990) *In-Depth Interviewing: Researching People*, Melbourne, Victoria: Longman Cheshire.

Murphy, J. (1991) *Restructuring Schools: Capturing and Assessing the Phenomenon*, New York: Teachers' College Press.

National Project on the Quality of Teaching and Learning (1993) *National Schools Project: Report of the National External Review Panel*, Canberra: Australian Government Publishing Service.

Noddings, N. ( 1987) 'An ethic of caring', in J. Devitis (ed.) *Women, Culture and Morality*, New York: Peter Lang.

O'Donoghue, T.A. (1990) 'The Roman Catholic ethos of Irish secondary schools,

## REFERENCES

1924–62, and its implications for teaching and school organisation', *Journal of Educational Administration and History* 12, 2: 27–37.

Payne, G. (1976) 'Making a lesson happen', in M. Hammersley and P. Woods (eds) *The Process of Schooling*, London: Routledge & Kegan Paul.

Perrow, C. (1970) *Organizational Analysis: A Sociological View*, Belmont, CA, Cal.: Wadsworth.

Peters, T.J. and Waterman, R.H. (1982) *In Search of Excellence: Lessons from America's Best-Run Companies*, New York: Harper & Row.

Plummer, K. (1983) *Documents of Life: An Introduction to the Problems and Literature of a Humanistic Method*, Sydney, NSW.: Allen & Unwin.

Pollard, A. (1980) 'Teacher interests and changing situations of survival threat in primary school classrooms', in P. Woods (ed.) *Teacher Strategies*, London: Croom Helm.

Purkey, S.C. and Smith, M.S. (1985) 'School reform: the district policy implications of the effective schools literature', *The Elementary School Journal* 85: 353–389.

Pusey, M. (1991) *Economic Rationalism in Canberra: A Nation Building State Changes its Mind*, Cambridge: Cambridge University Press.

Quality of Education Review Committee (1985) *Quality of Education in Australia*, Canberra: Australian Government Publishing Service.

Report of the Committee of Inquiry into Education in Western Australia (1984) *Education in Western Australia*, Perth, WA: Government Publisher.

Ribbins, P. and Sherratt, B. (1992) 'Managing the secondary school in the 1990s: a new view of headship', *Educational Management and Administration* 20, 3: 151–160.

Ritzer, G. (1983) *Sociological Theory*, New York: Alfred A. Knopf.

Rogers, C.R. (1951) *Client Centred Therapy*, Boston, Mass.: Houghton Mifflin.

Sachs, J. and Logan, L. (1990) 'Control or development? A study of inservice education', *Journal of Curriculum Studies* 22, 5: 473–481.

Schempp, P.G. (1993) 'The micropolitics of teacher induction', *American Educational Research Journal* 30, 3: 447–472.

Schlechty, P.C. (1990) *Schools for the 21st Century: Leadership Imperatives for Educational Reform*, San Francisco, Cal.: Jossey-Bass.

Schwartz. H. and Jacobs, J. (1979) *Qualitative Sociology: A Method to the Madness*, London: The Free Press.

Sergiovanni, T.J. (1994) *Building Community in Schools*, San Francisco, Cal.: Jossey-Bass.

Sichel, B.A. (1988) *Moral Education: Character, Community and Ideals*, Philadelphia, Penn.: Temple University Press.

Sikes, P. and Troyna, B. (1991) 'True stories: a case study in the use of life history in initial teacher education', *Educational Review* 43, 1: 3–16.

Sikes, P.J., Measor, L. and Woods, P. (1985) *Teacher Careers: Crises and Continuities*, London: The Falmer Press.

Simons, H. (1982) *Conversation Piece: The Practice of Uttering, Muttering, Collecting, Using and Reporting Talk for Social and Education Research*, London: Grant McIntyre.

Sizer, T.R. (1984) *Horace's Compromise: The Dilemma of the American High School*, Boston, Mass.: Houghton Mifflin.

Slavin, R.E. (1988) 'On research and school organisation: a conversation with Bob Slavin', *Educational Leadership* 46, 2: 22–29.

Smart, D. (1988) 'Reversing patterns of control in Australia: can schools be self-governing?' *Educational Research and Perspectives* 15, 2: 16–24.

Smart, D. and Alderson, A. (1980) *The Politics of Education in Western Australia: An*

REFERENCES

*Exploratory Study of State Education Department Policy Making*, Melbourne, Victoria: Centre for the Study of Higher Education, University of Melbourne.

Spradley, J.P. (1979) *The Ethnographic Interview*, New York: Holt, Rinehart and Winston.

Stake, R.E. (1978) 'The case study method in social inquiry', *Educational Researcher* 7: 5–8.

Stanley, W.O. (1968) 'The social foundations subjects in the professional education of teachers', *Educational Theory* 18, 3: 224–236.

Starratt, R.J. (1996) *Transforming Educational Administration: Meaning, Community and Excellence*, New York: McGraw-Hill.

Stenhouse, L. (1975) *An Introduction to Curriculum Research and Development*, London: Heinemann.

Stogdill, R.M. (1950) 'Leadership, membership and organization', *Psychological Bulletin* 47: 1–14.

——(1981) 'Traits of leadership: a follow-up to 1970', in B.M. Bass (ed.) *Stogdill's Handbook of Leadership*, New York: Free Press.

Strauss, A. and Corbin, J. (1990) *Basics of Qualitative Research: Grounded Theory, Procedures and Techniques*, London: Sage.

Sultana, R.G. (1991) 'Research in teaching and teacher education: qualitative methods and grounded theory methodology', *South Pacific Journal of Teacher Education* 19, 1: 59–68.

Taylor, S.J. and Bogdan, R. (1984) *Introduction to Qualitative Research Methods – The Search for Meaning*, New York: John Wiley and Sons.

Timar, T.B. (1989) 'The politics of school restructuring', in M.E. Goertz (ed.) *Politics of Education Society Yearbook*, London: Taylor and Francis.

Uhrmacher, P.B. (1993) 'Coming to know the world through Waldorf education', *Journal of Curriculum and Supervision* 9, 1: 87–104.

Verne, D.P. (1991) *The New Essay of Autobiography: An Essay on the Life of Giambattista Vico Written by Himself*, Oxford: Clarendon Press.

Waring, M. (1979) *Social Pressure and Curriculum Innovations: A Study of the Nuffield Foundation Science Teaching Project*, London: Methuen.

Western Australia. Functional Review Committee (1986) *A Review of the Education Portfolio*, Perth, WA: Government Printer.

Western Australia. Ministry of Education (1987) *Better Schools in Western Australia: A Programme for Improvement*, Perth, WA: Government Printer.

Western Australia. Parliament (1986) *Managing Change in the Public Sector: A Statement of the Government's Position* (White Paper), Perth, WA: Government Printer.

White, P.A. (1989) 'An overview of school-based management: what does the research say?' *National Association of Secondary School Principals' Bulletin* September: 1–8.

Wilenski, P. (1986) *Public Power and Public Administration*, Sydney, NSW: Hale & Iremonger.

Wolk, R.A. and Rodman, B.H. (1994) *Classroom Crusaders: Twelve Teachers who are Trying to Change the System*, San Francisco, Cal.: Jossey-Bass.

Woods, P. (1985a) 'Conversations with teachers: a potential source of their professional growth', *Curriculum Inquiry* 12, 3: 239–255.

——(1985b) 'Conversations with teachers: some aspects of life history method', *British Educational Research Journal* 11, 1: 13–26.

——(1992) 'Symbolic interactionism: theory and method', in M.D. Le Compte, W.L. Milroy and J. Preissle (eds) *A Handbook of Qualitative Research in Education*, London: Academic Press.

## REFERENCES

——(1993) 'Managing marginality: teacher development through grounded life history', *British Educational Research Journal* 19, 5: 447–465.

Woods, P. and Sikes, P.J. (1987) 'The use of teacher biographies in professional self-development', in F. Todd (ed.) *Planning Continuing Professional Development*, London: Croom Helm.

Yukl, G.A. (1981) *Leadership in Organizations*, Englewood Cliffs, NJ: Prentice-Hall.

# INDEX

Printed in the United States
by Baker & Taylor Publisher Services